Lawrence Verry Inc.

The house ~~that~~ the left built.
Inside Labour policy making
1970-1975

REVIEW COPY

Michael Hatfield

ISBN 0 57502471 2

LIST PRICE

$25.00

Publishers - Distributors - Importers
MYSTIC, CONNECTICUT
06355

THE HOUSE THE LEFT BUILT
Inside Labour Policy-Making
1970–75

THE HOUSE THE LEFT BUILT

Inside Labour Policy-Making
1970–75

by

MICHAEL HATFIELD

LONDON
VICTOR GOLLANCZ LTD
1978

MADE AND PRINTED IN GREAT BRITAIN BY
THE GARDEN CITY PRESS LIMITED
LETCHWORTH, HERTFORDSHIRE
SG6 1JS

*To my wife Margaret
and my two sons
Alex and James*

I use capitals to distinguish Fresh Thinking from the perfectly proper desire to keep our minds alert and adaptable. Perhaps a better term would be Socialist Revisionists. These are people who want to substitute novel remedies for the struggle for power in the State. . . . Now that we are once again engaged in policy-making, it is essential that we should keep clear before us that one of the central principles of Socialism is the substitution of public for private ownership. There is no way round this.

Aneurin Bevan, *Tribune*, 13 June 1952

It would be a shame, however, if the controversy over the proposal to take the large British corporations into public ownership should lead people, either in Britain or abroad, to overlook the remarkably progressive way in which Labour's Programme for Britain 1973 brings the problem of the large corporation into full economic and political focus . . . For this, however damaging its electoral effect, surely some will be grateful.

John Kenneth Galbraith, *New Statesman*, 6 July 1973

Contents

Acknowledgements

This book could not have been written without the co-operation of many people who gave up their valuable time to assist me in my researches, in a number of cases checking through their personal files for relevant documents. For obvious reasons much of the material had to be given on a confidential basis—to be used without attribution—and my one regret in accepting it on that basis is that it prevents me from expressing my warmest appreciation to named individuals for their help and kindness. Many actively encouraged me in my efforts by applying gentle pressure when the going appeared to be hard and progress was almost at a halt. For such bullying, my thanks!

However, there are others who are not covered by such restrictions and I would like to thank the staff in the libraries at Transport House and the Conservative Central Office for their assistance; also Dick Clements, Editor of *Tribune*, and Peter Stephenson, Editor of *Socialist Commentary*, for allowing me access to their files; and Diana Hayter, general secretary of the Fabian Society, for providing me with relevant Fabian pamphlets.

While I received advice from many quarters the book remains my own responsibility.

Author's Note

When the events described in this book were sufficiently advanced to expose the divisions within the Labour Party a backbench MP remonstrated that political journalists and commentators only reported the two wings of the party and forgot it had a body. He had to be told the unpalatable fact of life that it was the furious beatings of the right and left wings that kept the party aloft and in the public eye. Moreover, many a politician of the so-called centre had been known to climb out on one limb or another when he found the need to attract attention to his views.

In a sense this was unfair, but then politics, although fascinating, are rarely known for fairness. They also pose problems for the writer who conscientiously attempts to be objective in delineating the position of individual politicians in the spectrum of party politics. For example, where does one place a Labour MP who is against British membership of the European Community but subscribes to its military obligations to NATO on all the well-known grounds of collective security, who is doctrinally committed to a sweeping extension of public ownership but is critical of the failings of the nationalised industries?

It is a descriptive dilemma that can never be resolved to everyone's satisfaction and I cannot pretend to have done it here. Stylistically, however, it has been necessary to avoid the repetitious use of "right" and "left" and it will be seen that I have resorted to other convenient classifications. The former are social democrats and the latter democratic socialists. There is also a sprinkling, I hope not too liberal, of those over-worked and often misapplied words "moderates" and "militants". Somewhere there has to be a dividing line and it was graphically drawn by Harold Wilson at the Labour Party conference at Brighton in 1966 when he said : "We cannot afford to fight the problems of the 'sixties with the attitudes of the (Marxist) Social Democratic Federation, nor, in looking for a solution to these problems, seek vainly to find the answer in Highgate cemetery."

This book is about what happened in the early 'seventies, but the reaction of politicians to Wilson's statement is a reasonable guideline to where they stand ideologically (though the left would eschew the revolutionary theories of the SDF). Many of those who figure in this book will not accept entirely the labels that have been pinned on them because they may see the descriptions as being superficial. But they will accept that during their careers they have often argued their own positions, sometimes into the early hours, and have not always been consistent themselves.

INTRODUCTION

Introduction

18 JUNE 1970 not only saw the downfall of the Labour Government : for the Labour Party it signalled the erosion of the reformist social democrats' hegemony over the formulation of party policy. From the wreckage of the electoral defeat a small group drifted in on the ebb-tide of revisionist ascendancy and landed on fertile ground. Their aim was no less than to redirect the party towards what they believed to be its socialist objectives and from which it had been led astray. In this they were to be successful. Within four years the Labour Party was to produce its most left wing programme in thirty years. A central pillar of that programme was an economic-industrial policy which committed a future Labour Government, much to the dismay of some shadow ministers, to an unprecedented extension of intervention by the state. Two great issues, causes of fundamental divisions within the party, dominated the years in Opposition. One was how far a future Labour Government should intervene in the mixed economy and the other was Britain's continued membership of the European Economic Community. Throughout the period Labour politicians were to live through a paradox which never properly surfaced.

The unspoken paradox was this : the proposed planning agreements system between Government and individual firms and a state intervention agency, which the left wing was to force through as part of the industrial policy, was based upon continental models, but neither they, nor their rivals the centre-right pro-marketeers, could acknowledge this. For either side, the public admission of the inherent contradiction could serve to weaken the cause they served. The spawning ground for the growing conflict between the two factions was the committee system employed by the party for the formulation of policy. In total nearly 1,000 individuals served on over eighty committees and study groups between 1970 and 1974. What happened inside the key committees and how Labour finally came to approve its interventionist economic-industrial policy is the purpose of this study. The policy is traced from the drawing board to the Statute Book. The narrative is based on confidential papers and documents, minutes, and conversations with many of those involved. Its intention is not only to provide insights into the struggles of a major political party in evolving policy to present to the electorate, but also to show what happened when a significant change took place in the political balance.

The group which landed and successfully gained majority support for its proposals, while by no means tightly knit, was certainly politically motivated. It was a disparate group: middle class intellectuals, working class doctrinaires, trade unionists and academics. Their views on politics generally differed in many areas, but they shared one common conviction. This was the belief that successive Labour Governments had failed, and would continue to fail, unless there was a fundamental change in the balance of the public and private sectors of the economy. While not everyone believed in the eventual collapse of managerial neo-capitalism, they did agree that an ailing and inefficient private enterprise system undermined the objectives of achieving a planned economy and a more just society. In other words, the need for greater intervention by the state in the economic and industrial structure of the country was an essential prerequisite if a Labour Government was to fulfil its social and welfare aspirations.

Ostensibly, of course, none of this was new. Public ownership—or, to use the more politically motivated term, nationalisation—has always been seen by the left as the bedrock of the Labour movement. But the revisionists had held off this doctrinaire approach for over two decades. Revisionism came to the fore in the early 'fifties. Under the leadership of Hugh Gaitskell and the seminal influence of Anthony Crosland the party moved away from its socialist founding faith towards a programme of social reform and egalitarianism. The class-conscious, Marxist-influenced politicians of the left were reduced to fighting a rear-guard action. They could make little headway against the predominant social democrats and their projections of a classless society (or, more accurately, a middle class oriented society) and an economy based upon liberal Keynesian demand management principles. The success of the revisionists has been well documented: Crosland is rightly portrayed as pre-eminent, for he devoted his intellectual energies to pushing public ownership to the periphery of party policy. The revisionists won over the majority of the party to the concept of public *control* of the economy by Keynesian fiscal and monetary measures—the injection or withdrawal of money from the economy in order to stimulate or dampen down demand—rather than the public *ownership* of major sectors of manufacturing industry.

Yet six years of a Labour Government (1964–70) had shown these policies to be wanting, and no further progress had been made in solving the economic problems than had been achieved by successive Conservative Governments. At the same time the revisionists had been challenging one of the basic tenets of the party constitution: the public ownership of the means of production, distribution and exchange. Collectivist by definition, the Labour Party has never been able to share collectively the same dedication to the principle of nationalisation. Throughout its history the party has oscillated, with increasing intensity, over an ambiguous commitment in Clause Four of its constitution to "secure for the workers by hand or by brain the full fruits of their industry and the most equitable distribution thereof that may be possible, upon the basis of the common ownership of the means of production, distribution and exchange, and the best obtainable system of popular administration and control of each industry or service". It is arguable that Clause Four represents as much a consolation to the early left as an inviolable commitment. The constitution brought together the various socialist and labour groups into one national party. It was approved in 1918, when the ramifications of the Russian Revolution were still rumbling among socialists in Western Europe, and had intensified discussions within the Labour movement on methods for achieving industrial democracy and worker participation and control. Clause Four was one of the concessions awarded to the left for supporting the party constitution, however imprecise or vague the wording.

Nonetheless, over the years it has served as a plimsoll line on the party's fortunes. The leadership, in the main, has made obeisance to the sacred concepts while instinctively throwing overboard any socialist baggage when Labour's popularity is shown to be sinking dangerously fast. Labour Governments have brought in nationalisation measures for reasons not dis-similar to those that motivate Conservative Governments : the rationalisation of inefficient and bankrupt private enterprise. Within a decade of Labour approving Clause Four a Conserva-tive Government had nationalised the electricity grid system, forcibly merged civil aviation firms into a public monopoly before the Second World War and brought London Transport under public control. Attlee's Government brought into the public sector the railways, internal airways, road transport, gas, electricity, coal, iron and steel. It should be noted that neither Government, Conservative nor Labour, was greatly concerned with industrial democracy or worker participation. (It was not until 1966–67 that a Labour Government introduced the con-cept of worker directors into the renationalised steel industry.)

From the early 'fifties onwards the revisionist element in the party successfully resisted demands that public ownership should be carried into manufacturing, as distinct from basic and service industries. But the revisionists' belief in their intel-lectual triumph over doctrinaire leftism made them run too fast. Having persuaded the majority of the party that it must abandon its cloth cap image or be condemned to permanent Opposition, Gaitskell, unwisely and at personal cost, sought to jettison Clause Four from the constitution. The party was recklessly split and the majority rejected the proposition. In 1970, a decade later, the revisionists faced a different and more difficult problem. Their economic-industrial policies had been put to the iron test of Government and had not been a notable success. How, therefore, were they to maintain their dominant role in influencing party policy? This history tells how in the following years it was wrested from their grasp.

The shore upon which the group of state interventionists landed, to exhaust the metaphor, was peopled by trade union-ists and activists inside the constituency Labour parties. It was they who represented and articulated the widespread disaffec-tion among working class voters with the Labour Government. Traditional supporters, they had been estranged by what seemed unrelenting policies of deflation, controls on wages, proposed trade union legislation, and unemployment. At the same time, the cost of living continued to rise and the standard of living to fall. They were ready to hear an alternative to the apparently unsuccessful consensus approach to the nation's intractable economic problems. The left has always had a receptive audience; but for the first time in twenty years they were speaking in a climate in which it became apparent they could capture the ears of the majority of the party. The major trade unions, whose block votes can dictate the views of the annual party conference, had swung progressively leftwards in the 'sixties and there was a resurgence of left wing activity in the constituencies. The revisionists' declared inherent weakness was the left's strength. "Moreover," stated a Fabian pamphlet * on the social democrats' dilemma, "they have discovered, once cut off from the Marxist tap root, it is impossible to create a substitute philosophy through the agency of study groups and conference resolutions." While such an argument must remain unconvincing and defeatist, the left had no such problems. Their chosen ideological battleground has always been the committee room and the conference hall.

Policies worked out by the various committees have to be given the final seal of approval by the annual conference. The constitution states : "The party conference shall decide from time to time what specific proposals of legislative, financial or administrative reform shall be included in the party pro gramme." To avoid the obvious political challenge that the party's commitment to a policy could be based upon a bare majority, there is a qualification : "No proposal shall be included in the party programme unless it has been adopted by the party conference by a majority of not less than two-thirds of the votes recorded on a card vote." The annual conference is attended by about 1,500 delegates from the trade unions, constituency parties, socialist societies, Co-operative organisations, and Federations. While the number of trade union and constituency party delegates is roughly the same, there is a huge difference in voting strength. The trades union vote is based upon the number of their members affiliated to the Labour Party and on this basis the size of the total card vote can command up to almost 90 per cent of the total votes cast. Not all the unions will necessarily adopt the same line on individual policies but nevertheless their presence is formidable.

This can be reflected on the party's National Executive Committee : the supreme body which, among other functions, is

* John Gyford and Stephen Haseler, *Social Democracy: Beyond Revisionism* (Fabian Society: March 1971).

custodian of the conference decisions. The National Executive formulates policy for approval, prepares statements and submits resolutions to the conference. Before a general election it holds a joint meeting with Shadow Cabinet ministers (or Cabinet ministers if Labour is in Government), which draws from the approved programme the policies to be inserted in the general election manifesto. No conference decision, however, even with a two-thirds majority, has automatic right to be included. At the same time the joint meeting cannot contradict any programme item in shaping the manifesto. It can ignore the item, by failure to select, or decide that the item would be more suitable for a subsequent manifesto and therefore a subsequent Parliament. On this basis, the dominant faction inside the party may seek to have the full programme implemented while the minority may raise objections on grounds of ideology or electoral advantage and seek a compromise formula of words.

The balance of political views is invariably mirrored throughout the party structure. An exception is the constitutionally independent Parliamentary Labour Party, where the centre-right social democrats have always held the dominant position. The MPs elect the Leader and Deputy Leader of the party and the twelve members of the Shadow Cabinet. (To be strictly accurate, the twelve backbenchers are elected as the Parliamentary Committee; the Shadow Cabinet comprises these twelve members plus any other MPs or Peers the Party Leader chooses.) The party conference elects the National Executive Committee, the Leader and Deputy Leader being *ex officio* members. There are four divisions on the National Executive : twelve trade unionists, seven constituency party representatives, five women members, one socialist societies member, one Treasurer, and, since 1972, one representative from the Young Socialists.

Elections to the National Executive are not only a struggle between the rival factions but between personalities. Gaitskell used to complain that the reliability of some of his shadow cabinet colleagues diminished as they rediscovered their militancy in the run-up to the annual ballot. Richard Crossman, who was a member, describes in his Diary how Barbara Castle was obsessed with retaining her seat. Throughout the 1964–70 period there was a steady drift towards left wing representation. Dissatisfaction with the Government's economic-industrial policies was largely the cause. In 1964, the year Labour won the election, there were twenty so-called moderates on the National Executive and eight acknowledged left wingers; by the time Labour had lost office in 1970, the moderate representation had dropped to fifteen and the left had increased its strength to twelve. Although numerically this still gave the moderates the edge, the left gained the upper hand by their diligence at attending meetings. Put another way, some moderates displayed their notorious propensity to be absent from meetings and later complained at what was taking place in their absence.

This shift in the balance of power was of prime importance in the evolution of the economic-industrial policy in the 'seventies. The left wing representation was to increase in this period. There was therefore a corresponding increase in the left wing bias in the policy-initiating committees created by the National Executive. The principal policy committees are Home and International : it is the former that concerns us. The general secretary nominates the National Executive members of these committees, attempting to reflect the political balance of the parent committee. The Home Committee, in turn, sets up a series of sub committees to study various areas of policy and produce recommendations. Two of these, the Industrial Policy and the Public Sector Group, laid the groundwork for the challenge to previous Labour policy. Working directly to the committees is a party Research Department which is responsible for briefing, information and policy work on all aspects of the domestic programme.

When Labour lost the 1970 general election the Department consisted of a Research Secretary and eleven research assistants, most of them from universities and none of them well-paid. An office paper went before the Home Policy Committee which explained how the election defeat would affect the work of the department and the committee. In purely administrative terms the office would find itself spending more time on briefing party spokesmen and Labour MPs. The research programme, it was hoped, would benefit from the availability of National Executive members who were previously too occupied with Government to spare their time. After a period of adjustment many outside advisers who were unwilling to devote their time to the party when it was in Government would come back to work.

On the latter point, the inference was inescapable. It pointed up the fact that even party theoreticians (academics, trade unionists, and individuals from industry who privately advise the party) suffer the same disillusion that descends on party workers when Labour is in office.

The paper also asked the executive members to consider two proposals which concerned the formulation of policy : whether a more formal link with the Shadow Cabinet was possible; and whether the Parliamentary Labour Party might be invited to nominate members to the various advisory committees and study groups. Both propositions were to be accepted by the end of the year. They were not without importance for they were the beginning of the bridge-building exercise between the party outside Parliament and the Parliamentary Party. The man behind the operation was James Callaghan, who had been elected chairman of the Home Committee after the personal defeat of George Brown in the general election. Callaghan had been the principal casualty in the rift between the Labour Government and the trade unions over the proposed trade union legislation contained in the *In Place of Strife* White Paper.

Left out of Harold Wilson's "inner cabinet" because he did not agree with Government policy, Callaghan had created a new power base within the party. Political common sense told him, and others, that the first step to be taken after the election defeat was to heal the rift between the various wings of the movement. Restoring relations with the trade unions was to prove one of the more delicate operations. As we shall see, it was the trade unions allied with the left who were to impose the economic-industrial strategy upon the party. Wilson, for his part, spent the first six months out of office writing the initial draft of his "personal record" of the Labour Government. The general impression of his colleagues was that it took him a good eighteen months to readjust to leading the party in Opposition. Certainly, there is little evidence of his guiding hand. His party opponents would put this more strongly : Wilson failed lamentably to match up to his leadership responsibilities. Whether or not this was true, it partially explains why Wilson is not given a prominent role in the early chapters of this book. A second explanation is that Wilson did not directly involve himself in the early stages of policy making. If he had, there may have been a different story to tell.

ONE

Footings

THE LABOUR PARTY conference in 1970 was not the wake
it could have been. Six years in Government, the imposition of
a statutory incomes policy and threatened trade union legislation had severely strained relations between the political and
trade union wings of the Labour movement. There were no
bitter recriminations and none of the personality clashes that
were to materialise later. But nonetheless the disagreements
were there below the surface. The party met in Blackpool in
October after the general election defeat on 18 June. Labour,
having experienced majority government for the second time
since the Second World War, again had to re-equip itself for
Opposition and plan the way ahead. "This week we have
picked ourselves off the floor", commented Ian Mikardo, chairman of the conference, injecting the only public note of dis
cord within the National Executive by proclaiming the need
for an undiluted socialist programme in his closing address.
Departing delegates were informed : "We have looked around
to survey the damage and we have got the tool kit ready to do
the job of rebuilding."

Mikardo was to emerge as the undesignated clerk of works
for the left. Nurtured on Marxist philosophy, throughout his
life he had espoused the doctrine of public ownership. As a
relatively young delegate to the 1944 conference, he had rejected
the pleas of the National Executive to remit a motion asking
for the "transfer to public ownership of the land, large-scale
building, heavy industry, and all forms of banking, transport
and fuel and power"; moreover, the motion wanted appropriate legislation to ensure that publicly owned enterprises should
be "democratically controlled and operated in the national
interest, with representation of the workers engaged therein and
and of consumers". Mikardo won the majority support of the
conference. A ruffled Herbert Morrison said afterwards to
Mikardo, whom he did not know, that he had made a good

speech, but "you realise you have lost us the general election". Morrison's hyperbolic prophecy was to be proved wrong, although in retrospect his remark was a clear hint that the leadership would not accept the decision of the conference. "Socialism cannot come overnight as the product of a weekend revolution", stated the party's 1945 election policy programme *Let Us Face The Future*, "The members of the Labour Party, like the British people, are practical minded men and women."

The relationship between Morrison and Mikardo was not improved when, six years later, the latter was to win his way on to the National Executive. He has maintained his seat, apart from one year, ever since. Antagonism between the militant and moderate factions put down deep roots in the 'fifties. Edith Summerskill, when she chaired the National Executive, found it impossible to address Mikardo by his name : she referred to him as "the man in the brown suit". A man who physically gives the impression of permanently battling against a biting wind, Mikardo has collected his fair share of political enemies. But none of his detractors have questioned his competence, intellectual capacity and indefatigable energy. It seemed only natural that he should become chairman of the all-party House of Commons Select Committee on Nationalised Industries between 1966–70, winning the respect of politicians and civil servants alike. His left wing views and long-standing export business connections with Eastern European countries, however, have kept him from holding ministerial posts.

Mikardo's views can be stated briefly. They were set out in a document submitted to his National Executive colleagues. The Labour Party had, and has, four motivations for public ownership. The first, and the most dominant, was the desire to extend economic democracy as a counterpart to the extension of political democracy, by removing from small groups of largely self-selected directors, who were virtually accountable to nobody, the power to take decisions which affected the welfare of millions of people and to transfer that power to ministers who could be called to account for their exercise of it. By this means the key industries—the commanding heights—would be available for use as instruments of public policy, and particularly as levers of state planning and control.

The second of these motivations was to improve the efficiency of the industries. It was justifiably argued that coal-mining was inefficient because of its bad industrial relations which could not be put right without getting rid of the hated coal-owners; that the fuel industries as a whole were bedevilled by large-scale waste through duplication and overlapping of resources; that the railways were unviable through a combination of the burden of artificial capital debt and bad management; that steel needed massive investment which could not be financed from private sources; that the ports were being run by their customers in the interests of their customers and not of the community.

Mikardo went on to say that the efficiency argument was not the strongest of the four strands but was the most convenient because it was almost the only part of the case for public ownership which could be forcibly argued by non-socialists. "We have to remember [he continued] that most of the members of 1945 Government, which carried out most of the nationalisation programme at the 1944 annual conference, were executing it only because they were defeated at that conference. Many of them were keen, if grudging, admirers of the managers of big business, and believed that those managers had more initiative, imagination and go-gettery than could be provided by public servants, present or future. Morrison, in particular—and he was the key figure at the time—not only did not seek to controvert but actually echoed Tory incantations about 'the dead hand of the Civil Service'."

Mikardo's analysis proceeded in this fashion: the party landed itself in sometimes sterile and always irrelevant arguments about whether an industry was or was not efficient, and the thunder of these arguments drowned the still small voice of the case for socialism, economic democracy, planning, egalitarianism and industrial democracy. From that point it was a fatally easy slide to taking over only those industries which "failed the nation". So Labour backed the outdated, obsolescent, overburdened, loss-making industries, leaving the profitable ones to private owners, and giving the Tories a good case to argue that public ownership was wrong because it always made a loss.

The third of the four motivations seldom figured prominently in the party's presentation of its case: it was the egalitarian effect of taking from a small number of people and spreading throughout the community the gains resulting from an industry's self-generated capital appreciation. The fourth factor entered into the party's thinking a long while after the others, even though it stemmed directly from Clause Four. It was the concept that it would be easier to pioneer and develop the institutions and the operation of industrial democracy in a centrally controlled industry run in the spirit of public service than in a disparate one operated under the urge of the maximisation of profit.

Mikardo's document provides a concise description of the base from which the left was determined to proceed. Rebuilding the industrial policy could be approached from different directions : absorb the rising damp threatening Keynesian demand management principles or dig out the foundations and erect a dirigist edifice of state supervision and constraints upon the manufacturing industry, what Aneurin Bevan described as the "commanding heights of the economy". The policies of the outgoing Labour Administration had been to get an unspecified shift in the balance of the mixed economy and to weld the bunsen burner rhetoric of the "white heat of technology" into something more tangible. Unforeseen economic disasters, over which the Government was shown to have little control, had been partly responsible for the lack of success, but it was also true that ministers had never been able to reach a general consensus on the degree and character of interventionism.

The experience of Michael Shanks, who worked in the Department of Economic Affairs, was that "interventionism under Mr Wilson took place essentially on an *ad hoc* basis, as a reaction to crisis".[1] Largely, the Government had carried out policies initiated by previous Conservative Governments. Samuel Brittan, who had also worked in Whitehall, later wrote : "Much of the small print of the 1965 National Plan, and Mr Wilson's own 'purposive physical intervention' had already been enacted before Labour came to office."[2] Labour had entered Government with lots of ideas but, it materialised, few detailed plans. The 1964 general election manifesto had been prepared at a time when Labour was simply hell-bent on winning the election at almost any cost. Gaitskell's death and the retirement of Macmillan had brought about a new sense of unity at a time when morale inside the Conservative Party was beginning to collapse. Labour, consequently, maximised on the campaign platforms the issues on which everyone in the party agreed—notably spending programmes, such as pensions, education, housing, health and employment.

While the lengthy manifesto contained a good deal of analysis there were few substantial proposals to deal with many of the problems facing the country. Transport was to have an "integrated policy" in place of Beeching; fuel and power was to be "co-ordinated"; but there was nothing about fiscal policy if Labour faced a run on the pound. Incomes policy was agreed when Frank Cousins, general secretary of the Transport and General Workers Union (he became a Cabinet minister responsible for Technology), suggested the phrase "a planned growth of incomes". No doubt reflecting the views of the business community the *Financial Times* commented after Labour's 1970 election defeat : "The Labour Government greatly increased the degree of official intervention in many sectors of our economic and industrial life, but it never faced the problem of adapting the official machine to the new functions it was asked to perform."

Another commentator, Andrew Graham, found there was a failure to appreciate the complexities of its interventionist policies and to be over-optimistic about the size and speed of its effects. He wrote :

Moreover, once one intervenes within the market system all those conflicts which are hidden by the invisible hand become more obvious and the Government becomes the clear object for blame whenever expectations are not fulfilled. Nothing succeeds like success but the reverse is also true. The result was that once the business community became disillusioned all the difficulties—the delicacy, the differing views of what policy should be, the hostility to intervention, the role of the civil service, and the constant interaction between these—became worse.[3]

Graham's comments were contained in *The Labour Government's Economic Record 1964–70*, edited by Professor Wilfred Beckerman, economic adviser to Crosland when he was President of the Board of Trade. Crosland and Beckerman became deeply involved in the arguments of the Opposition Years. Crosland was far from uncritical of the Labour Administration. "Our record of economic growth has been lamentable", he told a Fabian meeting in November 1970. Britain's annual growth rate over the past five years of 2.2 per cent was lower than the previous decade, "an almost sufficient explanation of Labour's defeat last June". Four years later he was to be even more forthcoming : "Nobody disputes the central failure of economic policy. In 1970, unemployment was higher, inflation more rapid and economic growth slower than when the Conservatives left office in 1964." [4]

Former ministers were entitled to plead that they had experienced a buffeting from unforeseen economic winds and had been "blown off course" (it was coincidental that navigational metaphors became a vogue at a time when one of Labour's Chancellors of the Exchequer, Callaghan, was a former naval officer). But at the same time it is difficult to detect any co-ordinated belief in achieving the promises of a radically restructured industry and a mixed economy. There was minimal, if any, change in the balance. The Government introduced little public ownership. Steel was renationalised and parts of road haulage and public transport were taken into the public domain. Legislation was introduced in 1969 to nationalise the main ports and docks but was overtaken by the general election.* Reacting to crises, the Government took minority shareholdings in a number of manufacturing companies. One of them, Beagle Aircraft, later went into liquidation. Others involved were Rootes Motors, International Computers and the British Nuclear Power Group. But there was no fundamental change in the public accountability of manufacturing industry, despite the amount of taxpayers' money being poured in.

In reality, intervention was an extension of Conservative policies. Stephen Young, in his analysis of the period, points out that the watershed to a major extension of interventionism was crossed in 1962, with the creation of the National Economic Development Council and the National Economic Develop-

---

* The genesis of this proposal is not without interest. Wilson, Callaghan and Brown offered it as a sop to the left when it was feared that the wafer-thin majority of three in Parliament would mean delaying steel renationalisation. Transport House was instructed to form a study group and produce a report within three months. However, when Labour was returned with its massive majority of 97 in 1966, the new Labour Government appeared to be in no hurry to carry out the plans. Richard Marsh, the new Transport Minister, was not particularly enamoured of the idea.

ment Office.[5] His view was that the difference between the Conservative and Labour Governments was one of emphasis and scale rather than principles. This view is shared by, among others, Trevor Smith, who wrote that the new Labour Government carried on, for the most part, where the Conservatives left off.[6] Though the general direction remained the same, it was the pace that quickened perceptibly.

Relying on traditional macro-economic measures, initially at least, the Government used Keynesian financial controls and legal regulations to adjust the economic and legal framework in which firms operated. As Young observes, fiscal, bank rate and credit policies were used to alter the level of demand in the economy and the availability of labour according to whether inflationary or deflationary policies were pursued. Such regulatory and discriminatory measures were Corporation Tax, the Redundancy Payments Act, Selective Employment Tax (aimed at switching labour from service to manufacturing industries) and the Regional Employment Premium (in effect, an indirect subsidy to halt the growing imbalance of the regions). The NEDC's role was extended and more economic development committees were created with the optimistic objective of rooting out inefficiencies and increasing competitiveness. But, in the final analysis, this was exhortation not compulsion. Firms were free to ignore the blandishments of ministers.

The policies of intervention were proclaimed from a steel and plateglass office block, Millbank Towers, overlooking the River Thames. It was built on the site where the Wedgwood Benn family once had its home when Anthony Wedgwood Benn was a boy. After the collapse of the National Plan in 1966, the Government switched from its halting attempts at indicative planning to an industrial strategy of modernising and restructuring industry gradually. The main instrument was the Ministry of Technology (MinTech), housed in Millbank Towers where Benn now ruled. MinTech grew from a department responsible for the development of scientific and technological based industries—computers, electronics, telecommunications and machine tools—to one which became, in effect, a Ministry for Industry.

By 1970 MinTech was responsible for all manufacturing, mining and energy industries. Under Benn, the ministry had gathered over the four years unprecedented responsibility for a wide range of decisions covering the relationship between Government and industry. "The fundamental importance of the growth of MinTech was the institutionalisation of the principle of discrimination and the overturning of the traditional attitude of neutrality, or 'holding the ring'," wrote Young.[7] Graham Turner quotes a former Board of Trade official: "With this arrival of MinTech, the judgment of the bureaucrat replaced the judgment of the market." [8]

After the 1970 election defeat MinTech's interventionist role was set out by Benn when he refuted criticisms levelled at it by some of his Labour colleagues. Without intervention, he said in a letter to the *New Statesman*, the shipbuilding industry would have faced tragedy with the loss of tens of thousands of jobs; the British computer industry would have collapsed; at least two major heavy-electrical plant manufacturers would have suffered heavier redundancies than they had without reorganisation, and the nuclear industry would have stood no chance in export markets. Since Benn was to become the chief banner carrier for the new interventionist policy, his experiences as a minister are worth further quotation:

> MinTech, which only reached its present size last October, made its share of mistakes and had its failures, but to blame Labour's defeat on the fact that it did not evolve a magic wand for solving all our economic problems is a bit too fanciful. The task of modernising British industry, after a century of relative decline, will take a decade to complete . . . Having established Giro and the National DATA Processing Service as well as mixed enterprise arrangements in the computer, nuclear and shipbuilding industries, I am strongly in favour of further public sector developments.

Benn at that time did not know, or certainly did not declare, how far along the road he was prepared to travel in order to alter the balance in the public and private sectors of industry. We shall see in another chapter how he set down his first thoughts in a confidential paper to his colleagues. The group of like-minded interventionists were to build upon the experience of MinTech and the Industrial Reorganisation Corporation established by the Government in 1966. The IRC was a state merchant bank with powers to furnish industry with financial aid in order to bring about its restructuring. It was allowed to buy equity shares but had to dispose of them eventually. It had no permanent influence upon the firms. Its functions, as described by the Act, were to "promote or assist the reorganisation or development of any industry" and "if requested to do so by the Secretary of State, establish, develop, or promote or assist the establishment or development of any industrial enterprise".

The legislation provided the IRC with up to £150 million from the Exchequer funds to enable the Corporation to carry out its task. It was involved in some of the largest regroupings ever to take place in Britain. IRC's operation touched upon some of the highest peaks of the merger mania that developed during the period. But by the end there were ministerial doubts as to how it should be allowed to operate. The IRC was a statutory independent body and the Government, according to the former minister, Edmund Dell, found that "like Franken-stein, it had little control over its monster".[9] Dell also believed that had Labour returned to office after June 1970 it might have sought means of both increasing Parliamentary control and of freeing IRC of its statutory commitment to making mergers.

Labour had fought the 1970 general election on a limited extension of its interventionist policies. There was a commit-ment to create a state holding and development company which went beyond the IRC's principles. Its purpose would have been to promote joint ventures with private enterprise in the regions. The state holding company had first appeared in a party document, *Labour's Economic Strategy*, published in 1969. This had stated : "Labour's commitment to public ownership has not changed. We still believe that more and more of Britain's industries must move inevitably into public hands. . ." The function of the state holding company would have been to take a controlling interest in projects that private industry might be reluctant to take on its own.

The 1970 general election manifesto cited the examples of aluminium smelters and the Leyland bus-making plant in Cumberland. The 1968 aluminium smelter scheme had been a major project involving loans of up to £30 million to the

British Aluminium Company and up to £33 million to Anglesey Aluminium Metal Ltd (which included Rio Tinto Zinc) for development projects in Invergordon and Anglesey. The manifesto placed emphasis on the need for more intervention in both public and private industry to raise output. "Industrial reorganisation, with its emphasis on better management, is crucial to the success—even survival—of much British industry", it said. The Government planned to tackle on an industry basis, "where necessary firm by firm", the detailed problems of structure which existed in both public and private industry. The IRC, which up to the general election had been involved in thirty mergers, would have been provided with additional finances to develop its work. Here was confirmation, if it were needed, of the change of heart and mind of Labour ministers from macro- to micro-economic thinking, if not quite planning.

But the 1970 general election defeat halted Labour's economic-industrial programme. In Opposition the party could stand back and examine the direction in which it was heading. National Executive members were told in the July office paper : ". . . too much time has been wasted in 'consultation' with ministers, often to the detriment of our concentration on future policy matters." The hidden frustrations of the party when Labour is in office came shining through in the next two sentences : "This time can now be spent on serious consideration of issues. Similarly, for the Research Department there is the release from time-consuming activities of monitoring tiny areas of Government policy, often with no real political content whatsoever." Hopefully, it added : "This too will now allow a better focus on policy matters."

Labour's formulation of past economic-industrial policies when in Opposition is instructive and can be stated briefly. The party's 1964 programme had been formulated when the revisionists' period in the party had passed its zenith but it still commanded considerable influence. Whereas, for example, *Industry and Society*, published by the party in 1956, declared that British firms were "on the whole serving the nation well", by 1961 Labour was saying, in *Signposts for the Sixties*, that "with certain honourable exceptions, our finance and industry need a major shake-up at the top . . . the story of the last ten years is one of wasted opportunities and limping progress". This did not mean that Labour was suggesting a major shift away from the acceptance of a mixed economy. Instead of proposing the transference of some existing industries into public ownership (the doctrinaire formula) the party proposed to build up the public sector alongside the private sector by creating new public enterprises.

In 1963, Harold Wilson, by then Leader of the Party, stated in the *New York Times*: "Our plans to extend the public sector—to occupy the 'commanding heights'—consist mainly in the creation of new industries." These were to be science-based and "growth" sectors of industry. As we have seen, this never occurred. When Labour came to office, pragmatism overtook the programme. Politicians became preoccupied with saving the pound and lost the unity of the party. It was only when Labour was having to fight to remain in office in the 1970 general election that the party returned to the concept of offering some form of challenge to the private sector by proposing a state holding company. There was no disguising the despair of the left.

Tribune, the weekly left wing journal, thundered through the Opposition Years of the 'seventies. It was started in 1936 after the trade unions had rejected the left's motion at party conference for supporting the Spanish Republicans. Coming away from the debate, in which a massive majority had supported the Republicans but had been thwarted by the union block vote, a disconsolate group decided to launch their own paper. Among them were Nye Bevan, Jennie Lee, Stafford Cripps and George Strauss. Cripps, a wealthy barrister, and Strauss, who had independent means, and is now Father of the House of Commons, put up the initial £20,000. Bevan became its Editor during the war years, and *Tribune* pursued a highly critical line on many aspects of Government policy. Moreover, it never neglected the domestic political scene, keeping controversial home policies such as nationalisation of the mines before the public.

It has always revelled in the political battle. When Bevan resigned from the Attlee Government over the prescription charges of Gaitskell, who was then Chancellor, *Tribune* waded into the full-scale schismatic row which rent the party. In the 'fifties it became the principal propaganda agency of the left in opposing West German rearmament and campaigned for British unilateral nuclear disarmament. In the 'seventies the two main causes were opposition to Britain's continued membership of the European Economic Community and a positive policy of economic and industrial interventionism.

After the general election defeat in 1970, Labour backbencher Stanley Orme, whose politics matured in the engineering factories of Manchester, a breeding ground of socialists in the north-west, complained in *Tribune* : "In a situation where more and more public money is being poured into the private sector (something like £800 million a year), where mergers are becoming an everyday occurrence, where the international company is playing an ever-increasing part in our economy, it is time for a basic shift in control and ownership." It was this that the left were to push for in the early 'seventies. Hard, empirical experience had taught them that it was essential not only to win the arguments but to pin down a future Labour Government to a specific party programme. The rhetoric of the 'sixties had to be replaced by the detailed research of the 'seventies. Beginning a new decade with a stronger position inside the party, the left believed that it could write out the mortgage for the next Labour Government.

An office paper submitted to the National Executive members by the Transport House headquarters staff in July stated : "Our defeat at the polls means a radical recasting of the research programme now being undertaken by the Home Policy Committee. It is, however, extremely difficult to take basic decisions just three weeks after a general election, particularly when the moment falls so close to the summer break." Former ministers, in truth, were in no mood to plunge into the policy-making process. Tired and still suffering the withdrawal symptoms from office, their immediate thoughts were far removed from devising new policies for getting back in. When a policy document, *Building a Socialist Britain*, was eventually produced it was designed as much as anything else to meet the wishes of the demoralised party faithful at the 1970 annual conference. Its most controversial section was backward looking : a critique of why Labour had lost the general election.

Wilson, Callaghan and others thought that it was too radical and could open the door to dangerous controversies. Their ministerial record was still too near to be opened to public debate. The left, on the other hand, thought the statement too complacent. They wanted a serious inquest on the defeat, primarily so they could press for socialist policies. But Wilson was opposed to this: "There is no post-mortem when there is no body", he informed an interviewer on BBC Radio. When the Parliamentary Labour Party held a special meeting in July it was Callaghan who was left to reply to the debate, although Wilson was present. The only concession to the left in the statement to the conference was the dropping of an offensive phrase from the final draft which suggested that some form of incomes policy was essential. The party, pressurised by the trade unions, were to beat a retreat down that particular road of economic-industrial policy, although they were to discover much later that it was circular.

The industrial policy was to be built upon a paragraph in the statement which stated that the party must work "towards an extension of common ownership and a better balance between the public and private sectors of the economy". In a tacit admission of the ineffectiveness of the industrial policies applied by the Labour Government, it continued: "We shall also be concerned with the relationship between economic planning, the future production planning which goes on in most large private companies and the power these companies exert."

Building a Socialist Britain had been drafted originally by Terry Pitt, who had succeeded Peter Shore as head of the Research Department in 1964 and who took the side of the left in most internal battles, and Michael Mills, one of his assistants. But the majority of Executive members, when they saw the first draft statement, felt it dwelt too much on the failure to win the general election and compromised the credibility of the Labour Government. The final version was drawn up in September by a special sub-committee: Callaghan, Roy Jenkins, recently elected Deputy Leader, Benn, Mikardo, and Barbara Castle. In the same month, Executive members were told by Transport House that there was a whole host of policy issues which the Home Committee would wish to study in the coming months. "Our problem at this stage", they were told, "is to avoid the danger of failing to see the wood because of the trees." The office paper continued: "In deciding the new research programme this problem is a crucial one—we shall be tempted to devote scarce resources to the study of 'easy' subjects, but a strong political will is the only guarantee of including the need to prepare ourselves again for the most difficult subjects of government."

This was a direct challenge to former ministers that in future they must not be easily diverted from policy by civil servants. The paper also pointed out a number of areas which the Home Committee had wished to study in the past but had been unable to afford enough priority. They included : mergers, the pharmaceutical industry, and the aircraft industry. Among other proposals were "demand management"; how would a voluntary policy for prices and incomes be most effective, and how, within this, would a future Labour Government be able to present a better deal for the lower paid. The proposals reflected the growing unease within the party at the lack of any rationale behind the previous merger policy—bigger, it was discovered, was not necessarily better—and the desperate political need to get away from the hide-bound attitudes towards prices and incomes policy. But what about the manner in which "demand management" was gratuitously and nonchalantly dropped into the list without any further explanation? Was the tiger within the party about to slip from its unguarded cage?

After Labour's defeat in 1970 and up to the October annual conference, the left began to make its first demands for a socialist programme. While *Tribune* warned the leadership that the left would start campaigning for socialist policies at conference, the campaign, in an important sense, was muted because of other more immediate overriding issues. Having suffered curtailments on free collective bargaining under a Labour Government, and been threatened with trade union legislation from the Conservatives, the trade unions concentrated on securing higher wages and resisting the proposed legislation by the incoming Government. In this they were to be joined by the Labour Party, inside and outside Parliament. Unconsciously, the Heath Government was to become the marriage broker between the political and trade union wings of the Labour movement.

Wilson, in any case, was determined to resist any pressure from his left wing. Within a month of being out of office he stated that "there will be no lurches of policy from what we did in Government, but I hope there will be some healthy developments of new thinking".[10] But Michael Foot, who took over Bevan's mantle as the keeper of the left's conscience, and whose lightning flash, street corner oratorical style illuminated party disquiet, set out an alternative viewpoint. He wrote in *Tribune*: "what is needed is a strong shift leftwards"... "The Party in Parliament ought to start that process, but if it won't the party conference will have to do it for them." Foot was soon to find the strength of the left inside the Parliamentary Labour Party insufficient for the task. In July he unsuccessfully stood against Jenkins for the deputy leadership, blaming the "paralysing orthodoxy" of the Labour Government's economic policy as the major fundamental cause of its defeat.

Another bitter critic was Eric Heffer, a direct, intelligent, sometimes unconsciously but disarmingly pompous Labour backbencher from a Liverpool constituency. Heffer was a former joiner and, when Labour eventually returned to Government, the task of knocking the party's industrial policy into a White Paper would fall to him. But that was far ahead. In *Tribune* in 1970 he wrote: "It is in this situation we must develop our ideas on public ownership, industrial democracy, economic planning, the future of the welfare services, housing, education, political democracy, and a way to combat the financial interests in the event of sabotage following the election of a future Labour Government."

Heffer's views were to be carried through to a long conference motion from his Liverpool Walton constituency Labour Party, a "political extravaganza" in the words of National Executive member Bill Simpson, trade union leader of the blast-furnace men.* The motion asked delegates to confirm that "the only practical alternative to the Tories must be through Clause IV, Section 4, of the Labour Party constitution". It aimed to instruct the National Executive and the PLP to "reorientate the policy of the party towards the general socialist perspective of the Labour movement, to prepare a programme to take real economic power by bringing into public ownership the 280 monopolies, private banks, finance houses, and insurance companies, thus eliminating the power of the large private financial interests represented by the Tories".

Clearly this was too much for the National Executive to accept. Conference supported the platform by voting down the motion by 4,269,000 to 1,693,000 votes. However, the National

* Now chairman of the Health and Safety Executive.

Executive did give its approval to a second motion, from the National Union of Public Employees. This instructed the National Executive to present to next year's annual conference a programme designed to "secure greater equality in the distribution of wealth and income"; "to extend social ownership and control of industry and land by Socialist planning"; and "to develop industrial democracy and the role of the trade union movement in industrial, political and economic affairs". This was approved without dissent, but in giving the National Executive's blessing, Simpson added a qualification : it may not be possible to produce the programme for the following year's conference "because the job is a gargantuan one".

Building a Socialist Britain was introduced by Callaghan. He described the policy document as the National Executive's "first thoughts and our first words in a discussion that I trust will be carried on after conference in constituency parties and trade union branches". He expanded slightly the statement's views on industrial policy :

> The growth of the industrial giants results in them taking private planning decisions of such magnitude because of their size and scale, that they must seriously conflict with the economic policy of Government itself. Now this must be harmonised if we are to achieve steady growth, and we intend to study how to do it during the period of Opposition . . . it naturally follows that we must look again at the balance between the public and private sectors of the economy. We have now taken steel in public ownership, we have proposals to nationalise the docks, for North Sea Gas, for setting up a state holding company. We need now to work out how far the Labour Party intends to carry out these proposals and others in extending the field of public ownership.

The intentions of some were more determined than others. Callaghan added that there were other industries that would do better in the public sector, but it was not his "object here to draw up a shopping list". It would have been a sensation if he had. The very idea of shopping lists had been anathema to Labour leaders for thirty years. It echoed of days when Morrison had his iron grip on party management; the time of

Morrisonian "consolidation"—in other words no more national-isation—while the left was battering to break into the manu-facturing sector of industry. (Morrison, for his sins, was knocked off the National Executive in 1952, but was reinstated as an *ex officio* deputy leader under an ingenious proposal of the National Union of Seamen.)

Differences of opinion were still present in 1970, but the arguments were becoming more refined and more informed. There were those who viewed the necessity for public owner-ship on pragmatic grounds and others who felt strongly that history had now proved that a Labour Government was on shifting sands unless it was prepared to intervene in the "com-manding heights". A new spectre had also entered the dialectic : the advance of monopoly capitalism. In 1958, according to a study by the National Institute of Economic and Social Research, the top 100 firms accounted for 31 per cent of the United Kingdom manufacturing production, but by 1970 it was 45 per cent. Other figures were to be produced in the arguments in the Opposition Years.

Public interest required more direct intervention, it was argued, because of foreign control of British firms' inward investment by multi-national companies. Twenty per cent of total UK manufacturing assets were foreign owned, the pro-portion being substantially higher in such key areas as the electronic components business, where it was 49 per cent. What emerged at the end of the policy-making process was the pro-posed nationalisation of the ports, shipbuilding and ship-repairing, and marine engineering, and the aircraft industry. But it was an important deviation from the rigid application of doctrinaire nationalisation measures that was to produce the greatest movement since the Second World War towards public accountability of firms, particularly in manufacturing industry, who were the beneficiaries of substantial financial support from the state.

The gargantuan task of formulating policies after conference began inside the National Executive's sub-Committees. Soon after conference there was a change in the status of these com-mittees that was not without significance. It was designed deliberately to increase their influence within the party struc-ture. Since 1964 they had been designated "advisory" com-mittees, a decision by Peter Shore as Head of the Research

Department, before he became MP for Stepney that year. This downgrading had created suspicions among some members of the National Executive. They believed it had been done so that the sub-committees would be less of an embarrassment if they produced proposals which ran counter to Labour Government policy. When the proposition to increase the status of the sub-committees was first put to the Home Policy Committee in October after the 1970 party conference there was disagreement, not to say confusion. But by the next meeting, in November, the issue had been cleared.

The Home Policy Committee was told that the change offered an opportunity to set up high level committees important enough to attract outside advisers who were national figures. Before Labour's 1964 general election success these committees had been regularly attended by such notables as Lord Bowden, Mr Kaldor, Professor Richard Titmus, Sir Charles Carter and Professor Blackett. The view was expressed that it was unlikely that people of such standing would be willing to involve themselves in the work of *ad hoc* study groups which had little influence. The proposal also made sense in another way. If the National Executive was anxious to bring Labour's frontbench spokesmen early into the policy-making process then the sub-committees had to be reasonably high-powered. Seven sub-committees were created : financial and economic affairs, industrial policy, regional and local government, science and education, social policy, and agriculture. By November the terms of reference had been agreed.

They were to provide continuing and detailed review of particular areas of domestic policy and advise the Home Policy Committee and the National Executive on long-term and medium-term studies which needed to be undertaken. They would provide continuous advice on policy proposals and papers originating outside the movement as well as inside it— from trade unions, Labour parliamentary groups, and the TUC. There had to be subject specialists on each sub-committee. But there must also be representatives with responsibilities in the trade unions and the parliamentary wing of the party, so that party political and trade union interests could constantly react to the proposals of the subject specialists. It was inside these sub-committees that the seeds of the Social

Contract, the Planning Agreements system and the controversial National Enterprise Board were sown.

References

1 *The Times*, November 1970.
2 *Steering the Economy*, Samuel Brittan, Penguin 1971.
3 *The Labour Government's Economic Record 1964–70*, edited by Wilfred Beckerman, Duckworth 1972.
4 *Socialism Now*, Anthony Crosland, Jonathan Cape 1974.
5 *Intervention in the Mixed Economy*, Stephen Young with A. V. Lowe, Croom Helm 1974.
6 *Big Business and the State*, edited by Raymond Vernon, Macmillan 1974.
7 Stephen Young *ibid*.
8 *Business in Britain*, Graham Turner, Penguin 1971.
9 *Political Responsibility and Industry*, Edmund Dell, George Allen and Unwin 1973.
10 *The People*, 17 July 1970.

TWO

"New Candidates for Public Ownership"

IN 1971 THE party's approach to building an economic-industrial policy was speculative. The left fell back upon restoration work by tarting up old slogans. The right, when it did express an opinion, was inclined to slap preservation orders on the existing structure. "The objectives seems to me basically those which most Fabians have believed in for the last ten years or more", wrote Anthony Crosland.[1] He had left office as Secretary of State for Local Government and Regional Planning. It was the Heath Government which was to commence removing the tiles and allowing the interventionist rains to pour in. Benn and his colleagues, two years later, were to exploit the Conservative Government's assistance to industry and the drift towards corporatism. They called it "Heath's Spadework for Socialism".

Crosland, in providing an amorphous concept with an identifiable structure in the 'fifties, had become the architect of revisionism. Encompassed in his grand design was the argument that, contrary to traditional Marxist doctrine, the ownership of the means of production was no longer the key factor in imparting to a society its essential character. "Collectivism, private ownership or a mixed economy", he believed, "were all consistent with the widely varying degrees not only of equality but also of freedom, democracy, exploitation, class feeling, elitism, industrial democracy, planning and economic growth." [2] It was therefore possible to achieve the goal of greater equality and other desirable ends within the framework of a mixed economy, with public ownership as only one of a number of means for attaining those ends.

It was around such principles that the social democrats paraded but with quantitatively diminishing reliance upon the architect in the mid-'sixties. Richard Crossman once remarked that it was the Croslandites' air of "furious moderation" that had united them rather than any positive programme. Such activity was not apparent in Labour's early months in Opposition in 1970. Leading social democrats did carry out their own reassessment. Jenkins and Healey, and sometimes Crosland, were among those involved in private meetings to discuss the future of the party. But social democrats faced complications which had significant consequences for their approach to the shaping of Labour's programme.

Crosland's position at the end of 1970 was that he saw no analogy with the 'fifties. The evidence for this diagnosis, he told a Fabian Society meeting in November, was "a lack of ideological ferment within the party". This was certainly not the case, as we have seen. But in any event many social democrats had come to believe that Crosland had abdicated his leadership responsibilities. While it would be overstating his position to portray Crosland as the only intellectual force, the moderates in the party never found another influential theorist around whom they could rally in the dialectics with the left, apart from Roy Jenkins and the specific issue of the Common Market. Crosland's abandonment of his influential role was not sudden. His appearances, for example, at the monthly dinners of the Gaitskellites, started after Gaitskell's death in 1963, though never regular, were virtually non-existent after he became a Cabinet minister in 1965. His colleagues formed the view that they had seen him at his best as a driving force when he was a dissident on the outside track of politics. Crosland's politically debilitating insouciance did not lead to alienation within the ranks of the Parliamentary Labour Party. Between 1970 and 1974 he was in the top four in the elections to the Parliamentary Committee on three occasions. Outside the Parliamentary Party, however, the story was different. He failed on three occasions to win a seat on the party's National Executive Committee. Even the support inside the Parliamentary Party was qualified : when Jenkins resigned the deputy leadership in April 1972, Crosland flew home from a visit to Japan in the hope of finding sufficient support to get him elected to the vacancy and, automatically, to an *ex officio* seat on the National Executive. He received only 61 votes.

Those monthly dinners, at which the social democrats engaged in debates on politics in general and Labour politics in particular, were attended by former Gaitskellites such as Jenkins, Harold Lever and Bill Rodgers. The latter, a middle-

ranking minister, had already displayed his great talents as a
political organiser. He had a leading role in the Campaign for
Democratic Socialism which overthrew Labour's unilateral
nuclear disarmament commitment in 1960. Rodgers was the
Mikardo of the right : tactician, organiser, political wheeler-
dealer. At the end of 1970 he, along with others, rightly thought
that the first great challenge to the resources of the social
democrats would come over the application of Britain for membership of the European Economic Community. The Conservatives had a manifesto commitment to seek terms for entry.
Jenkins was to lead the social democrats' pro-market campaign
and Rodgers was a leading participant. But the complications
Rodgers encountered absorbed most of his organisational
talents. Not all social democrats, he discovered, were prepared
to embark upon a do-or-die struggle within the party on the
issue.

When not organising, Rodgers was investigating Government relations within industry, including the policies pursued
by the Labour Government. In 1971–72 he was chairman of
a sub-committee of the all-party House of Commons Expenditure Committee. He had been persuaded to join by another
social democrat MP, Dr David Owen. Rodgers was elected
chairman and the committee agreed they should examine
Public Money in the Private Sector. It was this area which was
to provide ideological conflict inside the party. Also Rodgers
was partly responsible for assisting the political career of a
young economist who was later to be the *bête noire* of the
social democrats. He brought on to the committee as a specialist
adviser Stuart Holland, who had been in Wilson's political
office in 1967–68. Rodgers had met him at an Oxford Seminar,
organised by *Socialist Commentary*, monthly journal of the
social democrats, in the summer of 1970. Rodgers was im-
pressed, an opinion he was later to revise. Today Holland is
seen as a renegade revisionist, the guru of Benn.

Rodgers, as a junior frontbench Opposition spokesman on
aviation supply, was invited to join the party's Industrial Committee in 1971, but quickly became disenchanted. Having
listened to what he considered an arid argument between
Mikardo and Dr Jeremy Bray—who had been dismissed by
Wilson as a junior minister in the Ministry of Technology for
writing a book critical of Labour Government policy—Rodgers

ignored the committee and concentrated on his two main pre-occupations. Bearing in mind his well-tuned political antennae and in-fighting instinct, it remains an open question whether the left would have been as successful if Rodgers had been fully operational and in a position to sound warnings. Bray, for his part, only served on the committee for one year. Its chairman, John Chalmers, a trade union member of the National Executive, found his lengthy and complicated expositions, unrelieved by a sense of humour, tedious and boring.

But before embarking on analysis of policy-making in 1971, reference must be made to the principal political dramas that dominated the year. The actions of the Conservative Government provoked reactions inside the Labour Opposition. Heath's determination to force through the Industrial Relations Bill helped more than anything else to stitch together the torn fabric of the Labour movement. He brought together the party, the Parliamentary Labour Party and the trade unions as a collective force, though the unions still harboured their suspicions. Vic Feather, then general secretary of the TUC, had been approached informally by Benn on a joint publicity campaign when they had met during a BBC "Any Questions" programme in November 1970. Benn, as the new chairman of the party's publicity committee, explained that he and some of his colleagues were working on the party campaign strategy over the next few months. With the possibility of an early general election, that might be fought on the trade union question or on Europe, they had to give some thought to the way in which the party would handle the matter. Benn said he had been authorised by the National Executive to approach the unions to see what assistance the party could give them in the campaign against the Bill.

Union leaders, however, were by no means unconditionally delighted at such an offer. Some of them were particularly annoyed at an invitation to attend a meeting of the party's publicity committee which had on the agenda a proposal "to consider the necessity for trade unions to take action to publicise themselves in a more favourable light". The unions felt they could look after themselves. " ... I think it a bit bloody cheeky," Feather wrote to a colleague, "if the party wants to put its nose into our affairs there might have been more

consultation." Feather suspected the "whizz-kid hand" of Benn.
The item was suitably amended. The TUC and the party,
nonetheless, co-operated in the challenge to the Bill. Michael
Foot afterwards wrote: "There is pleasure and instruction to
be drawn from the irony that the anti-trade union measure
which was to provide the instrument for destroying the Labour
movement has in fact supplied the lever for reforging its unity
and its chances of recovery." [3]

But in 1971 trade union leaders were hesitant about becoming
too involved with Labour politicians on policy matters. For
one thing, they were not sure what would best serve their
interests: dealings with shadow ministers or the National
Executive. Party and trade union leaders formed a Liaison
Committee to fight the legislation and discuss the possibilities
of an alternative, but it only met on three occasions in 1971:
January, March and July. (At a different level, TUC representatives assisted the parliamentary team, led by Barbara
Castle, in the day-to-day opposition to the Bill.) The TUC was
in no mood to co-operate in the Labour leaders' obvious desire
to broaden the scope of the discussions. At the July meeting,
Douglas Houghton, chairman of the Parliamentary Labour
Party, made a brave but abortive attempt. It is on record that
he suggested it was essential to ensure that in the next Labour
Government the trade unions would underwrite the actions of
that Government. He pointed out at the meeting that there
was no policy for prices and incomes or for industrial relations.
The TUC representatives—Vic Feather, Jack Jones, general
secretary of the Transport and General Workers Union, and
Alf (now Lord) Allen, President of the Union of Shop, Distributive and Allied Workers—were not pleased. The Labour side,
which included Wilson and Callaghan, were told sharply that
it was equally important that leaders of the Labour Party in
Parliament should recognise that the next Labour Government
had to take notice of what the TUC and the trade union
movement were telling them.

Nothing illustrates more graphically the long haul that faced
Labour if it was to get the agreement of the TUC on a shared
policy at the next general election. The July meeting was not
without interest in another respect. At the first two meetings
the composition was said to be representatives from the Parlia-

mentary Party and the TUC; it was only at the July meeting that the National Executive was given independent status. It was another indication that the TUC was only interested at that stage in co-operation to fight the Bill, particularly in Parliament.

Labour's unity over the Bill, however, was devastated by Heath's other measure : the application for Britain's membership of the Common Market. The consequences of Heath's initiative split the party down the middle to a degree not seen since the intestine battles over German rearmament and unilateral nuclear disarmament. Foot, for one, became a passionate anti-marketeer, propelled by the belief that entry would be a threat to parliamentary democracy and the chances of achieving a socialist Britain. He was prepared to press his passion further than most on the left : as a member of the Shadow Cabinet in 1973, he would even sacrifice, as an expedient, some of the left's proposals on state interventionism—on the grounds they could damage Labour's election chances—if it would facilitate the return of a Labour Government to take Britain out of the European Community. His earlier demands for a "strong shift leftwards" had to be trimmed in order to achieve the short-term, over-riding objective.

In the event his strategy was to come unstuck. These two issues—the inter-party struggle over the Industrial Relations Bill and the intra-party battle over the Common Market—dominated the political stage in 1971. But beneath the floorboards the party's policy committees began their work to prepare Labour's alternative programme. In this the Conservative Government was to prove more than helpful.

The Government's declared policy to "hive off" some of the profitable sectors of the nationalised industries brought out the Labour Party's atavistic instincts, but the fury it provoked was short-lived in some instances. Pragmatism overtook even the greatest proponents of socialist principles. The Labour movement reacted fiercely at the Tories' decision to create a second force airline at the expense of BOAC and BEA. Trade unions involved pressed the party for regular meetings to fight a rear-guard action. But as the trade union leaders saw union recruitment rise at Gatwick Airport, home of the private enterprise airline, their ardour subsided. Nevertheless it did not stop

Roy Mason, the Opposition spokesman, announcing in Parliament that the second force airline would be handed back to BOAC.*

Other Government actions had more lasting political implications. Faced with economic realities, the Conservatives found they could not allow all the so-called "lame ducks" to drown. The rescue of Rolls-Royce was a major demonstration of this policy reversal. "Interventionism" became, if not fashionable, at least politically respectable. The argument no longer rested on a question of principle but of degree. But this reversal of policy had the effect, in the intra-party tensions, of injecting a sense of caution among the social democrats. "The Labour Party will be very unwise if it is content to mock Tory performances and not do some hard thinking on the lessons involved for us all in this", wrote Harold Lever, a wealthy shadow minister who had excellent City connections that were useful to a Labour Government. Lever continued : "Clearly a more general disposition to favour state intervention can be as dangerous and damaging as the Tories' explicit hostility to it. We must evolve clear-cut and intelligible guidelines and principles to decide where and to what extent State intervention is justified." [4]

Lever argued that the party must evolve the means "within Government itself" to enable proper judgments to be made upon those questions. The alternative "is *ad hoc* intervention whose nature and extent are determined by the belly reactions or contacts of ministers". Was this a comment on Benn's tenancy of MinTech? Lever had been a junior minister at Millbank Towers. However, this was not the main burden of his message. He concluded : "The Rolls-Royce story highlights the Tory failure in Opposition to grapple with the real problems of our time. They evolved a number of doctrinal irrelevances pleasing the faithful but a hindrance to achievement in Government. We mustn't be their mirror image." In other words, policies, like knowledge, could be dangerous. Lever was to play a major part in circumventing those evolved by the left when he returned as a Cabinet minister and financial adviser to Wilson in the next Labour Administration.

Lever was not alone in his view. One principle upon which

* At the time of writing the Government has yet to honour this commitment.

most social democrats are agreed is that the pursuit of power—
not necessarily for personal ambition and advancement but for
social justice under a Labour Government—can be handi-
capped by having to carry too many manifesto commitments.
Moreover, it can be difficult and embarrassing for an incoming
Government to have raised the electorate's aspirations only to
find itself unable to fulfil the pledges. This was and remained
the view, for example, of Crosland. At the beginning of 1971 he
felt there was no need for "some great shift of direction".[5] This
empirical approach to politics determined the left to overthrow
the revisionists' dominance on the party's National Executive.
They did not share the social democrats' belief that only a clear
affirmation of agreed ideals was needed to reshape policies.
What were those ideals? Crosland's view was that they were
all fundamentally related to ways of distributing the country's
wealth and resources. Certainly he did not believe in the need
for fundamental rethinking or a mass of new policies. He
explained later: "Indeed, I think the constant call for new
policies or dramatic new statements is a sign of a rather
hysterical reaction to temporary electoral unpopularity." [6]

But this evocation of the revisionists' spirit raised more problems than it solved. How did governments achieve growth in
both wealth and resources? How could growth be achieved
without recreating the post-war dilemmas of inflation and
balance of payments' crises? And how was a future Labour
Government to achieve an enduring relationship with the trade
unions if they obdurately stood by the principle of free collective bargaining and abjured a prices and incomes policy? At
an industrial conference in New York in May 1971, Wilson
attempted to lay down the conditions for a solution: " . . . a
voluntary compact between Government and industry—both
sides of industry—in which Government can go forward boldly
with economic policies necessary to increase production, know-
ing that this need not lead to inflation so long as it could count
on industrial co-operation and restraint." Wilson and Callaghan, more than most, knew that eventually a deal would have
to be struck with the trade unions, but they also knew that
1971 was not the right time. Meanwhile the policy committees
had begun the foundations of the new programme.

The terms of reference of the policy-making committees, as
we saw in the last chapter, were sorted out by the end of 1970.

At the back of everyone's mind was the knowledge that some form of incomes and prices policy was essential, but the main strategy on this and its timing was left to the shadow ministers. The Shadow Cabinet, at a meeting on 17 January 1971, had agreed there should be discussion with the TUC about its latest economic document, but primarily the purpose was to explore the possibilities of ever reaching a joint policy on prices and incomes. We know that little advance was made during the course of the year. The policy committees started work in the spring of 1971, with the Industrial Committee, overlapping slightly with the Financial and Economic Committee, chaired by Jenkins. Mikardo was the only National Executive member to sit on both committees; in total, he sat on six policy committes in 1971, twice as many as any other Executive member. However, this ubiquity was less to do with organisational intrigue than with his role as chairman of the party that year. Mikardo found it useful as a means of witnessing how the social democrats were evolving their own stratagem, if any.

The original prospectus for the Industrial Committee was : industrial relations, state subsidies in the private sector, multi-national corporations, consumer power, the drug industry, the aircraft industry, and the motor car industry. Transport House staff, who drew up the list, were not only eager to encourage a left wing assessment after six frustrating years of Labour in office but were also ambitious apparatchiks. The head of the home research staff, Terry Pitt, helped steer the party on its leftward course. A former metallurgist, he had a sharp instinct for detecting hair-line cracks in the party. Sympathetic to the democratic socialist faction, he used his position as Research Secretary to influence the membership of the committees, the appointment of chairmen and the presentation of background papers. Legitimate advantage was taken of the procedure which allowed research staff to put before a committee a programme of work before the chairman had been elected at the inaugural meeting. Outline proposals before a committee were rarely challenged, although pressure of time enforced modifications. In April 1971, in consultation with some of the Industrial Committee members, the staff presented an obviously over-ambitious set of areas for study. To illustrate the momentum that was building up within the party they are set out below in detail.

The Public Sector The "philosophy" objectives and methods of operation of public enterprise; the relative importance of criteria such as the efficiency of the particular enterprise; the needs of the national economy; the fulfilment of certain social goals; pricing policies and the self-financing of investment, and its redistributive effects via public capital accumulation; the role of the consumer and industrial democracy.

New candidates for Public Ownership The drug industry; the aircraft industry; computers; insurance; motors. " . . . all have been mentioned in recent policy statements or discussion documents as worthy of investigation with a view to extending the frontiers of public ownership", but "what criteria are relevant here—efficiency by redistribution, or industrial democracy or certain social objectives?"

Planning and Interventionism Limitations and opportunities of both, in seeking efficiency and/or accountability, were worthy of study. The need for the co-ordination of statutory agencies, old and new, especially in the fields of investment, monopolies, prices and manpower planning, and for a comprehensive overhaul of *company law* geared to the requirements of the community and the workers. Opportunity of "attacking corporate secrecy, of ensuring greater accountability (e.g. public nominees on boards of all large companies) and a chance to provide additional legislative support to the concept of industrial democracy".

Multi-national corporations The need to understand the multi-national corporations and to make them socially accountable, not least in the field of investment and manpower planning.

Consumer Protection " . . . do we need a much tougher attitude altogether in this field, with a new comprehensive Consumer Protective (*sic*) Act and a new powerful protection body, independent of Government departments?"

State Holding Company This was necessary because of "The demise of the Industrial Reorganisation Corporation and the increasing need for a focus for stimulating new enterprises in the regions, co-ordinating the smaller public enterprises and as a possible 'reservoir' of miscellaneous equity shares obtained by the state in one way or another."

Presented with such an ideological *à la carte* menu, Harold Lever, if he had sat on the committee, would no doubt have suffered an attack of doctrinal dyspepsia. Crosland was co-opted on to the Committee and his digestion was not improved, but by the end of the three years most of the areas outlined in the paper were covered in the committee's studies. While the paper itself was not a commitment, it did set out a philosophy of the need for greater Governmental interference in vast and multifarious areas of British economic and industrial life. The first meeting of the Industrial Sub-Committee was held in the House of Commons on 28 April 1971. It was at this meeting that full employment and industrial policy were added to the list of studies and given priority. Unemployment in Great Britain was then 730,000 (including school-leavers and adult students, and not seasonally adjusted), a politically embarrassing figure for the period. Industrial relations was incorporated in the area of industrial and manpower policies.

We shall see how this priority enabled the committee to get a toe-hold in controlling economic policy and wresting it from the hands of the Financial and Economic Committee. No progress was made in 1971 in the complex field of industrial democracy. Part of the reason for this was the absence of any clamour from the trade unions. As one of the committee members put it to the author later: "Jack Jones saw industrial democracy at that time as strengthened plant bargaining and that was the end of it." When the committee came to present its final report to the full National Executive in September it was seen that the policy on industrial democracy had not been advanced from the position adopted four years earlier. Referring to a party document, published in 1967, the report said the basic approach was that workers should be involved in an ever-widening range of decisions within management and should do so on the basis of a "single channel of representation, one which did not hinge upon any distinction between subjects appropriate for bargaining and those appropriate for consultation". The document argued that this involvement must be closely identified with trade union organisation and representation. The emphasis was thus on the channel of *collective bargaining* and the objective was seen as extending the subject matter of collective bargaining to the point of developing within each enterprise a continuous system of joint determination.

After this lengthy quotation the Labour Party could only add the following observation in its report to the conference: "In our proposals to follow the repeal of the Tory Industrial

Relations Act, we shall clearly bear these recommendations very much in mind. Do they, however, go far enough? The straightforward bargaining approach does tend to rely on the willingness of workers to continually defend each and every advance made : the legal powers and initiative will still lie heavily with the management." At the annual conference in October the National Executive readily accepted a motion, from the National Union of Public Employees, calling for a joint NEC–TUC special sub-committee to formulate policy. Labour favoured an extension of industrial democracy; securing a collective approach, however, was a different matter.

Before the May meeting of the Industrial Committee there had been joint discussions between the Shadow Cabinet and the National Executive, on 16 and 17 May, at the Great Western Royal Hotel, Paddington, London. There was considerable unanimity on industrial policy at the meeting, principally because the issue of prices and incomes policy was sidestepped. Callaghan explained that prices and incomes would be put in the context of the total policies a Labour Government would have to follow. It would, he said, be part of a social compact that would have to be made. He added : "A compact of the kind envisaged by the Shadow Cabinet would involve concessions from both politicians and trade unions." Wilson, at the same meeting, also expressed the view that the party could have all the policy committees it liked in Opposition, but it was still liable to be overtaken by international financial and monetary events which prevented the party from doing what it intended. But he did add that more would have to be done to get on top of the "casino aspects" of the economy, like the banks and the Stock Exchange.[7]

Callaghan informed the press after the meeting : "We shall certainly want to look at whether the City institutions as they at present exist best serve the interests of the country." The left qualified their delight with the knowledge that Wilson and Callaghan would not be prepared to investigate very far. In 1970, when Mikardo was chairman of the Commons Select Committee on Nationalised Industries, the committee had produced a report criticising the management of the Bank of England. Callaghan said the Financial and Economic Sub-Committee would decide what to do but the problem did not rest with that social democrat-dominated committee for long, principally because no urgency was shown to do any preparatory work. If there had been, it probably could have saved Tom Bradley, a former Parliamentary private secretary to Jenkins, from the rough ride he experienced at the annual conference.

Bradley, an active moderate member of the National Executive, was put up by his colleagues to oppose a motion from the Hammersmith constituency Labour Party demanding that the next party election manifesto should "include proposals to nationalise all banking and insurance companies". It called upon the NEC to set up a working party to present proposals to the 1972 annual conference "for the public ownership of all the banks, insurance companies and building societies". It was more than chance that the motion should come from Hammersmith. The constituency party delegate, Jo Richardson, was not only secretary to Mikardo, but secretary to the *Tribune* group of Labour MPs. The motion, if carried, would take control of the subject away from the Financial and Economic Committee.

Bradley, who was also President of the Transport and Salaried Staffs Association, argued amid interruptions that the issue was already having active and detailed consideration by specialist sub-committees. "Conference must learn to draw a distinction between re-acquiring public assets which have been hived off and entering into new fields of public ownership", he declared above the rowdy reception he was receiving. The irony was not lost when Mikardo, who was in the chair, had to come to Bradley's aid after he had provoked further interruptions by remarking " . . . we have not yet become a confiscatory party". Bradley went on to add, in an attempt to win back the majority of the conference, that there was an adequacy or inadequacy of the various tools by which Governments exerted pressure on the system—changes in bank rate, calls for special deposits, or traditional open market operations; these were now being examined by a committee with a view to advising either on new controls or the introduction of full-scale public ownership, if it was thought necessary. Conference rejected his appeal for remission of the motion by 3,519,000 to 2,104,000. The executive was tied to setting up a study group which was to include Mikardo and Lever.

Bradley, in fact, was not correct in saying the issues were

being examined at the present time. The Finance and Economic Committee only had four meetings in the 1971 period up to the party conference and most of these were spent examining taxation policy and papers on the social services and the redistribution of wealth. Jenkins, as chairman, was not keen on holding meetings, as other committee members discovered. As Shadow Chancellor of the Exchequer, he firmly believed that economic policy making should be left to him in consultation with his shadow cabinet colleagues. He had already formed his own group of financial and economic advisers, an indication of his disdain at the quality and expertise to be found in the party organisation.

By November the left had plotted to unseat him as chairman, but failed, largely through the intervention of Callaghan. At the first attempt, with Benn proposing Mikardo and Shirley Williams nominating Jenkins, there was a tied vote inside the committee. Benn (together with Pitt, who had no voting powers) turned up a minute late at the reconvened meeting the following week and saw, to his astonishment, Callaghan occupying the chairman's seat. Callaghan admonished Benn for being late, and then informed him that voting had taken place and Jenkins had been re-elected as chairman. Mikardo was in the room, out-manoeuvred and looking abashed.

Jenkins' disdain for the party's policy making machinery was shared by many of his fellow social democrats, not least Crosland who voiced his opinion openly. In September 1971, he turned a press conference on housing at the Fabian Society's London headquarters into a vehicle for an attack on established procedures : "No one can say the party is in sight of formulating a better set of policies than we had in June 1970, when we were dismissed from office." The comment did not improve relations with his colleagues on the Industrial Policy Committee. He suggested that a new centre for Labour Party research might be able to tap resources such as foundations and trusts which at present were not available to the party's research department at Transport House. More importantly, he suggested that after the party's annual conference not more than six members of the Shadow Cabinet and the National Executive Committee should be deputed as a policy-making and steering committee to prepare for Labour's return to power. They should have the task of surveying the whole field of policy and deciding the critical areas in which Labour needed major policies and, above all, deciding where Labour needed new policies. His proposed centre could be headed by one of the younger Labour MPs.

This challenge to Transport House was too much for Pitt and his equally ambitious and social democratic colleague, Tom McNally, secretary of the party's international department. Protesting in the *Guardian*, they wrote : "The truth is that Tony Crosland is talking about research when he should be talking about policy-making; he is implying the absence of data when the real issue is political will." In other words, Crosland should be devoting his time to the work of the committees on which he was sitting rather than holding press conferences to make carping criticisms of the party's research facilities. While an influential participant in the regional and local government Crosland was an irregular attender at the Industrial Committee and meetings in the 1971 period, his one real opportunity of influencing a crucial area of policy.

There was little contact at the time between the various policy-making committees, and therefore Mikardo's multi-membership role was useful, if only on an informal basis. In July, within two months of the Shadow Cabinet–National Executive Committee joint conference, the Industrial Committee moved into the area of the economy without fear of challenge from Jenkins and his Financial and Economic Committee. After the joint conference the Industrial Committee agreed at its May meeting that they should produce a major paper on *Unemployment and Manpower Planning*. "We were fully conscious of the Labour Government's failure", a committee member told the author. It was actually stated inside the committee that as each area of its work was considered, adequate attention would have to be given to "where Labour went wrong" in that particular field of policy.

Barbara Castle, who had left office as Secretary of State for Employment, found her policies being challenged. Union members rejected her view that they, the unions, were the biggest obstacle to a major extension of retraining facilities. She had some support from two economists, Derek Robinson and Bill McCarthy, on this issue. Both were from working-class backgrounds and had worked with Barbara Castle at the

Department. Nonetheless, they were critical of the Government's failure to get a co-ordinated manpower policy. Robinson was a specialist in inflation and prices policy and had worked for the Organisation for Economic Co-operation and Development. In 1973, after consultation with some of his Labour colleagues, he accepted the post as vice-chairman of the Conservative Government's Pay Board and had to resign from the committee.

Robinson and one or two other committee members hoped that the debate on price controls would open up discussions on the need for an incomes policy, but they had little success.* McCarthy, from Nuffield College, had established his reputation when research secretary to the Donovan Commission on the Trade Unions and Employers' Organisations by producing a brilliant study on shop stewards. The other two economists on the committee were Professor Ken Alexander, of Strathclyde University, who had close associations with the Labour Party and trade unions in Scotland, and Richard Pryke, from Liverpool University, who had made a special study of nationalised industries. All four academics were interventionists to varying degrees.

John Chalmers, the chairman and number two in the hierarchy of the Amalgamated Society of Boilermakers, was a right winger with a leftish voting pattern because of his union's policies. Chalmers made few enemies but, on the other hand, he was never seen as a campaigning or effective chairman. His pliability served the purpose of the left until it was decided he should be removed from the chairmanship; that was in December 1972, when Benn was voted into the chair (although he was absent when the vote was taken). One of the important decisions taken at the May meeting was an agreement to hold a "conference of experts" in the fields relevant to the committee's work. This was planned to take place as soon as possible after the October annual conference. It was held in February 1972 at the Bonnington Hotel, London, and provided the foundation for the leftward swing in Labour's approach to economic and industrial policies.

The committee was involved in long debates over the problems

---

* It was Robinson's private briefing to industrial correspondents on the Board's report on mineworkers' pay relativities that Heath partly blamed for the Conservatives' defeat in the February 1974 general election.

of price control and its inevitable link to a viable incomes policy, acceptable by the unions. The hope was that by providing a credible system which would hold down price increases, and thus inflation, the unions would more readily co-operate in formulating an incomes policy, as expressed in the document presented to conference : "Once such an aggressive and comprehensive policy on prices was under way, the broad 'incomes' side of the equation could become a good deal more manageable." A future Labour Government, it said, "would seek to support this prices policy with restraints on rents, rates, by fair taxation and social policies, and by measures designed to redistribute income and wealth".

The overture to the unions was obvious, but when examined the proposals were no more than a declaration of intent. An Early Warning System needed to be re-established : on so-called "market power" the next Labour Government would "seek" to establish machinery "something" along the lines of Labour's proposed Commission for Industry and Manpower, and again "seek" to establish "some kind" of permanent but flexible system of price controls. These would operate at the point of production but would be concentrated on a select list of key products and services.

The extreme note of caution running through the price control proposals was a reflection of the debate inside the Industrial Committee. There was anxiety that the party should not be setting up an army of bureaucrats to police prices. An illustration of the experience of the French Office of Price Control was given to the committee : during the dispute with butchers over the price of beef the Office had carried out 500,000 inspections in nine months of 1964. In the end, the party was to propose the formation of a prices inspectorate on a less grandiose scale. The possibilities were examined by Robinson in a paper he submitted to the Bonnington Hotel "conference of experts".

In 1971 it was apparent that many in the party were not confident of evolving a policy that would win the support of the unions. The efforts by shadow ministers to open up discussions with the TUC on an approach to an incomes policy had not been very fruitful. At one meeting, two months before the party conference, Barbara Castle had suggested to the unions that they might discuss the Conservative Government's Code of Industrial Practice. Vic Feather refused. Labour politicians then attempted to give the initiative to the unions; the TUC, it was suggested, should make definite proposals so that they could be considered by the party. The TUC showed extreme reluctance and produced nothing before the annual party conference.

At this stage there were two approaches to an incomes policy. The first was the proposal that it was essential for the party to construct a deal on wages independently of other policy commitments. The second, and the one adopted by the party, was that an incomes policy should emerge from the unions after a Labour Government had undertaken a whole set of social and economic reforms. These would include policies for rapid growth and full employment, enlargement of the public sector, a wealth tax, and the repeal of the Industrial Relations Bill. It was the adoption of this second approach that persuaded the big unions—Transport and General Workers Union and the Amalgamated Union of Engineering Workers—to vote for the economic strategy document at the annual conference.

However, this is anticipating events. By the time of the June meeting of the Industrial Policy Committee there was pressure on the committee from the National Executive to prepare a draft document which could be presented to the annual conference. This, of course, would have to be approved by the full executive. Work began in earnest but the committee was running into difficulties. How was it possible to produce policies on the regeneration of the regions, manpower forecasting, and an approach to price controls in isolation from economic policy? The committee agreed it should recommend to the National Executive that a background paper be produced on unemployment and *economic strategy* (author's italics). It was the turning point politically.

A committee member said later that none of the social democrats were conscious at the time of a calculated manoeuvre by the left; indeed, there was unanimous agreement that economic strategy had to be considered by the Industrial Committee. Nevertheless they were aware that the initiative had been stolen from the right wing-oriented Jenkins committee. When Barbara Castle introduced the final document, *Economic Strategy, Growth and Unemployment*, at the party conference her sniping comment at Jenkins was not readily appreciated: "I also want to pay tribute to the lads from Transport House, Members of Parliament, yes, Clive Jenkins and the trade unionists, and the industrial policy experts, who helped us to try to hack out some solutions, while those esoteric chaps in the finance and economic policy group came limping along."

It was during the June meeting that the Industrial Committee bulldozed one of the psychological barriers towards a fresh approach to economic strategy, although it was the social democrats on the committee who were the driving force. A paper on "unemployment" raised the problems of the balance of payments and inflation : "To ensure that the balance of payments does not again become a major obstacle of growth, therefore, direct action will be needed, as necessary, on our terms of trade." This meant "a deliberate policy of adjusting the parity of the pound to accord with the basic facts of our trade balance, instead, as in the past, of waiting for a massive balance of payments crisis to force change upon us". The idea of abandoning the rigidities of a fixed exchange rate was broached. One year later, Anthony Barber, as Conservative Chancellor of the Exchequer, allowed the pound to float against other foreign currencies : devaluation by another name.

In 1971 such a proposition was not universally accepted by politicians, including some Labour leaders. Crosland was one of few to challenge the orthodoxy early on. In his Fabian tract he stressed a "willingness to make timely adjustments to the parity whenever the alternative would be serious deflation". Inside the Industrial Committee, one prominent right wing MP, Edmund Dell, a taciturn, highly intelligent Lancastrian whose abilities as a minister were much admired by Wilson, supported the proposal. Mikardo, however, was among the opponents subscribing to the orthodox view that the disadvantages outweighed the advantages. It directly hit the living standards of the workers. His view was that the balance of payments problem could best be overcome by reducing costs of exports through restructuring industry and increasing its efficiency. It was a familiar argument. In the first half of 1971 few Labour leaders were prepared to open up a public debate on the subject.

The reasons were numerous : Labour should not be portrayed as the party of devaluation and there was the risk of being attacked by the Government for talking down sterling.

An office paper produced in July mirrored the discussion inside the Industrial Committee : "In the context of a socialist plan for growth, however, this policy involves a number of serious difficulties." A parity change could involve changes in the distribution of real income whilst the price of imports is increased. It also involved problems concerning demand management and taxes "since room must be made in the economy for import substitution and additional exports". Most important of all, "it involves the very real danger of adding a dangerous twist to price inflation—the second of our major obstacles to growth".

There was an indication of these backroom hesitations when the document went before annual conference. Three options were given : " . . . there seems to us [the National Executive] only a very small number of ways in which to protect the country's payments position. First, the use of direct controls to curb or prevent any further rise in imports; second, attempts to obtain favourable changes elsewhere in the balance of payments, such as in capital flows; or third, to act directly to improve the competitiveness and profitability of our exports by changing the exchange value of the pound." The document then went on to talk about "an orderly re-alignment to our exchange rate", a carefully-worded phrase which did not, however, prevent it being called a "dirty float", with the parity of the pound fluctuating with little control. Essentially, the challenge to financial orthodoxy was no more than a proposal, a possible fiscal device. Jenkins' views at conference were interesting : "We should never again allow ourselves to be a prisoner of a rigid, over-valued exchange rate, and a currency which is a national status symbol and not an instrument of economic management", he told delegates, but he went on to warn : "We should not swing away from this into thinking that an easy series of devaluations, or a chaotic world monetary system, are the answer to our problems."

The Conservative Government's decision to scrap some of the machinery for intervention in the economy—the Prices and Incomes Board, the Industrial Reorganisation Corporation —served as a stimulant at the July meeting of the Industrial Committee. There was a general recognition that Labour had the opportunity of "starting from scratch" when considering fresh approaches. There was also strong emphasis on the fact that the possibility of entering the European Community would have to be taken into account when working out various aspects of Labour's strategy. The need to provide regions with a more flexible and discretionary approach to employment policies was felt to be important. Outside the committee the anti-marketeers played strongly upon the theme that British membership would prohibit the implementation of Labour's policies towards the regions.

None of the committee disagreed over the need for a state holding company : the arguments that developed were over its function and purpose. It was these arguments that the left were to win, much to the annoyance of Wilson, Callaghan, Healey and other shadow ministers. The Industrial Committee continued their discussions on the impact of Britain's membership of the EEC at a second meeting in July. Membership, it was thought, was another reason for expanding public ownership. It was felt that public ownership could well become the main reason for stimulating further economic activity in the regions.

By the September meeting, when their draft document *Economic Strategy, Growth and Unemployment* was submitted to the National Executive, committee members were considering extending the areas of public ownership. Although it was not finalised, there was a general agreement that the role and structure of public ownership should be discussed at the "conference of experts". The document spoke of a state holding company "backed by considerable funds ... For what has been lacking in past regional policies is a nucleus of management and entrepreneurial skills able not only to build up new production and service facilities, but to gear these to the markets that are available, and to seize new opportunities for expansion as these arise. With a State Holding Company these opportunities could be taken up, if necessary, by the acquisition of existing companies—and thus their skills, markets and facilities— or through joint ventures with existing firms in the private sector."

This was very much on the lines put forward in 1969 and supported by people such as Dell, but to allay any suspicions that a detour was being made around nationalisation the document stated that "Labour's commitment to public ownership remains as strong as ever". The methods of extending its frontiers, however, were likely to be more diverse than in the past.

There would still be cases where the outright nationalisation of a whole industry, or the bulk of it, would be appropriate. And there were a number of sectors in the economy which were ripe for a "major element" of public ownership. The document continued : "But given our diverse objectives in extending public ownership, we will be much more ready whenever necessary in the future, to bring individual companies into the public sector, as the Tories did with Rolls-Royce."

This declaration was open to countless interpretations. It was meant to be because by this means the policy statement could appeal to all sections of the party. The majority of the Labour leadership did not want to offer up hostages to fortune. The left had made a start but they had yet to achieve the binding commitments they sought. Judith Hart, a left wing member of the National Executive, wrote two months before annual conference that a Labour Government would succeed only if it consciously shifted the balance in favour of the unions and the people by substantially enlarging the public ownership of national resources.[8] It would have to give itself power to direct the economy and to redistribute wealth and incomes. "It is for this reason", she said, "that public ownership has again become central to Labour's economic and social policies."

Judith Hart was no recent convert to the need for an extension of public ownership. Like many of her close colleagues, the enemies she made were seen as milestones on the way to winning the argument. Although Judith Hart did not know it at the time, she was to become chairman of the Public Sector Group which was to challenge radically the consensus Keynesian approach to economic management. Her comments had been partly a response to the resolutions on the 1971 conference agenda which showed that over seventy had been tabled by constituencies and trade unions demanding the extension or restoration of public ownership. Many called on the next Labour Government to renationalise, without compensation, the profitable sectors of publicly owned industries that had been "hived off" to private ownership by the Conservative Government. The National Executive had in fact already committed itself to this policy earlier in the year, although it was to provide trouble later on. The conference agenda undoubtedly reflected the upsurge of left wing feeling in the constituency parties. The *Tribune* Group of MPs had not only been active in their own constituencies but elsewhere as well. The Group had issued a statement in September demanding that the stranglehold of the Treasury must be broken and the Bank of England be "truly subordinate" to the Government; they wanted substantial public ownership with the establishment of new enterprises. Conference debated four composite motions expressing these views. With the blessing of the majority on the National Executive all were approved by delegates on a show of hands.

References

1 *A Social Democratic Britain*, Anthony Crosland, Tract 404, Fabian Society 1971.
2 *Socialism Now*, Crosland, Jonathan Cape 1974.
3 Foreword to *The Class Struggle in Parliament*, Eric Heffer, Gollancz 1973.
4 *Lame Ducks Home to Roost*, Harold Lever, *New Statesman*, February 1971.
5 *A Social Democratic Britain*.
6 *Socialism Now*.
7 *Guardian*, 17 May 1971.
8 *Morning Star*, 3 August 1971.

THREE

The Year of Chairman Benn

ANTHONY WEDGWOOD BENN became chairman of the party at the 1971 annual conference on the well-established principle of Buggin's turn. Benn had been a member of the National Executive since 1959, apart from a lapse of one year. This was in 1960 when he resigned because of Gaitskell's refusal to accept the conference's majority decision on unilateral nuclear disarmament, a gesture he later regretted but at least it illustrates a certain consistency over decisions taken democratically by the party. Benn made great use of his year as chairman, annoying the social democrats by taking an unchairman-like partisan line. He was not so much the master-builder of the new interventionist policies as the enthusiastic entrepreneur, the sympathetic speculator. He encouraged fresh ideas whereas other senior Labour politicians approached them with caution, if not suspicion. While Benn naturally made contributions—his persistence over a referendum on the European Community was his greatest success, particularly infuriating to the pro-marketeers—it was in his second role that his presence was of at least equal importance.

The year of his chairmanship was the year that the real foundations for Labour's policy were laid down. He was, therefore, in an advantageous position to aid and abet those who, like him, desired to push the party further to the left. He was sympathetic to those with proposals which appeared to help resolve the dilemma facing the party as he and others saw it. Benn set about attempting to break down barriers which he felt had been erected along the channels of communication inside the movement. Not all of his exercises were well-judged for while he undoubtedly inspired the disaffected activists at grass roots level, his approach often angered his Shadow Cabinet colleagues and earned the distrust of some trade union leaders. It was one thing to articulate the dissatisfactions and unrest on the shop floor, but it was the trade union leaders who had to deal with that discontent in organised action.

Benn, as was shown, got off to a bad start with the unions over the question of publicity in the fight against the Conservatives' Industrial Relations Bill. But at the same time, he was one of the few shadow ministers who was anxious to open up immediately a dialogue with the trade unions. There was still a residual belief among some of his colleagues that *In Place of Strife* could have been successful and of lasting benefit to industry, for both management and men, if it had been accepted. It was also felt that an over-close relationship with the trade unions could be misinterpreted by the electorate and would be more to the disadvantage than advantage of the party at the next general election. Benn, however, was prepared to let his enthusiasms have a virtually free reign, often becoming their victim. Few have exploited the position of the chairmanship to better effect. By the end of his year he was seriously ranked as a potential leader of the party in the 'eighties. His cuttings files in newspaper libraries bulged beyond the aspirations of other publicity-conscious politicians, though half the references were non-complimentary.

Benn became a four-letter word which fitted comfortably into a single column in the largest type-face and symbolised the leftward shift of the party. "Bennery" was coined and assumed to be synonymous with demagoguery, populism, public ownership, syndicalism and workers' control. Yet the prejudicial approach towards his often tentative, exploratory, restless views blinded many to what he was seeking. That he was promoting his chances for the leadership need not be in doubt, but he wasn't the only one, and Wilson, after all, had openly challenged Gaitskell. Putting these personal ambitions to one side, Benn was also finding his way, examining the direction which the party should follow to maximise support in the country, turning over ideas which would get the disenchanted activists out of the pubs and back on the doorstep. Sometimes it was the wrong way: but one of the enduring questions asked by politicians is—what is the right way?

Essentially, Benn appeared to be following an old maxim of Aneurin Bevan and wondering how to put it into practice: the objective of political action is not to get power, it is to give it away. One clue to his development can be found in his

Fabian pamphlet *The New Politics*,[1] published in September 1970 shortly after the general election defeat. It was very much an exploratory essay, partly founded upon his experience at MinTech, and partly a distillation of his political thinking over a decade. His argument was that technology pressed industry, government and most forms of social organisations towards bigness, complexity, interdependence and centralisation. This, however, produced a reaction from the new citizen who was more formidable than the old because he was better off, better educated and had more access to information. Consequently, there were increasing social and political pressures for devolved power and decentralisation. Benn believed that only the Labour Party could provide the synthesis for this dialectical opposition. On the eve of becoming chairman, he told delegates at the party conference : "And therefore I say to this conference, the more rapid the technical change, the more need to protect the people, the greater the need to control the power. And I confess, frankly, having had those responsibilities, that the power I see generated by technology is too great for a Labour Cabinet to control unless the people are unleashed to control it themselves."

It is easy to see why the social democrats began to step back in alarm. This was on the path of "populism" and if the party continued in that direction it could leave itself open to every transient whim that captured public prejudice : hanging, flogging, stopping coloured immigrant student grants. Benn, of course, was not suggesting this. His record on social issues was as liberal as theirs, but where he sinned was by lowering himself down from the Parliamentary pinnacle and participating in grass roots activities, some of which were seen by his colleagues to be of a dubious nature. Before he became chairman he went to give support to the shipyard workers in their "work in" at Upper Clyde Shipbuiders ("the power of the workers that was negative has become positive") and was admonished by his Shadow Cabinet colleagues at their next meeting. The Parliamentary Party was also, initially, severely critical of the occupation. However, Wilson visited Glasgow and the shipyard workers soon after.

While chairman, Benn supported the "Pentonville Five", the dockworkers who had been imprisoned for contravening the Industrial Relations Act. Three days after this speech, the TUC called for a general strike if the men were not released. While the two events were coincidental, the men were eventually released. One of his colleagues observed during the dockers' strike : "His respect for the law is only exceeded by his respect for those who break it." Benn's final alienation from the majority of his Shadow Cabinet colleagues was his campaign for a referendum on the issue of British membership of the European Community. ". . . the whizzkid from MinTech, busily putting girdles round the earth like Puck in the play, seems to have a talent for sowing mischief and dissension wherever possible", an article complained bitterly in *Socialist Commentary*.[2]

The social democrats saw his referendum campaign as a device to embarrass colleagues such as Jenkins, Shirley Williams and Harold Lever, all fervent pro-marketeers. Benn refuted such allegations. He even invited Jenkins to his home (both live in the fashionable Holland Park area of London) to explain the rationale behind the referendum. Benn has also often quoted privately the remark of Callaghan, made inside a Shadow Cabinet meeting. "Tony has launched a rubber dinghy into which we may well all have to climb." Jenkins, for his part, had a deep distaste for Benn's brand of politics. Without mentioning names, he told a fringe meeting at the party conference in October 1972 : "What is populism? Clearly it cannot possibly be equated with democracy." Entitling his speech "Principles, not Populism", he concluded : "What I am against is talking left and acting right. I am in favour of acting as one talks."

Because of the antipathy he engendered and his effects upon policy-making, Benn's thoughts must be given closer scrutiny. These were best set out in a Fabian lecture he gave at the Caxton Hall, London, a month after he became chairman.[3] Crossman, who was sent a draft copy for his comments before it was delivered, remarked to a colleague that it was "bloody nonsense". But, in some respects, the two men were alike : they threw out ideas like a Catherine wheel, never sure where the sparks would land and what they may ignite. Encompassed in Benn's lecture were points about which he felt the instincts of the rank and file of the party and the trade union membership were right and the judgment of the Labour Government had been faulty. Spreading the doctrine of greater democracy within the party, he examined areas in which his theory could be borne out.

From 1964 to 1966, he said, the party instinctively disliked the idea of restricting economic growth to preserve the value of the pound. The Government, on the other hand, with access to inside information, thought it best to delay devaluation and put the balance of payments before growth. The movement had wanted an immediate end to the East of Suez policy so as to hasten defence cuts and release resources for use at home. The Cabinet, however, only reached its decision to end Asian military commitments after devaluation, and the process of withdrawal was not completed by the time Labour left office. The movement instinctively disliked what it took to be the Government's implied support for American policy in Vietnam, and wanted a clearer declaration of opposition to it. Ministers, however, argued that private representations were more effective and resisted appeals to speak out openly against the war. The rank and file greatly resented the prescription charges reimposed in the devaluation cuts, and were not convinced by ministerial arguments that these were an essential ingredient of the economic success the Government sought. The Labour Cabinet's industrial relations policy was still too close for it to be necessary to remind the party that the movement as a whole did not accept the way the Labour Government approached the problem. Benn's verdict upon this analysis was: "The Labour movement has often shown a surer instinct than the Parliamentary Leadership."

While Benn's senior Labour colleagues thought he was opening up a Pandora's box, the new chairman was anxious to provoke a great debate. In doing this he often over-simplified and was seen as encouraging the public belief that there were malignant forces in the Government apparatus and mass media. He told his Fabian audience that if the judgment of the Labour movement on major policy was as, or often more, right than that of Labour Cabinets with their access to the sheltered advice of their civil servants, how could the party make the movement more effective in setting the political objectives which were to be implemented by a future Labour Government? The only possible way to do so was by treating conference decisions with greater respect "because of their wisdom" instead of judging them on narrow and legalistic grounds.

Wilson, in fact, had suffered a defeat at the 1970 party conference on this issue, when he failed to get conference to remit a motion which stated, in part : "While appreciating that the Parliamentary Party must deal with matters arising in Parliament which had not been the subject of annual conference decisions, it deplores the Parliamentary Party's refusal to act on Conference decisions." Wilson set out the constitutional arguments : "A Prime Minister is responsible to the House of Commons and acts on the basis of Cabinet judgment as to what is necessary in the public interest in so far as and as long as he commands the confidence of the House of Commons, and he cannot be instructed by any authority from day to day other than Parliament." Conference carried the resolution by 3,085,000 to 2,801,000 which, it will be noted, was not a two-thirds majority.

Benn, in his Fabian lecture, appeared to be putting the counter view. He said the representative system must be made to work more democratically inside the Labour Party by making Labour leaders more accountable for their actions. "The fact is that those who exercise power in the Labour Party are not as accountable as they could or should be." Benn was not so much proposing solutions as consciously stimulating an argument inside the party, and an old one at that. Similar views had been expressed by the left at the time of the 1960 conference, the year that Benn had resigned from the Executive, but this time the arguments were being given a push by a leading figure in the Parliamentary Party. While his championing of the cause could widen the inherent divisions, Benn saw nothing fundamentally wrong in voicing his arguments. He viewed society as a mosaic of pressure groups. The historic function of a politician, he would theorise, was to capitulate to pressure; the role of the statesman was to capitulate to forces he himself had created. None of this appealed to the majority of his Parliamentary colleagues. He came a poor third (46 votes) in the deputy leadership elections in November 1971, about the time his lecture was delivered, with Jenkins (140 votes) coming top and Foot (96 votes) in second place. It was outside Parliament that he had his greatest successes, and some setbacks.

Participation 1972 was the National Executive's own idea of extending democracy within the party. In the words of Sir Harry Nicholas, party general secretary : "Policy research is one of the most important tasks to be undertaken by the Party as we prepare ourselves for the next General Election. The

NEC is anxious to give all party members the chance to comment on the issues we should study. Only in this way will our new Party Programme be comprehensive, relevant and forward looking." The quotation comes from a leaflet which the party sent to every constituency Labour Party, trades union, women's section and Young Socialist branch. Enclosed with it was a questionnaire listing twenty-four subjects which branches had to number in order of priority and also mark as "very important", "important" or "not so important". The aim, as explained by Sir Harry, was to ensure, with the help of the whole party, the biggest overhaul of party policy since *Signpost for the Sixties*. Benn was credited with promoting the idea, although in fact the participation exercise went back to 1969 when the party sent out a questionnaire on *Women and Social Security*. Terry Pitt, the head of research, copied it from a scheme launched by the Swedish Labour Party. (It is not without interest that a second questionnaire was to be sent out in 1970 with the hidden intention of bringing further pressure on Jenkins, as Chancellor of the Exchequer, to introduce a Wealth Tax, but it was overtaken by the general election in June.)

Benn and Barbara Castle, however, were the keenest supporters for *Participation 1972* inside the National Executive. Theoretically, it looked an admirable socialist act which extended democracy right down to the grass roots. Practically, it proved to be a time-consuming and not very worthwhile exercise. There were those who agreed that the methodology was wrong. How could thirty people sitting in a room reach a real consensus on the order of priority for twenty-four subjects, and on whether to add more? There were also strong opponents, particularly inside the Parliamentary Party. David Wood, Political Editor of *The Times*, was not alone in his view when he wrote : "*Participation 72* is not only an extraordinary confession of political bankruptcy. It is also a drumhead court martial of Mr Wilson and other principal members of the Cabinets he led, and consequently, as it will turn out, another seedy manoeuvre in the struggle to change the Labour leadership or put the Labour leadership in a straitjacket." And for good measure : " . . . It would be profoundly worrying but for the knowledge that when Labour comes back to power, *Participation 1972* will be seen for the bogus and highly disposable public relations exercise it is." [4]

Benn said he wanted to "see to it that as many people as possible are able to join in this policy-thinking, not only within the party, but even more broadly". By this he meant social pressure groups such as Oxfam, Shelter and Child Poverty Action. Pitt, in mock horror, remarked that "We'll be having homosexuals and Women's Lib in next". Yet at the beginning he was enthusiastic: "This is our chance to prove that our policy is made in the local parties and trade unions, and is not handed down on tablets of stone, as in other parties." He was to qualify his judgment when he gave his report to the National Executive in June. About 2,000 questionnaires were issued and Transport House received 600 replies. It was calculated that over 800 meetings were devoted to *Participation 1972* and at least 10,000 party members were directly involved in the discussion of policy. A number of groups were critical of the mechanics of the exercise. Criticism was focused on three points: the amount of time allowed to complete the questionnaire; its design; and the questions asked in the document. The compilers of the questionnaire appear to have studiously avoided the contentious issues: there was no mention in the twenty-four listed subjects of Northern Ireland, the Common Market, or incomes policy. Batley Borough Labour Party, for example, was "surprised and disappointed that no reference is made to incomes policy".

Pitt in his report said "it must be pointed out that with issues like Ulster and Europe it would not have been very illuminating to simply include them as such in the list". The report of the exercise that went before the National Executive set out a table of policy gaps identified by the respondents:

Policy Area	% Mentions
Prices and Incomes	12
Ireland	10
Land	8
Population	8
EEC	7.5
Financial Institutions	7
*Others	20

* This included discrimination against women (4 per cent), National Health Service reform—largely the abolition of private practice—(6 per cent), transport (5 per cent), immigration (2½ per cent) and fuel and energy policy (2½ per cent)—the latter coming largely from mining areas.

The one omission that was commented upon which pleased some on the left of the Executive was the 5 per cent who cited the adherence of the Parliamentary Party to conference as being of primary importance. The militant Thrapston constituency Labour Party wrote : "Unless the Parliamentary Labour Party is more directly guided by the mandates given by the Labour Party and TUC conferences, all activities, including this participation, can be considered as worthless." On average 48.6 per cent of the groups thought that economic policy was "very important" while 24.1 per cent thought it was "important" and only 12.3 per cent thought economic policy was "not as important". In the field of social policy 48.7 per cent of the questionnaire identified this as a "very important" policy area. The same policy area was seen as being "important" by 31.3 per cent of the groups and only 16.6 per cent saw social policy as being "not so important". In foreign affairs this general pattern was reversed. Only 20.3 per cent thought foreign affairs was "very important", 33.9 per cent as "important" and 43.1 per cent as "not so important".

When Transport House staff put the broad field of economic policy under the microscope it appeared that four out of five participants thought that the problems of unemployment, redundancy, retraining, etc. (summarised in the questionnaire as "Manpower policies and Unemployment") were "very important", but only one in five was prepared to give the same degree of importance to international trade, monetary reform, multilateral trade, and foreign investment ("The International Economy, Trade and Sterling"). Similarly only 25 per cent thought that the cheap food policy, formerly preferred by the Labour Party to the Tories' import levy system, was a "very important" policy field. This must have been somewhat of a setback for the anti-marketeers, their prime target of attack being the Common Agricultural Policy. Disparities of the same magnitude could be seen in the area of social policy. For instance, less than 15 per cent of the groups thought that the position of the consumer *vis-à-vis* the producer, and the potential role of the Co-operative Movement in this field of "Consumer Power", was "very important".

Nothing came of *Participation 1972*. It received only cursory mention at the annual conference in October. Although this consultation with the grass roots reaped little benefit—and Benn came to share this view—the development of contacts with trade union leaders, which was running parallel with the participation exercise, was of crucial importance. Without some form of understanding with the TUC the whole policy-making process would be politically valueless.

On 30 November 1971, Sir Harry Nicholas wrote to Vic Feather proposing a discussion between the TUC and the Labour Party on economic and industrial policy, with a view to involving trade union representatives in Labour's next general election programme. The Labour Party and the TUC had developed over the years an agreement whereby representatives from each body could attend the respective policy committees —Labour's Home Policy and the TUC's Economic Committee —but Labour leaders were anxious to establish a high-flown committee, on the lines of the Liaison Committee which had met to oppose the Industrial Relations Bill. Sir Harry's letter suggested that the starting base could be consideration of *Economic Strategy, Growth and Unemployment.* When the proposition went before the TUC's so-called "inner cabinet"— the Finance and General Purposes Committee—an argument developed. Some advanced the view that the real need was for meetings with the Shadow Cabinet, for this would ensure that any agreement reached would extend to the Parliamentary Party (suspicions of the National Executive were just below the surface), but others argued that although this formula was right for industrial relations, it would be wrong to insist on this approach for other issues.

Two days earlier, on 6 December 1971, at a meeting of Labour's Home Committee, the general view had been that there should be one channel of contact and that the Parliamentary Party should be excluded. (Mikardo, incidentally, challenged Callaghan for the chairmanship of the committee at that meeting and was beaten by nine votes to seven.) David Lea, TUC research secretary, had attended the meeting and advised Feather that it was none of the TUC's business who represented the Labour Party; on the other hand, the TUC had to be clear who it was talking to and on what subject. Moreover, there had been some trade union leaders, Jack

Jones in particular, deliberately seeking to involve the Shadow Cabinet in broad discussion on economic planning issues.

The final outcome was that the National Executive, Parliamentary Party and TUC, representing the three wings of the movement, constituted the Liaison Committee. While Benn, as party chairman, claimed credit for being one of the principal bridge builders between the political and trade union wings, it will be seen that many hands were involved in its erection. The membership of the three groups was : Parliamentary Labour Party : Wilson, Callaghan, Jenkins, Houghton, Mellish, as Labour Chief Whip, and Lever; National Executive : Benn, Castle, Chalmers, Mikardo, Kitson, an executive officer with the transport workers, Nicholas, Gwyn Morgan, the party's assistant general secretary, and Pitt; TUC : Jones, Scanlon, President of the Engineering Workers, Feather, Lord Cooper, then general secretary of the General and Municipal Workers Union, Sir Sidney Greene, then general secretary of the National Union of Railwaymen, and three officers from Congress House, Len Murray, Ken Graham and David Lea.

The moderate-minded Shadow Cabinet team provided an effective counter-balance to the left-dominated National Executive group, although Barbara Castle was declared virtually *persona non grata* by the trade unionists after she had attempted to impose *In Place of Strife* on them in the name of socialism. The first meeting took place on 21 February 1972, shortly after the mineworkers had won their post-Wilberforce Report massive pay award. National Executive representatives were curious to know the TUC's attitude to collective bargaining, " particularly in the light of the successful conclusion of the miners' strike". But the trade unionists would not be drawn on specifics. Shadow ministers saw an opportunity. Treading delicately on a highly sensitive subject, they obliquely opened up a discussion on wages, although the phrase incomes policy was hardly mentioned.

The trade unionists were informed that it would not be a happy situation to approach the next election with a rate of 10 per cent inflation without specific ideas to counteract this. The TUC representatives, however, were listening to a different tune. They pointed out that the main difference between Britain and other countries was not wage rates so much as output rates, and there should be much more emphasis on the waste of output caused by unemployment, and the attendant adverse effects on unit costs. One specific proposal they did come up with was the negotiation of cost of living threshold clauses. It was apparent that there was a long way to go before a semblance of agreement could be reached.

Benn had not served on the Liaison Committee of the PLP and the TUC which met in 1971, and which was discussed in the preceding chapter. His chairmanship of the party now ensured him a place on the new committee. Before becoming chairman the greatest influence upon his thinking about relations with the trade unions had been a series of meetings he had with the Transport and General Workers Union in his Bristol constituency. These meetings had taken place shortly after Labour's 1970 general election defeat, and he encountered extraordinary bitterness against the out-going Labour Administration. The feeling of betrayal engulfed the first meeting. Benn was left with the impression that they wanted the union to disaffiliate from the party and from a trade union party. While recognising that this was an over-reaction, it was nonetheless a frightening indication of the state of morale among party activists.

Over-reaction probably bred more over-reaction. Benn's immediate instinct was to get deeply involved with the trade union rank and file. He tackled it with characteristic missionary zeal. It was this involvement which eventually led him to Glasgow and the shipbuilding workers. While not being one of them, he felt it essential to be seen to be with them. As party chairman in 1972 he delivered the fraternal address to trade union conferences and meetings, which stressed the need for greater worker participation, industrial democracy and an extension of public ownership. It was no wonder that the left warmed to him. "We're not in the mood to kick converts in the teeth", said Marxist Ken Coates, a leading light in the left-oriented Institute for Workers Control, at the time of the UCS occupation, "I don't want to put words into his mouth, but I think if Mr Wedgwood Benn keeps on this track he will find himself among friends in certain sections of the Institute." [5] Benn was later to feel the warmth of their embrace when he attended seminars organised by the Institute.

While the centre-right were incensed at the way Benn appeared to have broken with the tradition of an impartial chairman, to live with him was exciting, inspirational, sometimes dangerous. When he first became chairman he astonished his National Executive colleagues by reorganising the seating arrangements to give the impression of meeting round a Cabinet table. The staff at Transport House initially took to him, but this support tapered off after Benn had placed his casting vote in favour of Ron Hayward succeeding Nicholas as general secretary. The staff had wanted Morgan, the other main contender, to win.

Benn moved around committees and conferences giving encouragement to the left. He was a member of the Industrial Committee from the outset, although not present at every meeting. There was one occasion, in June 1971, before he became chairman, when he set down his thoughts *Towards a Socialist Industrial Policy* in a document for discussion by the committee, but he failed to attend the meeting. It was placed on the agenda for the following month, but never discussed. Nonetheless, it is worth quoting, if only to illustrate how experience at MinTech had developed his thinking : "In recent years most discussion within the Labour movement has been about economic policy and industrial relations. The development of an industrial policy within the Ministry of Technology was much less fully debated, and has been more discussed in recent months when the instruments which the Labour Government created were being dismantled."

Public ownership, he continued, had tended to be seen in isolation and was now being considered as part of a rear-guard action to protect the public sector from the Conservative Government's attacks upon it. Benn argued that the party should consider a future Labour Government introducing a Bill for general use which would allow it to buy shares, make loans, acquire assets and take whatever steps were necessary to run the businesses concerned under the Companies Acts. This procedure, he maintained, would dispense with all the cumbersome machinery associated with nationalisation measures and would cater for all the situations for which the Industrial Reorganisation and Industrial Expansion Acts were intended. He wrote : " . . . any money that Government wishes to put in to help declining industries, finance advanced industries or cope with the consequences flowing from the economic collapse of vital industries could be injected in such a way as to expand the

public sector and create a public portfolio and central management unit that would profoundly shift the balance of power
in favour of the public sector."

Although little of this was to appear in *Economic Strategy,
Growth and Unemployment*, policy-makers were eventually to
formulate a Bill on these lines. But that was a long way ahead.
After the 1971 party conference they were to get down to
detailed study. It was Benn who replied to the Industrial debate
at the 1971 conference and he was given a tremendous reception. It was not by accident that the UCS shop stewards were
standing behind and above him on the platform. Benn stressed
that the National Executive was seeking a new partnership
between the industrial and political wings of the movement in
the country and in the Parliamentary Party. The party wanted
industry in the public sector to change the power structure of
society. A much more flexible method of extending the public
sector was needed with common ownership taking many forms,
one being a state holding company. It was due to the National
Executive's exploration that the divergent views appeared and
the deep-rooted divisions over economic policy were exposed.

What lay behind the rationale for a State interventionist agency?
"It is a sad thought", Wilson told the 1971 annual conference,
"that so much of the legislation of the first two years of the next
Labour Government will be of an anti-vandalistic character."
His comments were directed at policies being introduced by the
Conservative Government, at the dismantling of the Industrial
Reorganisation Corporation and at the potential of the Industrial Expansion Act. However, he went on to promise that the
agency would be carried through simultaneously with measures
to extend the area of public ownership, as was made clear in
Economic Strategy, Growth and Unemployment. "Just as—if
we are to attack our endemic problems of declining investment
—we shall reassert the principle of industrial intervention", he
continued. "We shall establish a State Holding Agency on the
lines of IRC—but written large this time, and with clearer
power to ensure that where society invests in private industry,
society will stake a claim in the profits."

This was meat and drink to the delegates. When reflected
upon, however, the phrase was characteristically Wilsonian. It
was open to several interpretations. The party as a whole

recognised that the machinery the previous Labour Administration had laid down for the IRC was insufficient and inadequate. But what was the new state agency going to do? In its economic strategy statement published in 1969 the party declared that "the dynamism which characterises the Italian public industrial structure is completely missing from the British scene, and it is in order to develop this that over the past few years the Party has considered the establishment of a new State Holding Company along the lines of the Italian IRI (Industrial Reconstruction Institute)". The questions now being begged by Wilson and *Economic Strategy, Growth and Unemployment* were these : what size? what economic power? and for what purpose? It was in providing answers to these questions that the policy-makers became divided. Towards the climax of the argument Wilson went beyond the party constitution by threatening that the Shadow Cabinet would exercise a veto if the left persisted in pushing through its proposals.

The initiative for a State interventionist agency belonged as much to the right as to the left wing of the party. In fact, initially many of the left were highly dubious. They suspected it was a device concocted by the social democrats to deflect the party from its commitments to nationalisation. Its antecedents also aroused suspicions. The model for various experiments had been the Italian IRI, whose beginnings damned it in the eyes of many socialists for years. When three of the main private banks were threatened with bankruptcy because of the depression in Italy from 1930 to 1933, the Fascist Government set up the IRI as a temporary salvage company. It was only years later, when the concept of a state holding company appeared as a useful economic instrument (and consequently attained respectability), that IRI's pedigree became worthy of further inspection.

Its first director was Alberto Beneduce, an ex-social reformist minister who had worked with the Turati and Amendola group in the early 'twenties when the group had recommended opposing fascism with force. He had also been responsible for the nationalisation of insurance in Italy before the First World War. It was only after the Second World War that IRI developed into an agency for helping solve the structural and regional problems in Italy. In the early years after the war it had been criticised by the Italian Socialist and Communist parties. They did not consider it fascist, since its independence from the mainstream of fascist corporatism was generally recognised, but they wanted the traditional form of public ownership. IRI had partial control of many companies in different industrial sectors. The Socialists and Communists wanted monopoly public ownership of the sectors concerned.

By 1956 the IRI had achieved permanent status in the framework of Italian economic policy. This was partly the result of a three-year Parliamentary inquiry into its activities which reduced the pressure for its dismemberment and partly the demonstration of its capacity to contribute to national economic growth through the creation of an indigenous ore-based Italian steel industry in which it had a holding. Another reason was Government recognition that the IRI could play an important part in the regional development of the south of the country, a region of some 18 million people with an average income per head of only two-fifths that earned by some in the more developed north-west area of Italy. Previous government measures to promote the industrialisation and modernisation of southern Italy through investment grants and infrastructure expenditure were proving ineffective. Moreover, the "clearance" of the IRI came at a time Mattei, the flamboyant entrepreneur who was later killed in a mysterious air crash, had secured the establishment, in 1954, of a second holding company. This was the National Hydrocarbons Corporation (ENI) which was based on the exploitation of natural gas deposits in the Po Valley.

Both IRI and ENI have since shown a variety of ways in which State holdings can serve economic and social ends of Government policy. Nonetheless, British socialists held strong reservations for years. There was a wide belief that the IRI operated as a state within a state, maintaining its existence because of an inefficient Italian civil service and unstable Italian governments. It really had little to do with democratic socialism. And, in any case, why embark upon an alien concept when the party should not only be extending the frontiers of public ownership but carrying out a fundamental reappraisal of how the existing public sector could be improved both in performance and management.

Crosland and some of his colleagues had advanced the idea

of competitive public enterprises to act as price-leaders and pace-setters in the mid-'fifties, but it was never made clear how they would fit within the framework of a planned economic policy. Two economists, Michael Posner and Richard Pryke, in their 1966 Fabian pamphlet *New Public Enterprises*, rightly stated : "What hitherto has been lacking in Britain, and what advocates of competitive public ownership have for the most part failed to suggest, is machinery by which new public enterprises can be brought into existence and controlled." [6] They argued that the holding company would pool the financial, administrative and technical expertise of enterprises in which it had interests. It could offer specialised services to small firms to avoid the diseconomies of small-scale operations. It could select new areas for public enterprise and expand into them. Moreover, it could ultimately act as a channel for the re-allocation of investment funds between different enterprises within the public sector "so operating, as in Italy, as a device for the socialisation of the capital market".

The guiding principle of Posner and Pryke was : "There should be no iron curtain to put public enterprise out of the newer, more profitable, more extensive and continually expanding territory which has hitherto been the exclusive preserve of private enterprise. In a truly mixed economy there should be no signs along the border stating that this ground is reserved for private firms and that public trespassers must be kept out." Posner and Pryke wrote their pamphlet in the year that the Labour Government created the Industrial Reorganisation Corporation. The belief that its terms of reference were too narrow and inhibiting proved to be prophetic, but they did state that there was nothing, apart from doctrine, to prevent it evolving into a state holding company. However, by the time ministers and Labour policy-makers began to explore ways of broadening its scope to assist regional development and create new enterprises they were overtaken by the 1970 general election defeat.

When the Conservatives came to power they looked upon state agencies with abhorrence. The Government's decision to scrap the IRC squared with its "lame duck" philosophy. But, when examined against the general climate at the time, the decision also appeared at variance with its views on Britain becoming part of the European Economic Community, particularly as one of the reasons was to stiffen Britain's industrial competitiveness. European experience generally pointed in the direction of the need for some form of para-governmental agency or agencies. 1970 had witnessed governments taking closer interest in the concept, even though they differed on its scope, size and control.

In January 1970, a bill was introduced in the Swedish Parliament for the establishment of a single state holding company, the Statsforetag, which would be responsible for all state companies. Thirty-one companies were involved, including such sectors as mining, shipbuilding, banking, distilling, tobacco and state catering. The French Industrial Development Institute (IDI) was formed in March 1970 with the role of promoting new activities. These included the development of the national telephone and telecommunications network, the expansion of the national motorway system, and the expansion of investment in engineering, agricultural equipment, food processing and electronics. In West Germany, Alex Moller, then the Finance Minister, proposed in April 1970 the creation of a "super holding" to permit better management of a variety of holdings which the Government held in industrial companies. The object of the Moller proposals was not better use and management of taxpayers' money in the private sector but more private finance for the public sector. There was strong pressure in Belgium from the socialist parties for a para-governmental agency with the right to create firms as well as promote mergers between existing companies. The following year, 1971, the Agency for Industrial Development (Office de Promotion Industriel) was created.

This is necessarily an over-simplified account of developments in the continent at the beginning of the 'seventies. However, what more fitting conclusion than the fact that in 1972 the Conservative Government was obliged to have second thoughts and brought in the Industrial Development Executive, which was larger than the IRC it had killed off. The main differences were that it was located inside the Department for Trade and Industry and came under the direct control of a minister.

It was not only Labour politicians who regretted the abolition of the IRC. In May 1971, the TUC submitted a memorandum to the Bill Rodgers' Trade and Industry Sub-Committee referred to earlier. It stated, in part :

> A single agency on the lines of the Italian IRI should be established with terms of reference for the promotion of industrial, technological and regional development. It would have the power to provide private loan capital and to purchase private company equity so as to acquire either a minority or a controlling share. It would also be empowered, subject to parliamentary approval in a particular case, to set up new public enterprises.

When questioned, Vic Feather, the then general secretary of the TUC, envisaged the new organisation as a public investment agency with initial access to public funds of perhaps £500 million. It would differ from the IRC in that where the IRC was limited to short-term finance, the TUC visualised its agency as a permanent public stake, or permanent extension of the public sector.

The TUC, to quote from the sub-committee's report, saw the agency concentrating on regional development, technological advance and areas of rapidly growing world trade. Asked why the money market should not be capable of recognising the profits to be gained from this third category, the TUC thought that the market preferred to invest in something already established and likely to provide quick returns. The agency would have the national motivation of developing the country's economic growth and resources, a function which the City did not and should not have. The agency could accept the obligation involved in the need for social development. Although this might not bring the best immediate financial return, the TUC thought it would in the long term. The sub-committee reported that the TUC spoke at first of the agency being financed from public funds only and qualified this later by saying that while no private equity capital would be allowed the possibility of private loan capital was not excluded.

But what of other witnesses before the Committee? Sir Anthony Part, Permanent Secretary of the Department of Trade and Industry, which was the Whitehall link with IRC, was decidedly sceptical about para-governmental agencies. In one of those moments which raise the atmosphere of committee proceedings, Sir Anthony, under pressure to give his own personal view about such an agency and not shelter behind what was debated in Parliament, said : "I do not think it is essential." The sub-committee report recorded other witnesses who thought an agency unnecessary, either in itself or for a particular purpose. Lord Sherfield, chairman of the Industrial and Finance Corporation, saw no need for a general agency. Sir Frank Figgures, Director-General of the National Economic Development Office, believed that selective aid to the private sector could basically be handled within the appropriate Government department, which gave greater scope for *ad hoc* treatment. Sir Alec Cairncross, formerly head of the Government Economic Service, thought that the problem of restoring a particular industry which had difficulty in surviving was better handled direct by the Government than through an agency. Ronald Grierson, who was the first managing director of IRC, told the committee that the job of gingering up sleeping managements was not a task for any agency so much as for shareholders and other interested parties. His successor Charles Villiers, on the other hand, was in favour of para-governmental agencies, although he did tell the committee that the IRC should have been based on selective investment (seen as a secondary role) rather than on restructuring and mergers.

Lastly, the Confederation of British Industry : they saw a role for an agency although it should be "somewhat more distant from Government than the IRC". The committee reported that the CBI in their evidence seemed to speak in terms of private money only, though later they agreed that part of the funds could be public. Not surprisingly, this contrasted with the TUC which envisaged that the major source of funds in their agency would be public money. Rodgers' committee was able to conclude : "The evidence we received from Industry and the City was on the whole rather more favourable to the idea of a para-governmental agency, or of particular attributes of an agency, than might have been expected." It added : "We believe that the advantages an agency may be able to bring of flexibility, initiative and industrial expertise should not be lightly written off, and deserve closer consideration."

Bill Rodgers was to follow through his chairmanship of the sub-committee by introducing a Bill in Parliament, in February

1972, for a Regional Development Corporation. Nor was he the only social democrat who saw the desirability of maintaining the initiative. Edmund Dell had proposed a motion in December 1971, and in March 1972 John Smith, Labour MP for Lanarkshire North, was to introduce a Bill to create a Public Enterprise Development Agency. All of them were designed to serve the same purpose : to promote investment and employment, particularly in the regions. In December 1971, the social democratic monthly *Socialist Commentary* ran three articles on public ownership, one of them a review by Dell in which he paid tribute to Pryke's book *Public Enterprise in Practice*. "It is to be hoped that Mr Pryke's book will encourage the Labour Party to be less timorous about public ownership", wrote Dell.

Another contributor was Stuart Holland, at that time seen as a young protégé in social democrat circles. His article was on the need for a state holding company. In Dell's view Holland was the "foremost of those who have argued the relevance of this idea to this country".[7] Holland was to assist Roy Jenkins in his major speech on public ownership delivered to the North Western Area conference of the National Union of Mineworkers in May 1972. It was only the following year, when Holland's essentially Marxist approach to economics became obvious, that he was abandoned by the social democrats. The protégé, in their eyes, had become a parvenu.

Holland and Pryke were brought together in January 1972 to prepare a background paper on the state holding company for the Bonnington conference the following month. They had first met when they served in the Cabinet Office after the 1966 general election, although Pryke's term was of short duration. He resigned within the month when the Government introduced the July "squeeze" and wrote off the National Plan. Pryke earned the enmity of Lord Balogh, special economic adviser to the Cabinet, by stating publicly his reasons for resigning— "you little fool"—which were later expanded in a book *While Cowards Flinch*. Pryke argued the case for devaluation and the need for further public ownership.

When Pryke and Holland joined forces to write the background paper Pryke was seen to be further to the left; the latter's confidence and Marxist approach was to grow during his membership of the Public Sector Group and the Industry

Committee. Pryke could be temperamental and obstinate; Holland cautious and, in the early months, anxious not to give offence. Pryke was familiar with the inner workings of the Labour Party : he had been a research assistant at Transport House and had resigned when he was beaten by Pitt for Shore's job as head of the department. Holland was a newcomer to party policy-making. What they did share in common was a resignation from the Cabinet Office (Holland left in 1968) and an awareness that there was a lack of any strategy, with the Civil Service an obstacle to change. Both of them had a special desire to see the expansion of public ownership. Pryke had completed his *The Nationalised Industries* during the 1970 general election campaign.

The Public Sector Group, which they were asked to join, was formed by the Industrial Policy Committee after the 1971 annual conference. It became the principal engine for driving the party into examining wider areas for public ownership. Judith Hart volunteered to form the group, whose recommendations would have to go back to the Industrial Committee for approval and thence through the Home Policy Committee to the National Executive. Judith Hart was an enthusiastic recipient of the ideas brandished inside the committee, in particular by Holland, even if she was not seen by everyone as holding a tight rein in the structuring of the committee's deliberations.

Hart, Holland and Margaret Jackson, a research assistant at Transport House and this committee's secretary, worked closely together. Margaret Jackson, like Pitt a former metallurgist, eventually became Labour MP for Lincoln. Coincidentally, she was first approached by officials of the Lincoln Labour Party at Labour's annual conference in Blackpool in 1973, the year the party programme, including the state holding agency, was debated in detail for the first time, and approved, by delegates. Having sacked the social democrat Dick Taverne, the leftish Lincoln officials were looking for someone with a contrasting democratic socialist background. Margaret Jackson fitted the bill.

Judith Hart formed the group with Pryke and the late Lord Delacourt-Smith, of the Post Office Engineering Union, in December 1971. Her commitment to the need for paragovernmental agency went back at least ten years. She was a member of the unofficial group formed by the late Richard Crossman in 1963–64 which worked on policies for science, industry and education before the 1964 general election. They produced a paper at that time on the need for a Public Investment Trust, a forerunner of the agency upon which she was now embarking. Although less far reaching, the proposed Trust had similar functions as the state holding company, especially in relation to new public enterprise in the regions.

Holland was invited to join the Public Sector Group in January 1972, the month that he and Pryke were asked to produce a background paper on the state holding company. This would go before the "conference of experts" in February. It was not until May 1972 that the other members were invited to join the group. They were: Lord Balogh, the old Cabinet Office boss of Pryke and Holland, Mikardo, Jim Mortimer, a former trade union official but at that time the Labour Relations Director of the London Transport Board (who pursued a highly philosophical line for further public ownership and doubted whether profitability was high priority), Derek Robinson (an infrequent attender but who developed, like Pryke, a scepticism at what was being created) and Tony Banks, a young researcher with the Amalgamated Union of Engineering Workers, who broadly adopted the view developed by Hart, Holland and Jackson. Later, when Labour returned to office in 1975, Holland and Banks were to become Judith Hart's paid special advisers, and Margaret Jackson her parliamentary private secretary.

When the Public Sector Group was being formed, Judith Hart disputed with Pitt over the size of the working party. The general Transport House line was to have large committees so that a broad spectrum of party attitudes were involved, the principle being that although the policies that resulted would inevitably be compromises it did reduce the dangers of rows within the party afterwards. Judith Hart took a contrary view. She wanted a small, homogeneous group, debating the methodology of a state agency rather than becoming bogged down in time-consuming ideological disputes. She won her argument over the size, but the controversies involving the Industrial Committee, the National Executive and the Shadow Cabinet were to follow in the wake of the group's recommendations. Judith Hart and her close co-operators were to welcome if not provoke the confrontation. Throughout the debates and arguments that flowed from the work of the group, Judith Hart was to play a prominent part. She was instrumental in getting ideas off the ground and in pushing them through the tangled layers of policy-making machinery.

References

1 *The New Politics: a Socialist reconnaissance*, Fabian Society 1970.
2 *A Tribune of the People? Socialist Commentary*, October 1972.
3 *The Labour Party and Democratic Politics*, Fabian Lecture (unpublished).
4 *The Times*, 3 January 1972.
5 *Financial Times*, 3 January 1972.
6 *New Public Enterprises*, Posner and Pryke. Fabian Society 1966.
7 *Socialist Commentary*, May 1972.

FOUR

State Holding Company: an Ideal

THE RUSSELL HOTEL, red-brick and terracotta, overlooks
Russell Square in the Bloomsbury area of London. Near by
lies the more modern Bonnington Hotel. They were the
venues of two conferences organised by the National Executive
for February 1972. On 25 February, twenty-two Labour politicians, trade unionists and academics met in the Russell Hotel
to discuss the party's future economic policy. Industrial policy,
to be debated at the Bonnington Hotel, was held during the
two succeeding days. The party had done little towards re-
examining economic policy in the previous twelve months, as
was shown in a previous chapter. Roy Jenkins, chairman of
the Finance and Economic Policy Sub-Committee, preferred
to confer with his own small group of advisers. They included
Dell, Lever, Taverne, Lord Diamond, a chartered accountant
who had been Chief Secretary to the Treasury throughout the
1964–70 Labour Administration, and David and Judith
Marquand, the former, Labour MP for Ashfield and the latter
an economist with the Treasury, all of whom were co-opted
members of the Finance and Economic Committee.

Among the academics who had been co-opted were the two
Hungarian economists, Lord Balogh (who was thought to be
past his best in contributing ideas; he published a Fabian Tract
Labour and Inflation in October 1970 but it had little impact
on policy-making, particularly since he was an advocate of
incomes policy), and Nicholas Kaldor (who proved to be too
individualistic and, in the view of some, too inconsistent to
provide a driving force for an independent centre of policy-
making). The only two National Executive members who took
an active interest in the Finance Committee were Shirley
Williams and Mikardo, who challenged Jenkins for the chairmanship and lost and who soon became preoccupied with the
financial institutions. All of them attended the Russell conference. The TUC was represented by Sir Sydney Greene, of

the National Union of Railwaymen, and the then Mr Allen, of the Union of Shop, Distributive and Allied Workers.

Little came out of the conference, although Lord Diamond's comment that the Labour Cabinet "did not work as a team" and that the Labour Government "was a time of departmental conflict between ministers" was not a view which former ministers were prepared, at that time, to state openly. Dell introduced an office paper on "demand management", which was not revealing in itself although Dell showed that he believed macro-planning to be more important than micro-planning, an economic approach which former ministers did not want to explore in great detail, even eighteen months after the general election defeat. Non-ministerial members had become increasingly conscious of this fact. "Planning" was seen as almost a dirty word, the principal cause was assumed to be an over-reaction to the disasters of Labour's commitment to planning in the early 'sixties. But by the summer the Industrial Committee was to launch a re-examination of planning with a more positive commitment.

To revert back to the Russell conference. The participants were naturally concerned at the increasing level of unemployment. It was Judith Marquand who put forward the then unfashionable view that the increase in public expenditure in the latter years of the Labour Government had contributed to unemployment. Lord Diamond, who as Chief Secretary had been responsible for public expenditure and therefore spoke with authority, stated that public expenditure had been rising too fast up to 1967. Jenkins' contributions from the chair were that wage increases did not depress demand in the economy as a whole and that unemployment may not go down much when demand picked up. He doubted, however, whether the unemployment situation contained any new factors. In order to overcome unemployment, Jenkins favoured IRC-type policies to revitalise industry and promote growth in the regions. But the Jenkins committee was not in a position to develop this theme. The basis of a new governmental agency was being considered by the Industrial Policy Committee, which could accurately be described as a rival. Jenkins was to set out his views on an agency in a speech in May.

The final session of the conference was devoted to financial institutions. Mikardo, as chairman of the study group examin-

ing the institutions, introduced the discussion. Two papers
by Transport House staff and economist Roger Opie were
before the meeting. Little came out of the debate. It was left
to Makardo, who questioned the institutions' non-accountability,
and his group to come up with proposals. In the end the group
failed to reach a common agreement.* The two papers, nevertheless, formed the basis of their deliberations and should not be
passed over. The revival of demands for public ownership of
banks and insurance companies "ought to be taken very
seriously indeed", said the office paper. They arose after strong
condemnations of the inadequacies of the present regulation of
finance through the Bank of England by the Select Committee
on Nationalised Industries (it will be recalled that Mikardo had
been the chairman). And, secondly, said the paper, these
demands came at the end of a decade which had seen many
changes in the structure and roles of Britain's various financial
institutions.

These changes had made the significant degree of control
which could only be achieved by ownership more important
than ever before for financial institutions. In particular, there
had been a remarkable growth in the importance of institutional investors throughout the 'sixties, with life assurance and
pension funds playing a key role. Pressing hard its case, the
Research Department continued : "The failure to include the
private pension funds in the conference resolution should not
deter the Financial and Economic Sub-Committees from studying how control of the investment policies of these funds can
be incorporated into the framework of publicly owned banks
and insurance companies." The most important benefit which
a Labour Government would enjoy from the public ownership
of the banks and insurance companies, the paper argued, would
be the increased ability to plan adequate national and regional
investment and industrial reorganisational policies.

The enormity of the task facing the working group was set
out by Opie. For a start the City "is wholly and implacably
hostile". In an understatement, Opie wrote : "This is more
than mildly annoying." It was important, first for the effect
that "confidence" could have on the volatile elements in the
balance of payments (a danger not fully eliminated by floating);
and secondly, for the sort of monetary policy which operated

* See Chapter Eight.

by informal influence or so-called "moral suasion". Opie remarked that the hostile elements were extremely active; they had great political influence behind the scenes and were very vocal in front of them. All the institutions were closely linked in temperament, prejudice, background and control. They were important because they had a dominant influence on the flow of funds and allocation of credit.

This influence was exercised on the basis of, first, the success of a given institution; secondly, its irrational and historical prejudices about "proper" types of business and "proper" types of customer; and, thirdly, its judgment of the conflict on profitability and illiquidity. The Clearing (or High Street) Banks had a near monopoly of the money transfer mechanism. This was based on the public's preference for cheques and transfers from and to current accounts as a means of payments; the banks' monopoly of the Clearing House; and the Bank of England's refusal to allow any takeover of an existing Clearing Bank by a non-clearer or by a non-bank. All the institutions were enormously sinuous and fertile. Their spontaneous spawning of new institutions or new activities, or both, was not easily contained by a set of rigid controls.

Opie stated that this increase in influence and power of the High Street banks throughout the economic community was both a challenge and an opportunity for the next Labour Government. The challenge was the concentration of irresponsible power; the opportunity was to use that power responsibly. He did not agree with the outrage, expressed in the Research Department paper, about "financial dictation to companies". After all, he argued, had someone done some financial dictating earlier, Rolls-Royce might not have got into the mess it did. More generally, this was only one aspect of shareholders' control and it "would be dangerous to argue that active intervention by knowledgeable shareholders is never to be preferred to sleepy, inefficient management". Opie stated he would certainly argue that financial dictation was not necessarily bad and that Britain could do with a great deal more of it in the private enterprise sector.

He stated that the group ought to divide its analysis into three parts: Why do anything? What to do? How to do it? The first question included the threat of a greater concentration of power; the present and prospective behaviour of financial institutions in the allocations of credit; the monopoly of clearing houses and hence of the payments mechanism; and the nature of the competition in which they indulged. Question two demanded different treatment for different layers of institutions. Why should the Bank of England's relationship to the financial institutions be different from that of, say, the Ministry of Agriculture and Fisheries to the farmers? The Treasury was satisfied with the present position, but that was merely an objection to change, not a judgment. Building societies ought to be nationalised, although he did not share the view of the Research Department that "a policy of nationalising the building societies [ought] to be an integral part of housing policy and not financial policy".

On the third question, Opie stated, the clearing banks could most effectively be influenced by firm Bank of England control (which in future should be Treasury control) and by injecting a non-like-minded source of competition. The Giro may be effective on the liabilities (deposits) side. Opie concluded his "first thoughts" by stating: "But to improve overall performance, I would recommend that one clearer should be nationalised, and operated as a catalyst of efficiency and price competition." The left, in the end, was to go much further than this.

Policy-making then moved to the Bonnington Hotel, where the Industrial Committee held its two-day conference. Holland was not present: he was singing in a performance of Brahms' Requiem in Brighton. Where Marxism influenced his economic thinking, music dominated his relaxation: he could have become a professional singer while he was studying at Oxford. Crosland was also absent, having a previous commitment. Crosland, in fact, had been given the opportunity to influence thinking when the Industrial Committee suggested that he might like to prepare a paper on *Monopolies and Mergers*, but Crosland, for some unaccountable reason, did not deliver. Instead, Dell produced a ten-page paper on *Competition Policy* which threw up important political differences.

Among the participants were Jim Mortimer, Lord Balogh, McCarthy, Robinson and Dell. That there should have been differences was not surprising. The party has never been able to come to terms with a policy on competition : intrinsically it means a recognition of private ownership. It appears as a threat to a worker's vested interest in his job. As Dell pointed out, the Labour Party had therefore sought for a collectivist rather than competitive means of achieving the same objects. But he argued that these different means did not have to be in conflict. A competition policy which was also *laissez-faire* was a contradiction in terms. *Laissez-faire* would tend to eliminate competition. The preservation of competition required Government intervention of various kinds. Governments should act not just to preserve competition but to create jobs. Existing jobs could be threatened by new technology and by international competition as much as by domestic competition. He argued that the next Labour Government would need to make a calculated use of market forces to get results : competition policy would play a part in this.

Dell concluded in his paper that there was a need for a more vigorous competition policy, creative as well as regulatory, and the need for a Department of Consumer Affairs. Wilson was to create such a Department in the next Labour Administration, although not wholly on the Dell model. Dell's reasoning was that it was "desirable" that consumer protection should be brought together with competition policy under one minister. Given the giant departments, this minister might be in charge of a separately identifiable administration within the Department of Trade and Industry. But the existence of such an administration "if not a separate Ministry, would give impetus to an aspect of policy that tends to lag within our great industry-dominated departments, DTI and the Ministry of Agriculture and Fisheries".

While he received few objections from the participants to this idea, it was in pressing the logic of his arguments on competition policy that he ran into trouble with some of his colleagues, particularly doctrinaires such as Mikardo and Hart. Dell argued that the next Labour Government would need to make a "calculated use of market forces to get results". Competition policy, he believed, necessitated three functions. The first was "regulatory" (through the Monopolies Commission and the Restrictive Practices Court) with what he described as an *underlying presumption* in favour of competition when dealing with monopolies and mergers, although this could be operated fairly pragmatically. There was, secondly, the "creative" function, involving the use of the proposed state holding company. Thirdly, there was a "consumer protection" function based, perhaps, on his proposed Department of Consumer Affairs, which would be responsible not only for the competition policy itself, but also for company regulation and consumer protection. The *presumption* in favour of competition, however, came under attack. The view, particularly from the left, was that consumer protection was a somewhat less important consideration in merger policy than the needs of the economy as a whole and the relevance of the overall structure of industry to those needs. Labour's old Industrial Reorganisation Corporation, it was suggested, was perhaps more relevant than the Monopolies Commission. While no decision was reached it became clear that the policy-makers had a long way to travel before they could even reach a compromise.

The same judgment can be applied to the discussion on a prices policy, which was based upon a paper submitted by Derek Robinson. As we saw earlier, Robinson strongly supported the need for a prices policy, not only in its own right but as a way of bringing back discussion on an incomes policy, which he believed to be a necessity. In his paper he was specific : "Every form of price policy is at the same time a form of wages or incomes policy. It is unrealistic to believe if prices are controlled wage determination can continue as though the price controls were not present." There was little discussion on "incomes" however, although one trade unionist, Frank Chapple of the electricians' union, said price controls, which he did not think would work but must be tried, would lead to a prices and incomes policy. Robinson, to avoid using the contentious word, resorted to the phrase "prices and thing policy".

Even the discussion on prices showed up considerable differences of view. Robert Sheldon, Labour MP for Ashton-under-Lyne, who was on the Parliamentary party's economic and finance committee, and became chairman of the general subcommittee of the Commons committee on expenditure in 1972, said price control would fall down on quality. The United Kingdom was a consumer society and prices were related to the fundamental objectives of industry, i.e. profit. Price control would require too many civil servants and all the party could do was to lean on key prices. Lord Balogh thought price control would strike at the fundamentals of capitalism but as there was not perfect competition there must be price controls.

Robinson asserted that prices policy had to be multi-dimensional. No single approach would deal satisfactorily with all aspects of prices. Various measures should be seen as interlocking and complementary. The particular measures adopted would be influenced if not determined by the general economic policy framework.

Robinson went on to suggest that there would appear to be advantages in setting up a similar sort of agency to the abolished National Board for Prices and Incomes. He also supported the creation of a Central Purchasing Agency responsible for the bulk of the public sector purchases. He quoted as an example that the fragmented purchasing policy which operated over large sections of the National Health Service was obviously inefficient because it prevented the realisation of the advantages of large-scale buying and impeded the exercise of the full degree of purchaser power which could be available. To obtain the benefits of large-scale buying, or import substitution, it would be necessary to limit some of the powers of the decentralised decision-making units. Robinson recognised that this "would lead to a considerable outcry but should not on this account alone be rejected".

Another Robinson suggestion was "a price inspectorate", along the lines operated in Finland. There, about 100 groups of domestic products and twenty groups of fees were subject to the price stop. Any consumer could complain to a price inspector. If the charge was proved the enterprise could be ordered to refund to the state up to treble the amount of excess charged and in serious cases to pay additional fines and serve a maximum of three years' imprisonment. Robinson met criticism that such a policy would lead to charges of Whitehall "snoopers" by saying these would be outweighed by the advantages of giving the public a fair deal against unjustified price increases.

Figures produced by Robinson showed that there were 48 price inspectors in Finland at the time. In 1969 about 700 enterprises voluntarily surrendered excess charges when discovered and 73 cases were pased for prosecution. In 1970 the figures were 300 and 56 prosecutions and in 1971, 209 and 108 respectively. Robinson concluded from these last figures that enterprises were less willing to voluntarily surrender excesses or the authorities were getting tougher as the policy ran into increasing difficulties.

In a post-conference paper produced for the Industrial Committee on some "unresolved problems" it was quite obvious that the committee was faced with enormous difficulties in reaching a tenable policy on prices. "We cannot, it seems," stated the paper, "properly consider the operation of price controls without taking some sort of view on profit margins and self-financed investment, both from an economic viewpoint (the demand effects and the effect on investment finance) and from the viewpoint of the distribution of income and wealth (existing shareholders own the new assets financed from profits)." It was recommended that the problem should, at least, be passed over to the party's Capital Sharing Study Group, under the chairmanship of Tom Bradley. However, little came of this.

A second "unresolved problem" was this: any system of price control would involve "taking a view of some kind on particular increases in pay, and hence on the existing relative levels of pay". The dilemma was explained further: with any given pay increase some employers would be able to absorb the increases; others, especially in the public sector, would not be able to do so. "Do we need to commission some work on this aspect of price control?" asked the paper somewhat unnecessarily. The answer was "yes".

Dell, as we saw in the last chapter, was a keen adherent of the need for a state holding company; but he and the rest of the social democrats could not anticipate how far the left were to push the concept inside the Public Sector Group. It is to the state holding company we must now turn. Before the conference Pryke had written to Judith Hart stating that his views on both its *raison d'être* and administrative structure were set out in the pamphlet he had written with Michael Posner, and he did not have any fresh thoughts on the subject. This could well have been a factor which helped Holland to push through his own ideas. Pryke, however, admitted in his letter that there was one problem which he did not face up to in the pamphlet and "which I can now see more clearly than when I wrote it".

The problem was the difficulty of getting the holding company into operation within a fairly short space of time. He gave two reasons why this was necessary: first, the problem of regional employment, to which the holding company should be able to make a major contribution, was so serious that it was clearly undesirable that precious time should be wasted;

secondly, there was a need to build the holding company up to such an extent that the Conservatives would find it impossible to unscramble it if they were returned at the next general election but one. "Size is a great obstacle to denationalisation, factories which are in course of construction are not readily saleable, and if the holding company is already making a contribution to solving the regional problem its liquidation will be politically unpopular."

Pryke admitted that it would not be easy to get the holding company off the ground within the space of a single Parliament. It would obviously take time for the necessary legislation to get through, for the company to find the necessary personnel and then acquire private companies to serve as the basis for expansion. These views were incorporated in the paper that Pryke and Holland presented to the conference. If a future Labour Government planned to use the holdings as a macroeconomic instrument, he told Judith Hart, it could not afford to get off to a slow start and wait for private companies in difficulties to approach it for help.

At a very minimum, Pryke said, it would have to approach leading companies with an offer of investment funds in return for both a shareholding and an influence over the strategic investment decision-making of the companies concerned. The holding company would have to consider seriously whether or not compulsory powers should be made available to it to fulfil the function of securing a foothold within the main manufacturing sectors—even if such powers would be very rarely applied. The paper suggested that compulsory powers would be used sparingly because firms would have a stronger motive to co-operate with both a state shareholding and the strategic growth sustaining or promoting investment which the company was remitted to undertake on the Government's behalf.

The background paper did not recommend compulsory purchase because it was one of a number of areas where Pryke and Holland held divergent views. It was Holland, later to become the more militant of the two, who initially proved hesistant over compulsory purchase; at that stage he was more in favour of buying equity shares through the Stock Exchange. Pryke, however, put the alternative argument in the paper. It had to be recognised, he said, that it may be difficult for a state holding company to negotiate the purchase of suitable firms at a reasonable price. There were objections to it becoming involved in a series of disputed take-over bids which might result in an excessive payment in order to gain control. The reasoning was that once it was known that a state institution was bidding, directors and shareholders would probably expect a much higher price than they would if the bid was being made by an ordinary company. Not only would their political prejudices come into play, Pryke said, they would stand out for a very high price in the knowledge that the resources of the holding company were exceptionally large because it was backed by Government money. To guard against the challenge that his proposal would be labelled as draconian by political opponents, Pryke suggested restrictions. It could be written into the act setting up the company that the power would lapse after three or four years. Arguing through mixed metaphors, he said compulsory purchase would be needed only while "the industrial foundations were being put in and before shareholders and directors have learned what type of animal they are dealing with".

Holland and Pryke agreed they were entering a politically sensitive area with their state holding proposals but they saw it in a different light. Pryke, as we have seen, argued for its creation in the late 'sixties and at the time of the joint background paper he was still convinced that a state holding was a means of the Government managing a miscellaneous portfolio. In other words, his view was still a "management" philosophy approach : it was this which led him naturally to believe in the need for a Ministry of Nationalised Industries. Holland, on the other hand, saw the state holding company as a major economic instrument. He wanted to harness the power of profitable leading companies in a comprehensive planning context.

It was this idea adopted by the Public Sector Group, and then pushed through the Industrial Committee, which was both new and contentious. Holland and Pryke eventually came together on the issue : if they had remained opposed the row over the state holding company may have been different. Both recognised there would be challenges to the proposal of using a state holding company as an instrument of macro-economic planning, with equity shareholdings or compulsory purchase used to acquire a foothold within the main manufacturing sectors.

One challenge would certainly be the claim that the standard techniques of Keynesian demand management and investment allowances or grants were sufficient not only to iron out the trade cycle but also to enable the economy to attain sustained growth at its natural rate. The other could be that the prospect of extending public enterprise throughout private manufacturing—even if only in one or two companies in the main manufacturing sector—would be, to use their phrase, "politically difficult if not the best gift to the Tories since the Zinoviev letter".

Holland's concept of the state holding company as being a major macro-economic instrument was based upon his examination of the Italian IRI. In his memorandum for the Expenditure Sub-Committee he had set out six areas, these were based on the Bonnington Paper. They were :

1 The location of soundly based and competitive modern companies in less developed regions.
2 The channelling of Government expenditure into directly productive activity as growth promotion or counter-recession instrument.
3 The supplementing of macro-economic trade and exchange rate policies on a permanent and anticipatory basis through investment which is import-substituting or export-promoting.
4 The reinforcing of competition through state firms which can restrain price increases through their own competitive pricing in sectors which are not wholly exposed to foreign competition.
5 The undertaking of investment which private industry either is or is not willing to commit, or unwilling to make, on a scale or time horizon sufficient to meet long term growth requirements.
6 The provision of an instrument which can cope with the major problems posed for national or regional enterprise by foreign multi-national companies.

The Bonnington Paper recognised that the advocates of Keynesian demand management techniques were still to be found, but Holland argued they were shrinking under recent conditions of stagnant investment, rising unemployment and marked inflation in both the United States and Britain. Those who remained close to Keynesian techniques would also have to maintain that the natural growth potential of the British economy was the $2-2\frac{1}{2}$ per cent increase in GNP at which the country had grown over the last twenty years. Holland, who wrote this particular section of the paper, said this was not the argument which underlay the forecasts and hopes of the National Plan, nor the argument which in itself would constitute a strong pull to the polls for Labour's natural supporters.

He stated that Keynes (as opposed to Keynesians) never shrank from the principle of public expenditure as a direct means of reflating an under-developed economy. It had mainly been since the war that the orthodoxy had become established that the appropriate instruments of Keynesian policy were monetary and fiscal measures, i.e. indirect Government intervention. The trouble with indirect forms of government intervention to sustain or promote macro-economic growth—and thereby the general case for the introduction of a direct instrument such as a state holding company—could easily enough be generalised, maintained Holland.

Holland's analysis proceeded along the following lines. In a market economy system in which management investment decisions were decentralised, with management alone responsible for the internal profitability of its company and not responsible for the external effects which its decisions may entail, there was no mechanism to ensure that indirect incentives to increase investment actually resulted in increased growth. Even investment grants equal to the total value of the investment concerned would not necessarily persuade management to undertake a particular investment project if it was not convinced that the increased capacity would not be matched by increased demand. "The resulting surplus capacity—well enough publicised for large companies by the financial press—would be taken in business circles and boardroom comment as an example of business incompetence", wrote Holland.

The paper recognised that the problem was not endemic to capitalist systems alone, but would equally obtain for a market economy system in which there were publicly- or worker-owned and controlled enterprises, as in Yugoslavia. Besides, in the British case, management had become accustomed to Governments of both parties heralding the new dawn in industrial investment, and disbelieved it as a routine factor in their investment planning. And there was little reason to blame them, granted the failure of that dawn over twenty years.

For those who remained persuaded that the market system had political as well as economic benefits over total state control of investment decision-making the instrument of a state holding company offered a middle way. For those who believed in market economy socialism, but realised that it could only be achieved through a transitional period of a mixed economy, a state holding company offered a major transitional instrument for the economic basis of social change. It also gave a dimension to Government economic policy which might well be necessary if the main structure of ownership and control were to pass from private to public hands.

It is important to recognise at this point that Holland's arguments represented a significant departure from doctrinaire nationalisation measures, the state take-over of a whole industrial sector. A state holding company need not control more than one or two leading companies in each sector of the whole spectrum of manufacturing industry. Put another way, it was seen as a multi-sectorial instrument of intervention. As we shall see, this was to cause some doubts among the traditional left which was suspicious that Clause Four was being by-passed by clever and articulate young academics who were swamping the committees with quasi-marxist economic analysis. The fears were not unlike the early reactions of the Italian socialist movement to the IRI.

If the holding company was to be effective and to get off the ground within a reasonably short time, the party argued, it was vital that it should, from an early date, possess a large industrial base in the form of factories operating in a wide range of industries and in most parts of the country. Holland and Pryke rejected the transference to the holding company of the diversified activities of the nationalised industries as a suitable base. They believed that it would not be a very extensive or useful spring-board for expansion. There was also the not inconsiderable factor that the party was being highly critical of the Conservative Government's policy of hiving off sectors from the nationalised industries.

Holland and Pryke did suggest the possibility and desirability of the holding company being a minority shareholder in some of the nationalised industries' diversified activities so that it would have access to their managerial expertise and personnel. Alternatively, it might be possible to provide the holding company with the firm foundation it needed by vesting it with the state's existing shareholdings in independent or semi-independent firms and it was this approach that was adopted. The principal firms they named were British Petroleum, in which the Government had a 49 per cent stake, Rolls-Royce 100 per cent, and Short Brothers in Northern Ireland 69 per cent. Pryke, in particular, looked to the significant role played by ENI in the development of public enterprise in Italy as the model for British Petroleum.

There were, however, important differences. British Petroleum was an international company with a relatively small proportion of its refining capacity located in Britain. ENI was highly diversified with its subsidiary activities being major sources of employment. Among the diversified concerns were chemicals, textiles, plant construction, mechanical engineering and cement. Holland and Pryke were not discouraged : that BP was not a diversified concern did not mean that such opportunities did not exist. It may simply mean that the concern was unadventurous and conservative. Nonetheless, they recognised the need for a detailed study of BP to establish what scope for diversification existed and how far it could assist in regional development.

They went on to argue that if BP did become a subsidiary of the holding company the latter would have to appoint a majority of its directors. This would necessitate the Government having to increase its stake in BP, a logical but not inexpensive operation. In July 1971 British Petroleum's equity had a market value of nearly £2,250 million; it would cost the Government about £400 million to increase its stake to about two-thirds.

The authors were also keen to exploit the insurance companies by nationalising them and vesting the voting rights in their shares in the holding company. At the end of 1969 insurance companies owned 12.2 per cent by value of the ordinary shares of quoted British companies, and pension funds owned a further 7.6 per cent. The proportion of equity held by insurance had been slowly increasing and if this continued the insurance companies' stake would be about 14 per cent by the end of 1975. Moreover, the insurance companies' holdings tended to be concentrated in particular companies. They argued therefore that the holding company would find it automatically possessed a stake of around 25 per cent in a substantial minority of firms. They believed this to be a strong case for nationalising insurance. Not only would it make the holding company's task much easier, but it would be a major step towards remedying one of the principal weaknesses of the large private corporation —the divorce of ownership from control.

Holland and Pryke, in conclusion, stated that their primary object had not been to prepare a blueprint but to raise possibilities and state the arguments for and against various courses of action. The danger of this approach, they recognised, was that since there were always objections to doing anything no firm policy would be adopted, and all options would be kept open until every option was closed. It had to be realised that the holding company would be still-born unless it was able to acquire a number of private firms at an early date. It was ridiculous to assume that the company could commence operations by building factories to produce markets of which it had no experience and for which it had no established market. It had long been recognised that there were formidable barriers to entering most manufacturing industries and the Labour Party could not ignore this fact. What must be avoided was the adoption of some non-solution such as joint ventures in partnership with private enterprise. True joint ventures were only possible where the holding company had something, apart from money, to offer its potential partner.

Three years later, when Labour was in power, Benn was to develop the theme on institutionalised investments. He was sacked as Secretary of State for Industry and was responsible for the Department of Energy when he presented, as a National Executive member, a paper to the party's Industrial Committee in 1975. Together with co-authors Francis Cripps, his economic adviser, and Frances Morrell, his political adviser, Benn looked to the institutions for additional finance for lagging investment by industry. The main source of new funds in the private capital market was life assurance and pension funds contributions paid by or on behalf of working people, their paper stated. The net increase in these funds, over £3 billion each year, was about the same level as total investment expenditure in manufacturing industry. Yet only about one-quarter of the money accruing to these funds had in recent years been invested in the public sector or in private manufacturing industry. The growth of these institutional savings had shifted financial power in the private sector away from wealthy owner-managers into the hands of financial companies in the City, and the reinvestment of private savings was increasingly controlled by the decisions of a small financial community. This shift of power to the City had been responsible for the growing volatility of financial markets and recent massive speculation in land and property.

However this is looking ahead. At the Bonnington Conference, Mikardo, not surprisingly, approved the idea of nationalising the insurance companies. But Robert Sheldon raised objections. Sheldon was Opposition spokesman on the Civil Service and the machinery of Government, and an old Parliamentary colleague of Dell, who, it happened, did not participate in the discussion on the state holding company. Sheldon's view was that insurance funds were a "sensitive area" and that the party must take into account the feelings and reactions of small savers. There would be the inevitable danger of these savers believing that a future Labour Government was planning to rob them of their money.

He strongly supported the view that the state holding company should be used on problems which had faced the previous Labour Government. Sheldon specifically mentioned large sums of money spent on incentives to force industry to do what it did not want to do. Next time the money would be better spent directly through the state holding company. James Dickens, former Labour backbencher and one of the brightest minds in the *Tribune* group, was then employed by a nationalised industry, The National Freight Corporation. He believed the party had to state explicitly that the state holding company was a means of extending the public sector and extending socialism.

The weekend conference was not expected to reach conclusions and it didn't. The general view was that the SHC was seen as a public enterprise company of some size and weight, which would be fast growing and innovatory, able to move quickly and flexibly to fill the gaps in Britain's industrial and regional structure, and co-operating closely with the Regional Boards and the proposed National Labour Board. Two out-

standing issues emerged from the conference and went to the
Public Sector Group for further study : the holding company's
powers of acquisition; and whether it should come under a new
Ministry for the Nationalised Industries, or under some kind
of "Ministry of Planning and Finance". The policy-makers were
serious and rejected taunts of playing Governments in exile.
We shall return to these issues later.

At this stage it was impossible to disentangle the essential areas
of disagreement which were to split the left and the right over a
state holding company. The contributions to the debate were
conducted on a philosophical level. They were propositions for
discussion not policies. There were no reasons why the two
factions should part company and argue over a political-
economic divide. If, in retrospect, there was an absence of
realism in the debate it was because no one had got down to
rationalising the thoughts and imposing conditions on the
degree of state interventionism. For all its validity as an
economic instrument, the state holding company had yet to
become, in part, a symbol of the intra-party rivalries and the
direction that Labour should follow.

Holland was still nearer to the social democrats than the
Tribune left. He could work with Jenkins, and Jenkins was
happy to receive his advice. About the time of the Bonnington
Conference Jenkins had decided to embark upon a series of
major speeches, wrongly dubbed by suspicious politicians and
some political commentators as a bid for the leadership. Ironi-
cally, within a month of making his first speech in February,
he resigned the deputy leadership over the majority view of the
National Executive and the Shadow Cabinet towards the
Common Market, and in particular, the proposed referendum.

Holland, as we saw in the last chapter, assisted Jenkins in
his speech to the north-west mineworkers on 5 May. As Jenkins
became one of the strongest opponents of the proposals for the
National Enterprise Board, the state holding company proposed by Judith Hart's Public Sector Group to which Holland
made the major and most controversial contributions, it is
important to set down Jenkins' views at this stage.

The theme of Jenkins' speech was "Socialism and the
Regions". His analysis was along the following lines. Fifteen
years ago, when national full employment seemed secure and

regional inequalities could plausibly be regarded as a hang-over from the past rather than as a continuing problem for the future, it was widely thought that future extensions of public ownership would have more to do with equality than with economic control. Keynesian techniques, it was believed, could maintain full employment; indicative planning could ensure balanced growth. Public ownership would, no doubt, be used from time to time as one instrument among many, but its role in future would be far less central than it had been between 1945 and 1950 or than the pioneers of the Labour Movement had foreseen it. (It is almost unnecessary to state in parenthesis that the left would and did not share this analysis; however, few disagreed that he was on better ground with his projections.)

Jenkins told the mineworkers that time had again moved on, new problems had arisen and old ones reasserted themselves. It was now clear that techniques for managing the whole economy could not solve detailed problems—even when the problem was that of a whole region rather than a single firm. General demand management must be supplemented by more rigorous policies of direct intervention than those which Labour used between 1964 and 1970. "We relied principally on a mixture of bribery and cajolery—on lavish grants supplemented by some Government pressure on the more public spirited or politically exposed businesses", he said. "These weapons were far better than no weapons at all, and their results should not be underestimated, but they have not nearly solved all the problems which we face in this field of regional policy."

Jenkins stated that for too long the question of public ownership in Britain had been dominated by dogma from both sides. He went on to praise the performance of the nationalised industries, especially in terms of productivity, which had been "outstandingly good by comparison with our other industries, and also good by comparison with the corresponding industries in other countries". Because the nationalised industries had been managing their affairs rather well over the last ten or fifteen years, they had built up a pool of able managers. In view of this record, he continued, in an attack on the Conservative Government's policy, it was both foolish and discreditable that the present Government should seek to hive off parts of the nationalised industries and return them to the private sector. "We should move firmly in the other direction", he said. "We should seek to hive off parts of the private sector, and encourage the nationalised sector to diversify wherever it sees a good opportunity."

Although Jenkins was not being revolutionary, it certainly wasn't the revisionism that the left had come to know and hate. There was more to come. The facts, both here and abroad, he told the mineworkers, all indicated that the remorseless pressures of a highly industrialised economy lead towards the need for greater public ownership. Jenkins went on to destroy the "myth" that only private ownership had the managerial ability, entrepreneurial flair and marketing skills to run modern industry by relating continental experience.

Renault, wholly Government-owned, competed only too effectively with our own cars, even in Britain. And the French Government had, through a national policy of industrial location, been able to build a major new plant to boost local employment in Normandy. Alfa Romeo was wholly owned by the Italian state holding company IRI. Volkswagen was Government-owned throughout its formative years of mounting success. The Italian IRI and ENI controlled some 370 companies, from Motta and Alemagna in food processing to oil refineries and steel mills. Moreover since 1968 the Italian Government had decreed that all new projects undertaken by the state holding companies should be in the Italian Development Area, the South. Sixty per cent of gross investment undertaken by the holding companies had to be located there.

Jenkins is worthy of lengthy quotation because not only did his speech reveal his personal position, it also demonstrated that the Labour movement was marching on a broad front towards the necessity of greater Governmental intervention. Jenkins thought it worth examining the Italian experience with state holding companies, not that the situation was directly comparable, but it could show the practice of active state intervention in a mixed economy. He stressed that if a state holding company was to be effective it had to represent a broad spectrum of industry. Only in this way could it afford to adopt an unusually long time scale for some of its projects, or to take risks too large for most ordinary companies to contemplate. Except for special subsidies where the state holding company might be asked to undertake an unprofitable venture for the social benefit it would bring, it should otherwise be expected to operate like any commercial undertaking and to earn profits. Its diversity would enable it to earn profits.

Jenkins put forward the now familiar thesis that the state holding company would have to grow steadily from existing public holdings in private industry, referring to the ownership of 49 per cent of BP, 100 per cent of Rolls-Royce and the Government's stake in International Computers Ltd and a number of other companies. These, supplemented by a *limited amount* (author's italics) of selective nationalisation, should provide good bases from which to diversify into the labour-using industries which the regions required. Its scarcest resource was likely to be experienced, yet adventurous, management and this was likely to set a limit on its rate of growth.

Jenkins, finally, staked out his own personal concept of public ownership. Since the fulfilment of the 1945 Government's programme of basic nationalisation he had always believed that public ownership should be judged more by its results than by abstractions and preconceived views. He had not been convinced that it contained the key to the elimination of injustice between individuals. Nor did he think it necessarily solved the problems of injustice between different groups of workers. He was, however, increasingly convinced that injustice between the regions could not be dealt with except by significant expansion of the public sector.

Yet the proposals that the Public Sector Group were to bring forward to the National Executive—and which were approved —were too "dogmatic" for Jenkins. He did not think them "remotely sensible". These comments, however, were to come a year later when the Public Sector Group had published its Green Paper on the National Enterprise Board.

FIVE

Birth of the Social Contract

BY MARCH 1972 the Labour Party had entered into a number of commitments. These had been given either through decisions at the party conference or statements by shadow ministers or the National Executive. That month the party's policy co-ordinating committee—comprising representatives of the National Executive and the Shadow Cabinet—had before them a document setting out the areas of commitment since the 1970 general election.

The *Economic Strategy* document had promised a Commission for Industry and Manpower, a National Labour Board, statutory early warning systems for redundancies, compulsory notification of all vacancies, regional industry boards, a state holding company and the introduction of new public enterprise to help the less prosperous regions. Wilson, in a debate in the Commons on 24 January 1972, had pledged the party to the reintroduction of investment grants in the regions, the re-establishment of the IRC, public investment boards similar to the Shipbuilding Industry Board and the establishment of Development Authorities. The 1971 Labour Party conference had come out wholeheartedly in favour of the repeal of the Tory Industrial Relations Act, and there had been subsequent pledges by the National Executive Committee or shadow ministers to return, without compensation, routes transferred to British United Airways–Caledonian, and the "re-nationalisation without compensation" of any industry de-nationalised.

On top of all this there were commitments in the areas of housing, education and health and welfare. Labour would repeal the Conservative Housing Finance Bill 1972, there would be private rent allowances for unfurnished and furnished tenants and security of tenure for furnished tenants. In education there would be the restoration of free milk "to those deprived of it by Mrs Thatcher", in the words of a National Executive statement in December 1971, the integration or abolition of public schools and "action" over direct grant schools, and abolition of museum charges. The 1971 annual party conference also pledged the party to reform the National Health Service and "end" private practice.

It will be seen that a tangible proposal for the trade unions and an industrial policy was not mentioned. Without it the credibility of any programme would look distinctly hollow. Repeal of the 1972 Act would not in itself constitute a policy. The electorate would demand substance rather than shadow. And, in any case, the unions were seeking a framework in which they could live and operate without the constraints imposed by the Conservative Government. Party and union leaders had begun talks but something positive needed to emerge.

The breakthrough came from an unexpected quarter, although the initiator was in the forefront of the trade union campaign. The *New Statesman* on 18 February 1972 carried a signed article by Jack Jones. Jones set out by attacking the Conservative Government for performing a "pretty massive confidence trick on the British public" in the publicity efforts it made supporting its industrial relations legislation. The Labour Party, by its conference decisions, was already pledged to repeal the present legislation and re-introduce the principles of the 1906 Act and other legislation favourable to the unions which had been wiped out by the Industrial Relations Act.* "But", he went on, "that alone will not be enough. A well-thought-out forward-looking policy can evoke support from the electorate because of its inherent sense of fair play and thus help an election victory."

Between these comments on the two main political parties, Jones made a proposal : the Labour Party "in presenting, as it must very soon, a comprehensive industrial relations policy to counter the Tory legislation should place special emphasis on the development of voluntary conciliation and arbitration—available quickly at both local and national level". In essence Jones was proposing an agency independent of the Govern-

* The 1906 Trades Dispute Act restored to the unions the immunity they thought they had as a result of legislation in 1871 and 1876. It prohibited all actions tort (civil wrongs other than a breach of contract) against trade unions; legalised picketing; and attempted to remove liability for actions of civil conspiracy from institutional trades unionists or their leaders involved in a strike.

ment, in particular the Department of Employment which, as the Ministry of Labour in the past, used to hold the ring between embattled trade unionists and employers. An independent conciliation and arbitration service would give far more force to any future Labour Government's appeals for restraint in the use of the strike as a weapon.

The proposal had enormous attractions for the politicians. It would remove Labour Prime Ministers and economic ministers from the role of parties in industrial disputes. This was felt necessary because ministerial intervention of this nature undermined union trust and confidence in a Labour Government. The TUC submitted a document to the TUC–NEC–PLP Liaison Committee in the April and by July the creation of an agency on the lines suggested by Jones passed into Labour Party policy. By coincidence it was in the same month that the Conservative Government and the TUC began talks which were eventually to break down in November when statutory controls on wages and prices were introduced by Heath.

The left was fully in favour of the conciliation and arbitration service. The inquest they had sought after Labour's electoral defeat in 1970 never came off, in the sense that it was unconstructive. Foot, who was wanting a strong shift leftwards in the aftermath of that defeat in summer 1970, was offering an explanation in April 1972 why the inquest never took place. "It was a dangerous moment", he wrote. "The left within the Labour Party could have demanded a grand inquest on all the delinquencies of 1964–70, could have mounted a furious attack on the leadership." [1] The result, he suggested, would have been disruption and fragmentation of the Labour movement in the face of the "most hard-faced Conservative Government since Neville Chamberlain". The Heath assault on the trade unions, the publicly-owned industries and the welfare state would have been all the more encouraged to penetrate even deeper.

Foot said the proper course for Labour after 1970 was to repair the damage, to refortify the base. That had been the one major purpose of the Labour Opposition throughout the past twenty-two months, and was the meaning of the extremely well-conducted opposition to the Industrial Relations Bill, and several of the issues which emerged in those discussions which were smothered at the time. Foot went on : "But, let it also be added, to anticipate objections, such a strategy does not mean that Labour's political leadership must accept dictation from its industrial paymasters, according to the tedious vulgar jargon of the Conservative Central Office. It does mean that an over-riding sense of confidence and common purpose must be restored between the leaderships of both sections of the movement and between the trade union and constituency party rank and file who fortunately happen to be the same people. Much more has been achieved in this direction over the past two years than might have been expected . . ."

By this time, April 1972, Foot was shadow leader of the House of Commons, having been appointed by Wilson in January, primarily to strengthen the Opposition's team fighting the Government's Common Market legislation. The party was now in complete disarray over the issue. Jenkins had resigned as deputy leader, and Lever and George Thomson had quit the Shadow Cabinet. Wilson had a serious split on his hands. There was talk in the newspaper columns, encouraged by some Labour politicians, of the social democrats breaking away and forming their own party. Much of it betrayed an extraordinary ignorance of the structure of the party and the nature of politics. No one appeared prepared to ask the fundamental question . where would they go to? They would not be able to commandeer the party's organisation, headquarters, funds, or win over majorities in the constituency parties. There was no doubting, however, the dismay of the pro-Europeanist social democrats. They had lost their leader, Jenkins, from the Shadow Cabinet, and the left at the same time had succeeded in chalking up another victory. This was the decision of the Shadow Cabinet, after weeks of vacillation, to accept the possibility of a referendum on the Common Market if a Labour Government were returned to power.

The emergence of Foot was part of this seething debate within the party. Ambition had come to him late in life and it was an ambition of a limited kind. His objectives were to keep Britain out of Europe and improve the balance of power within the party from the point of view of the left. Benn also shared these objectives. But he was also seen as being prepared to humiliate the social democrats within the National Executive and the Shadow Cabinet. This, at any rate, was the reasoning of his opponents who bitterly resented his personal drive to get a referendum accepted as party policy.

Foot was the natural heir of Bevan, but he was a reluctant leader. While he relished trumpeting the cause of the left, and in this he had no peer as an attraction, he had no taste for the minutiae of the struggles for power and influence. He was involved in the bitter intestine battles in the later 'forties and had no wish for a repetition in the early 'seventies. Although he stood, successfully, since 1970 for the Shadow Cabinet, he had shown no desire, up to 1972, to seek re-election to the National Executive on which he had last sat in 1950. It was said of him, by some friends as well as enemies, that he was more interested in his literary pursuits and taking his dog for a walk on Hampstead Heath. But the pressures grew upon him to accept the leadership of the left. In November 1971, and again in April 1972, he stood for the deputy leadership of the party. Although he failed on both occasions—against Jenkins and then Edward Short—his vote showed he had considerable support within the Parliamentary Labour Party.

"I am not in favour of bitterness between left and right because I don't believe bitterness is the way to solve difficulties", he stated when he became shadow leader of the Commons. He added : "The left is prepared to go much faster carrying the logic of their Socialist policies much further. But because we have left and right it does not mean we should state these policies in terms which distract from the policy issues themselves." [2] Foot was pressed to stand for the National Executive at the October 1972 annual conference. He came top of the poll in the constituency section. The annual report in an uncharacteristic display of emotion recorded : "The following people are elected after three recounts : Foot M. [applause], Benn A., Allaun F., Castle B., Mikardo I., Lestor J., Healey D."

Foot, nonetheless, arrived too late on the scene to have significant influence on Labour's *Programme for Britain* which was being prepared during the year as consultative document to put to conference. He was not on any of the policy groups. His membership of the Shadow Cabinet allowed him to attend the joint meeting with the National Executive at the Charing Cross Hotel in May, but this was the only occasion he was directly involved. He was not even a Shadow Cabinet member of the tripartite Liaison Committee involving the NEC, PLP and the TUC. This body, as we saw earlier, rapidly approved the TUC proposal for a conciliation and arbitration service. But this was not the only area where the political and trade union wings of the movement were searching out areas of a common approach. It was in these meetings that the birth of the Social Contract began, although none of them were fully aware of the chemistry that was taking place at the time and had certainly not dressed the discussions in quasi-Rousseau-esque clothes.

The unions, however, could not allow themselves to be too politically ambitious because they had to maintain the increasingly strained relationship with the Conservative Government. The politicians, on the other hand, doubted the party constitutionality of the meetings. Or, at least, some of them did. It was thought there could be a substantial row if the Parliamentary Party and the TUC were seen to be muscling in on the rights of the National Executive to prepare policy which would form the foundation on which the next general election manifesto would be built. Callaghan was one of those who was aware of the dangers, although he was a strong advocate of the tripartite discussions. When David Lea, of the TUC, had first proposed that the meetings should be tripartite rather than bilateral he had been warned by Gwyn Morgan, the party assistant general secretary, that they would have to proceed with caution for they were treading on a thousand principles.

But there is no doubting the success of the tripartite meetings. A degree of harmony between the political and industrial wings of the Labour movement was being restored, even if only gradually. The breakdown in the talks between the Government and the TUC in November 1972 clinched an agreement between the Labour politicians and the trade unionists. The trade unionists felt less inhibited in producing a joint statement of aims with the Labour Party. But this is anticipating future events. What was important to both sides was the agreement, in February 1972, that they should hold discussions on the basis of the documents the two bodies had produced separately. These were *Labour's Economic Strategy, Growth and Unemployment* and the TUC's *Economic Review*, published in February.

The Labour Party, at the same time, increased activity on its consultative document. The resignation of Jenkins had a bearing on this. As he was no longer deputy leader he lost his *ex officio* membership on the National Executive and in consequence had to relinquish the chairmanship of the Finance and Economic Committee. Healey, as the new shadow spokesman on Treasury affairs, took over the chairmanship. Jenkins' departure also meant that two of his closest colleagues, Lever and Dick Taverne, left the committee. They were there in their capacities as PLP frontbench economic spokesmen, but they had lost their jobs. Dell, however, stayed on the committee. He had resigned as a frontbench spokesman as early as October 1971 over the issue of Europe and Jenkins had made sure he was retained on the committee as a co-opted member. Healey brought on to the committee the new Labour frontbench spokesmen : Joel Barnett, Bob Sheldon and Brian Walden. But the National Executive members continued to take little interest in the committee, except, that is, Healey, Mikardo and Shirley Williams. The other members included : Douglas Houghton, chairman of the Parliamentary Labour Party, Tom Bradley, John Roper, a young Labour MP and an economist, and the Marquands.

Healey was new to the whole field of economic policy and was frank about his lack of expertise. This lack of experience meant he treated the committee as a forum in which he could hear the differing views of economists. However, he had other forums. From the commencement of his shadow chancellorship he held meetings with a small group of academic economists with varying degrees of commitment to the party. He was also to prove cautious and conservative in his approach. At its April meeting the committee was presented by the office staff with a draft paper as a contribution to the party's consultative policy document. One of the items was a proposal for the public acquisition and liquidation of some of Britain's privately owned overseas assets. The proposals had been pushed inside the Labour Party, particularly from the left, since the mid-'sixties. Healey sat on the idea. With the backing of the majority on the committee he would not even allow the proposal to go before the senior Home Policy committee for discussion. It was felt that borrowing from overseas central banks would only be a satisfactory counter to speculation on the pound when the underlying balance of payments position was sound.

The draft paper was extensive, covering a wide area of economic and finance policy which had not been touched by the committee. When Healey, the newcomer, was informed that this was the case he told members that they had only themselves to blame. Several areas of policy were to emerge from the two meetings held in April. The committee turned down a draft paper proposal that all investment grants should be discretionary and—more controversially—agreed that the commitment to a wealth tax was too firm and should be less specific. The draft had sought a commitment that the next Labour Government would impose an annual levy on the large concentrations of private wealth. It was suggested the tax would be graduated; perhaps starting at the rate of one per cent where net assets amounted to more than £50,000 and rising to a top rate of 5 per cent.

The committee also rejected a proposal for a payroll tax on top of Value Added Tax. Again, because of possible international financial repercussions, the committee turned down a proposal for paralleled exchange markets, as had occurred in France. It was thought that such a proposition at times of international exchange rate instability should not be dealt with in a statement of long term policy. The paper also contained a section on prices. It included items already discussed in an earlier chapter : a statutory early warning system on all proposed price increases in both public and private sectors; a statutory system for the control of key prices of essential items of household expenditure, at the point of production; the establishment of a small mobile inspectorate to investigate prices at retail level, and the strengthening of policy on monopolies to cover all areas of abuse or market power by companies supplying the home market. It looked like a belated attempt to claw back an influential role for the committee over policy on inflation and the economy. But the committee was told that it could not deal with prices in detail. The subject was being left to the Industrial Policy Committee.

The Industrial Committee was pressing ahead. It held two meetings within the space of a week in April, the 18th and 25th. Before the first meeting was a paper prepared by office staff, which brought together the areas of discussion at previous meetings. The committee began amending it for inclusion in *Programme for Britain*. One of the earliest decisions taken was that the language in the paper should be toned down and less firm. It should be more a "Green Paper", i.e. it should be less positive in its commitments. The *Programme*, after all, was a consultative document. But this did not imply there was any back-tracking by the committee. It was agreed that specific proposals should be "floated", with more or less firmness depending upon the particular issue. Mikardo reminded the committee that the overall *Programme* was seen by the National Executive as the *basis* for resolutions to conference. Although never openly stated, the principle adopted became an unwritten invitation to grass root activists to mobilise the constituency parties to furnish leftist resolutions for debate. The Green Paper was seen as part of a continuing process and would be amended and "rolled forward" after each conference. The committee also decided that a major theme of the industrial policy section should be the "erosion of economic inequality".

These decisions gave the committee considerable room for manoeuvre in shaping policy. By not specifically committing the party it avoided a fight with the less interventionist-minded members. The policies that were "floated" would undoubtedly win the approval of the activists at the party conference. However the section on prices was substantially changed. The committee, for example, agreed that the party should be less specific about subsidies and make it clear that not all price changes would be subject to scrutiny. In the draft paper it had been argued that the party would have to consider seriously the possibility of short-term subsidies, or of meeting a firm's capital needs from public funds. The paper tentatively accepted that the proposed system of price controls had very serious implications for incomes of all kinds. A failure by a firm to obtain permission to increase prices could "affect the incomes of shareholders, managers *and* workers".

The inherent problems of securing a viable and acceptable prices control policy was considered in greater length at the subsequent meeting. But before seeing what was discussed then, one further decision taken at the first meeting must not be overlooked. Holland, who had been brought into the party's policy-making process on the Public Sector Group, was co-opted on to the Industrial Policy Committee. Holland's influence on the committee can be exaggerated; but by the same token it can be underrated. He was singled out among the ideological right as being troublesome; Benn, from the other side of the party's political spectrum, was to admit after the policies were finally approved that much of it was due to the contributions of Holland. Holland worked tenaciously but quietly. He was virtually unknown outside a limited circle of politicians and academics, although they did not deny his increasing influence. There were many members of the Parliamentary Labour Party who had not heard of him.

When Holland was invited on to the committee some of his close associates on the committee suggested he should prepare a paper on *Planning and Policy Co-ordination* for the next meeting, if time were available. Within the week he had produced a 15,000-word document. There is sufficient evidence to show that a degree of preparatory collusion was involved. Holland had been working on the paper before he was invited on to the committee and he was in regular contact with Geoffrey Bish, research secretary of the Industrial Policy Committee.

Dropped into the draft Green Paper prepared by Bish and others on the staff, which went before the first April meeting, was a section on "Planning and Programme Contracts". This was the first time the subject had been mentioned inside the committee. It was to prove highly contentious. What, therefore, was it all about? And what were the political implications? It was imperative, said the paper, for the next Labour Government to commit itself to planning on a *continuing* basis, "through a ministry armed with interventionist teeth". It continued : "But planning on this basis is impossible without the basic information, with the plans of leading companies being provided on a continuing and rolling basis." This was to be the beginning of the party's commitment to a Planning Agreements System, later to be strongly challenged by the Conservatives and industry. The proposal came from Holland, drawing on his experience and studies of industrial policy on the continent.

The draft Green Paper proposed the adoption of the programme contracts procedure used by the French Finance Ministry, and adopted by Italy and Belgium, in which leading companies were "invited" to submit advance programmes to the government covering key aspects of their strategic activity. These included prices and location of investment. The paper added : "And should we choose to adopt this system, we should ensure that firms 'invited' to provide this information do so, and do so promptly—thus enabling us to plan for the first time with reliable, up-to-date information."

This small passage had far-reaching effects. It helped strengthen the interventionist arguments of the left and establish Holland's influence. Backed by Hart, Mikardo and others, his theoretical and ideological contribution to the policy-making process increased. The committee agreed, at the instigation of Hart and Mikardo, that it should delete the various references in the draft Green Paper which pinned down too closely the role of the proposed state holding company. They had their own reasons for doing this. The Public Sector Group, on which Hart, Mikardo and Holland sat, wanted the group to be unencumbered and free to come up with its own proposals. The committee had already helped further their ambitions by agreeing that the state holding company should be given a different title, one that was more *accurate*. In other words, one that would recognise that the concept being worked out by the Group was not fettered by the circumscribed structure imposed upon the old Industrial Reorganisation Corporation.

Another implication was that the committee was looking at planning as a major objective of a future Labour Government. The proposition awakened old fears. The reservations held by many members of the Industrial Committee was implicit in their initial reaction to the draft Green Paper. The majority thought the party needed to be "fairly modest" in its claims for any new planning system, particularly when they saw the contribution made by Holland. Before examining his propositions it would be useful to set them in the context of the various brands of planning that have dominated thinking in post-war Western Europe. Andrew Shonfield has described them :

There is first of all the intellectual approach. It is "indicative" planning—the system which relies on pointing out desirable ends rather than on giving orders to achieve them —in its purest form. The plan is made to work because the quality of the analysis done by the planners convinces the men wielding economic power, in the private and public sectors alike, that the conclusions offered to them provide good advice. On this showing, the plan does the same sort of thing as watching the market normally does for managers of enterprises, only better : it provides them with additional signals to guide their decisions.

Secondly, there is the approach which relies on reinforced governmental powers. The state controls so large a part of the economy that a planner can, by intelligent manipulation of the new levers of public power, guide the remainder of the economy firmly towards any objective that the government chooses.

The third approach, by contrast, eschews whenever possible the use of direct governmental intervention, and places its reliance instead on the corporatist formula for managing the economy. The major interest groups are brought together and encouraged to conclude a series of bargains about their future behaviour, which will have the effect of moving economic events along the desired path. The plan indicates the general direction in which the interest groups, including the state in its various economic guises, have agreed that they want to go.[3]

Shonfield noted that the British approach in practice has been very largely a combination of the first and third brands, even under a Labour Government. Under Labour, however, a major attempt was made to plan the public sector as a whole, and to fit this plan clearly into an overall picture. But what the left needed was a "very considerable" move towards the second approach, reinforced by governmental interventionist powers. In the phrase used by Holland in one of his subheadings, it needed to be "more than indicative if less than imperative". Holland explained in his *Planning and Policy Co-ordination* paper : "Unlike the British National Plan, the successive French plans were not merely indicative." Quoting from Shonfield, Holland wrote that planners were "part industrial consultant, part banker, and part plain bully". They could be this, Holland stated, by going below the level of individual sectors, and messing their hands with individual firms— normally the leading firms within those sectors. The lessons from the National Plan experience was hard but clear enough. Indicative planning alone was doomed when it started. Nonetheless, it was the means rather than the will which was lacking. Holland, not altogether convincingly, argued that the means were already available from those policies to which the party was already committed. He stipulated the proviso that the party would have to appreciate that a future Labour Government "will probably have to extend the frontiers of planning in a market economy system rather than imitate a French experience under different conditions from those obtaining in France".

When Holland submitted his paper to the second meeting, committee members such as Hart and Mikardo had already been primed. It is a customary practice that minutes and documents are circulated to committee members at least a week before a meeting takes place. Mikardo was quick to realise what Holland was offering. Like-minded committee members were alerted by Mikardo to absorb the Holland paper and thoroughly brief themselves to get it through the committee.

The paper explained the programme contracts procedure. The crucial area was prices. But the forward planning of prices for such produce of key firms meant that the Finance Ministry secured information over a far wider range. It covered the scale of investment projects, the rate and scale of innovation of new products and their substitution effects relative to produce which would be displaced, and import and export ratios anticipated in the period concerned.

On the prices' front alone, Holland argued that the advance information process on a systematic basis from companies which were themselves price leaders for their sectors was a considerable advance on some of the best work already achieved in the United Kingdom by the Prices and Incomes Board. (This was the Board set up by the 1964–70 Labour Administration and scrapped by the Heath Government.) It was a "considerable advance" because the information was consciously used by the Finance Ministry in its global planning, and because the firms themselves benefited from greater certainty in forward company planning and from clearance on price increases, once these had been granted by the Ministry.

Advance information from leading companies in the private sector, the paper stated, would bring with it information on those companies which constituted the bulk of our export performance. By the same token, advance information on what they anticipated as the pattern and rate of imports could give information on trends in the sectoral composition of imports. Both sources of information could permit the planning authorities to map out trends in export bottlenecks and import gaps. It would help to identify those sectors in which efforts should be concentrated to secure a higher rate of export promotion or import substitution. In investment terms, the same information process would assist the planners in identifying which crisis in company boardrooms, or tired admission of another "stop", was greater in particular sectors than in others, and how much the rate of investment would have to be increased to fulfil even a "deflated" growth target.

Holland accepted that a programme contracts system alone could not ensure either maintenance or redirection of investment and growth. But he argued that it would prove a forward step on an exclusively macro-economic policy if pursued through leading companies on a widespread and continuing basis. However, there was the fundamental problem of getting the agreement of industry. Holland commented that judging by the difference between the conditions under which planning had been introduced on the continent and its possible re-introduction in the United Kingdom, there appeared to be a strong case for making programme contracts compulsory rather than voluntary.

It was to be this very idea of compulsion which was to make the moderates baulk at the proposal. Wilson, as will be shown later, had the compulsion element removed from the draft White Paper which Benn, when he became Secretary of State for Industry in 1974, submitted to the Cabinet committee in the late summer. Holland stated that compulsion would mean requiring the leading firms by law to submit a true report of their medium term projects, prices, imports, exports, finance, employment, innovation, product substitution and location. Where firms had no such projects—or claimed they had not— the law would require them to elaborate on them. The problem of deceit was relatively simple to counter, he said, if the Government was serious about the policy.

Holland suggested that providing the legislation specified that the companies concerned must inform the Government in advance of any change in their plans which affected the outcome of their programme contract, no company could afford to diverge dramatically from what it had informed the Government. A firm which submitted in its programme contract that it would undertake investment on a particular scale in a specific location with a given labour force, but later did something else, would be hard put to avoid penalties imposed on it by the Government planners for breach of contract.

The concept of "Programme Contracts" procedure received a fifty-word reference in *Programme for Britain*. The committee had agreed that it should be fairly modest in its claims for any new planning system. The *Programme* described the procedure as "attractive". There was no commitment at this stage, for good reason. A joint meeting of the National Executive and Shadow Cabinet, held in the Charing Cross Hotel on 19 May—a month after the Industrial Committee meeting at which Holland's paper was considered—called a halt to further policy decisions to be included in the *Programme*. The reason was straightforward. The National Executive Committee had committed itself to publish the consultative document in July. Any further policy proposals after May would hold up the redrafting that had to be done before the *Programme* could go to the printers. The senior Home Policy Committee had already sifted and debated all the policy proposals from the various sub-committees, including finance and economic and industry. They had then gone before the joint meeting. The proposals were now the property of the National Executive. There were no substantial changes, though Wilson suggested at the joint meeting that the party should look at the possibility of the public ownership of urban land as one way of preventing the continuing escalation of land prices.

On prices generally, we saw earlier in the chapter that the Industrial Committee was wrestling with the problem of reaching a viable policy. The committee recognised the crucial importance of the investment and profit link with prices. It was argued, for example, that to ensure the higher rate of investment needed to sustain a higher rate of growth, profits may need to go up faster than wages. This would be true, it was suggested, whether or not companies raised the necessary capital internally from retained profits, or externally from the capital market, meaning that profits would need to take a bigger share of Gross National Produce. At the time lack of investment was not due to lack of funds. But it was accepted by the committee that under full employment investment would compete.

The arguments that developed turned full circle—the committee was back to the question of the whole nature of private ownership of capital. For the left it underlined the relevance of public ownership and policies on redistribution. It was agreed that the area of investment-profit-prices would need more study and that a pricing policy was central to any realistic planning policy. The experience of the French planning system seemed to bear this out. It was also agreed that the Prices Inspectorate proposal would need to be in greater detail. The committee felt that the Inspectorate would have to be a Government body rather than be assigned to local authorities, since the odium attached to inflation would always accrue to the Government. When *Programme for Britain* appeared the Party was understandably unspecific in its proposals.

Labour's *Programme for Britain* was launched officially at a press conference in Transport House on 6 July 1972. The previous day there had been an $8\frac{1}{2}$-hour session of the National Executive Committee to ratify the finalised document, which ran to over 50,000 words. The issue which engaged most attention (the debate lasted over three hours) was the bitterly contentious policy towards the Common Market. The arguments involved have been documented elsewhere and fall outside our scope. Essentially the left was opposed to British membership of the European Economic Community because it could impose unacceptable restrictions upon the future Labour Government's freedom to plan the British economy. The treaties demanded a degree of economic integration, it was argued, that would take control of the economy out of the hands of the British Government and put it in the hands of European industrial and economic interests. This view was challenged by the pro-market social democrats as a gross distortion of the realities, but the left, who wanted a socialist planned economy, was unrelenting in its attack upon the Common Market. Yet they had failed over the past two years to commit the party to a withdrawal from the Community. The National Executive agreed a fudged compromise that a future Labour Government would seek to renegotiate the Brussels Treaties. If these renegotiations did not succeed Labour would not regard the Treaty obligations as binding. The Government would "consult" the British people on the "advisability of negotiating our withdrawal from the Communities", through a general election or a referendum.

The press conference was conducted by Wilson, Callaghan and Benn. In the latter's view, it was "the most radical and comprehensive programme ever produced by the Labour Party". The document stressed that it was "not a manifesto", though it contained proposals that would go into a manifesto. There were proposals in some fields which could not be carried through in a single Parliament. Some objectives set out could not be attained in five years through lack of resources. "It is at the same time a document more ambitious than a manifesto, and yet one in which the NEC is still aware of important gaps", it stated. It was being published as a basis for discussion throughout the country in time for debate at the annual conference. The document continued : "In the light of the debate and decisions at Conference, it will be our intention to place before next year's conference [1973] a shorter document which will recommend, for consideration by Conference, the priorities for the next Labour Government."

The substantial gap in the document was the relationship between the party and the unions. For a variety of reasons there could be no explicit common approach. Two days before the press conference the TUC had embarked upon a series of discussions with the Conservative Government.* The *Programme* stated : "By the end of July we hope to issue a joint statement on these subjects [voluntary machinery to improve industrial relations and industrial democracy] for consideration by the TUC in September and the party annual conference in October. We shall then go on to consider the wider issues of economic and industrial policy." Wilson confirmed that he hoped for an agreement on 24 July, at a meeting of the tripartite Liaison Committee, on some of the economic questions vital to Britain's future. He said the party leaders and trade unionists had virtually agreed the heads of a Bill on industrial relations, although the Bill had not been drafted. (This followed on from the firm commitment to repeal the Conservative Industrial Relations Act.) They had also agreed on the conciliation and arbitration service proposed by the TUC. Moreover, they had agreed to sit down and work out all the implications of inflation and the best method for dealing with it.

Wilson, however, doubted whether all the work would be

* These were to break down in November when the Government decided to introduce a standstill on incomes. See Chapter Six.

completed on a "compact" between the Labour Party and the unions before the party conference in October. The reality behind this was that the trade unionists could hardly enter into wide-ranging agreements with the Labour Opposition when they were involved in discussions with the Conservative Government. Callaghan, replying to a questioner, said: "We also attach considerable importance to a voluntary incomes policy, with the accent on co-operation and not the bludgeon, and a redistributive taxation policy and a progressive social policy." If prices were to be squeezed, how would the next Labour Government achieve the investment necessary for a high rate of economic growth? Callaghan answered: "If the key control of prices means there are not sufficient funds available for investment, then we should expect the state to intervene with the necessary funds, perhaps in exchange for some holding—equity or otherwise—in the concern."

The reaction of the press to the document was not surprising: "The Smith Square socialists ride again", declared the *Economist*. Its view was that the document "is very much what one would expect from a Labour Party in Opposition when the left wing is in the ascendancy". *The Times* headlined its leader: "Equal but Incoherent." It said: "The whole tone of the document is very strongly egalitarian; this raises issues of principle which will no doubt be an important matter at the next general election." The paper's Political Editor, David Wood, commented: "Nothing in the document commits the next Labour Government yet. It points directions, but leaves the pace of advance and any possible detours to be decided later. It is at once venturesome and cautious, socialist and pragmatic, hard-shelled and soft-centred. It is a document intended to create impressions rather than to hook Labour leaders on specific commitments."

The Times and the *Observer* agreed on one particular point. The former said: "The whole document shows how seriously the Labour Party is missing the presence of the Labour Europeans in the Shadow Cabinet. A Party cannot humiliate and force to resign its best and most experienced people without serious loss of understanding and intellectual grasp." The latter concurred: "It is instructive to compare the scrappy and ill-digested quality of this document with the carefully considered material in Mr Roy Jenkins' recent speeches. His hand and that of Mr Harold Lever are sadly missed, particularly in the economic section of the document." The truth, of course, was that the social democrats let the party's economic policy slip through their fingers twelve months earlier. Viewed from the other side of the political spectrum, the Communist *Morning Star* commented: "This programme is not for Socialism, but for the continuation of capitalism."

Eric Heffer, who had been brought on to the Industrial Committee in 1972—and was to fail by only 4,000 votes to get elected on to the National Executive in October at the party conference—offered the view: "There is no doubt that the draft programme... is a recognition that the party has moved and continues to move left." It was also a tacit recognition, he wrote in the *Morning Star*, that during the last Labour Administration the left was correct and the right wrong. But the character of the programme made it difficult to pin down precisely what the commitments were, he complained. Heffer instanced the "vital" question of public ownership of banks, insurance companies and finance houses.

The *Programme* stated: "The public today own a substantial proportion of the economy, yet crucial levers of financial and economic power are still in irresponsible and private hands." It added that "our commitment to public ownership and control in this area is, of course, firm and definite". But Heffer complained that later in the document a number of indefinite proposals were spelt out that, unless improved upon, could mean a "tinkering with the edges of the problem, rather than all-out ownership and control".

Heffer was to prove an enthusiastic member of the Industrial Committee, strengthening the position of the left, particularly when the crucial arguments started later in the year over the state holding company. His comment on the SHC in his article was: "It is proposed to establish a state holding company which will in various ways and degrees incorporate private firms and industries into the public enterprise sector. The weakness of this approach to the subject of public ownership is that it begins to take the right road, but draws back at the decisive moment."

But while these diverse comments were being made the most important aspect at the time was being overlooked. This was the remarkable degree of similarity in the thinking between the party policy-makers and the trade union leaders. Not only did the political and industrial wings of the movement reach accord on a conciliation and arbitration service on 24 July, as Wilson promised, but there were also whole areas of policy where they shared a common approach. This was not really surprising. Trade unionists sat on the party's policy-making committees and study groups. Conversely, some party members attended TUC study groups and the Economic Committee. There was a constant exchange of views between Transport House and Congress House. Proposals thought worth considering were placed on the separate agendas. There was a continuous cross-fertilisation of ideas. All of this occurred at varying levels in the two organisations, with the tripartite Liaison Committee being the supreme body linking the two sides of the movement.

References

1 *The Leadership Labour Needs Now, Sunday Times,* 30 April 1972.
2 *Birmingham Post,* 17 January 1972.
3 *Modern Capitalism,* Andrew Shonfield, Oxford University Press 1965.

SIX

1972—Advance by the Left

"The General Council are unanimous in their belief that the Government have made a major error of judgment." With these words, by the TUC on 6 November 1972, the structure of co-partnership between the Government and both sides of industry, designed by Heath, collapsed. The TUC statement added : " ... The General Council have taken at its face value the Government's claim that it was prepared to enter into a real partnership with both sides of industry in the management of the economy. ..." Whatever the ramifications for the Heath Government caused by the breakdown, the way was now open for more formal and concerted co-operation between the TUC and the Labour Party.

The causes of the walk-out by the trade union leaders, and the reasons for the protracted talks between the Cabinet and the TUC, need further explanation. Since the beginning of the year the Government had felt compelled to reverse its economic and industrial strategy. It had found itself in an inflationary recession, with rising prices and unemployment, and stagnant investment. Public money was poured into the regions and industry. Its earlier, partially successful, attempt to lower by degrees the level of pay settlements ended with the first miners' strike in February. Before then the rate of annual increases in earnings fell from the high point of 14 per cent in November 1970 to just under 9 per cent in January 1972. By the spring of that year the annual movement was almost back to 12 per cent and by the autumn it had climbed to around 16 per cent.

Wages were not the sole cause of rising inflation. In June the Government had decided to shore up Britain's failing " competitive position" by floating the pound, a disguised devaluation. The inevitable consequence would be increased costs for imported basic raw materials and rising prices. In order to get some degree of control on the economy the Government had begun talks with the TUC and the Confederation of British Industries. The TUC Congress met at Brighton from 4 to 8 September and union leaders made it abundantly clear that a policy on incomes could not be considered unless it was part of an economic strategy covering control of rents, profits, dividends and prices, and designed to secure a redistribution of income and wealth. Jack Jones informed delegates : "We have said 'No' to wage norms in our talks with the CBI and the Government, but we do say 'yes' to redistribution. Our Movement has never objected to fiscal measures to ensure equality of sacrifice, if sacrifice is necessary."

When the TUC saw the Prime Minister on 26 September at Chequers, Heath proposed that pay increases over the next twelve months on past increases should be limited to within a cash sum of £2. Trade union leaders were decidedly unhappy. They pointed out that the figure would result in wages and salaries rising more slowly than profit incomes (incomes from profits, self-employment, professional fees, rents and capital gains). Moreover, the arrangements the Prime Minister proposed for prices appeared quite inadequate to control those actually being charged in shops. In addition, the Government seemed to be making no proposals about the increase in council rents which would come into operation under the Housing Finance Act, the increase of food prices that would result from the adoption of the EEC agricultural policy, the present inflation, and house prices. The two sides were never to reach an agreement. On 6 November Edward Heath made his statement in the Commons in which he announced Government proposals to take statutory powers as soon as possible to freeze prices and incomes.

These deliberations were watched closely by Labour. *Programme for Britain*, which had been completed long before the Government–TUC talks began, was understandably vague on incomes policy. It stated :

We therefore intend to supplement our strict price controls, in both the private and public sectors, with a voluntary incomes policy—the objective of which must be to ensure that the growth of the nation's wealth is accompanied by steadily rising real incomes, with sharper rises for the lowest paid. This will be in the context of a redistributive taxation system and a progressive social policy. If inflation is to be overcome, then *all* sectors of society must co-operate in a necessary adjustment. . . The extent of Government intervention will have to depend on how successful voluntary efforts are. There will be no behind-the-scenes discrimination against workers in the private sector, nor will there be statutory intervention into wage negotiations.

On 6 August, when Heath was about to begin his talks with the CBI and the TUC, Harold Wilson published "my cure for inflation".[1] Wilson repeated his flat opposition to a statutory incomes policy, and stated why. It could be invoked only in conditions of dire national emergency, and only for a short period. "With the greatest difficulty it can be accepted, but only if those concerned, particularly the unions *and their members* accept the need for it, and are satisfied that the Government is taking correlative social and fiscal measures to provide reasonable equality of sacrifice and the required 'climate of social justice'." A statutory policy produced anomalies injurious to industrial relations in the months and years following. Even if severe restraint was exercised for a further period, the time would come when too great a head of water was battering against the dam. Wilson stated that a voluntary system must satisfy, just as much as a statutory policy, the necessary requirements of fairness and justice. Prices must be controlled and seen to be controlled. Provocative increases— in top peoples' salaries, for example—must be avoided. Effective action must be taken to deal with even more provocative get-rich-quick adventures in housing, property or land speculation. The workers asked to participate in a voluntary system were concerned with their own household cost of living index. Action on prices without action on rents, school meals, fares and other household out-goings was meaningless. Higher charges in these areas were just as much a reduction at source as PAYE.

This is what the TUC had been arguing. The day before the TUC saw Heath at Chequers, and was faced with a proposal for a limitation on wage increases, Jack Jones, Vic Feather, and other trade union leaders had attended a tripartite meeting of the Liaison Committee. They had not met since the July meeting. The politicians, who included Wilson, Healey,

Benn and Houghton, were anxious to hear the comments of
the trade unionists on the *Programme*. It was out of these discussions that the question of wage negotiations arose. The trade
unionists welcomed the fact that there was a close agreement
on several policy areas in the *Programme*, particularly on industrial, regional and taxation. But they pointed out that it would
be a mistake to believe that the industrial and political climate
was the only consideration. Jones and Feather stated that the
realities of collective bargaining could not be ignored and told
the politicians that it was important that the Labour Party
should not have too simple an approach in the area of wage
negotiation.

The politicians agreed, but informed the trade unionists that
the TUC ought to be more specific about some of the problems
in wage negotiations. This was so that the Labour Party could
dispel the idea that it had nothing useful to say about the problem of inflation which was uppermost in the public mind. The
Labour Party, it was stated, fully understood the context in
which the TUC was talking to the Government and on that
front, too, it would be helpful to the party to have a clear
appreciation of the TUC's approach.

Jack Jones and his colleagues were not as specific as the
politicians would have liked. It was difficult, stated the TUC
representatives, to assess how far it would be possible to go in
defining concrete problems and solutions in the field of wage
negotiations. Indeed, the TUC had regularly drawn attention
to the complexity of wage negotiations. Anything which was
agreed at national level would require interpretation in terms
of plant bargaining which had become a typical method of
negotiation in many industries. They gave as an example the
movements towards measured day work which often gave the
appearance of establishing very much higher rates of pay
whereas, in reality, the earnings secured under the previous wage
negotiations patterns were often not significantly lower. The
politicians proposed that a joint working party might examine
the range of issues, but were unable to persuade the trade
unionists, who preferred further discussions by the whole committee. But at least a delicate area between the two sides had
at last been broached. The meeting, amicable and co-operative,
was the most crucial the Liaison Committee had had since its
commencement in February. For the first time the two sides

were prepared to go beyond industrial policy and approach the highly sensitive area of incomes. Although no great advance was made, a dialogue had opened up. In other areas there was little fundamental disagreement. The production of the *Programme*, though not fully realised at the time, laid the foundation for the Social Contract. It was out of future meetings of the Liaison Committee that it was to emerge.*

When the Liaison Committee met on 20 November, under the chairmanship of Jim Callaghan, the TUC representatives circulated copies of their printed report of the Chequers and Downing Street talks which had ended in the breakdown on 2 November. The TUC had told the Government that they would not insist on statutory control on all retail prices so long as the Government could give a guarantee that food prices and rents would be limited to a 5 per cent increase. But the Government had been unwilling to give such a guarantee and consequently lost the TUC's acquiescence to wage limitations. The politicians on the Liaison Committee informed the trade unionists that they recognised the Government's major problems in the coming period were over prices and rents. The difficulty for the Government in keeping prices down in the light of their policies on rents and food was quite apparent. It was made even more difficult by the trend of import prices since the downward float of the pound. The Government's only hope was to find the scope for sharp reductions in indirect taxation at the time of the next Budget.

Both sides agreed with the proposition that the critical problem was not only the policing mechanism for prices at retail level but also the need for policy changes on the part of the Government, particularly on rents and food prices. An open-ended subsidy to keep food prices within the given figure— even if this did not fall foul of Common Market considerations —might lead to a very high Exchequer expenditure commitment, to be financed by taxation. There was general agreement that the problem of price control was one of the points which the two sides should try and cover in a joint document, but this work would need to be part of a wider remit to include such items as housing and land, policy on poverty and pensions, and policy on industry and investment. Labour Party

* For a detailed analysis of the foundation of the Social Contract, see *Appendix*.

committees, of course, were considering these issues and the TUC was also doing work on them. The two sides also felt that it was important to focus attention on the policies already agreed, as spelt out in the *Programme* and the *Economic Review*.

The two sides then turned to the issue of wages and salaries, when reference was made to the emphasis that the Government claimed to be placing on help for the low paid. The trade unionists pointedly remarked that it remained to be seen how far the Government were committed to making real progress on this issue. Moreover, it was doubtful whether any agreement at Downing Street would make a real impact if it were not reinforced by effective progress in trade union organisation and pressure at local level among the workers on the shop floor. It was felt it would be wrong for policy on collective bargaining to concentrate on the TUC–Government level. Nonetheless, the issue of wages, prices and the national income was one which could be the subject of further work. It was recognised that the question of how these matters would be arranged between the TUC and an incoming Labour Government was a vital one, but the trade union side asserted that it would depend to some extent on the specific circumstances of the economy at the time. Both the politicians and the trade unionists agreed that this view presented a difficulty in laying down a policy towards the initiative taken by Heath, but at the same time they were conscious that some progress was being made towards a viable Labour policy on prices and incomes, something which had been absent for two years.

Over the next two months the Liaison Committee, either formally or through informal contact, worked towards publishing a joint declaration of aims. The agreed document was to become a landmark, for it brought together publicly the political and industrial wings of the Labour movement for the first time since the schism of the late 'sixties. Wilson and Vic Feather solemnised the "great compact" (Wilson's phrase) at a press conference on 28 February to launch the document *Economic Policy and the Cost of Living*. Labour rejected statutory wage controls, Wilson said : "On the simple ground that history has shown that in democratic countries you can only do this once." [2] He added : "Each time you try a statutory freeze it diminishes in value and acceptability. The case for statutory freeze has been destroyed by Mr Heath because it is accompanied by manifestly unfair and unworkable policies." Both sides were offering up the hope—they could do no more than that—of voluntary restraint by the unions under a favourable economic climate created, partly, through price controls. The document stated : "In this way the next Labour Government will prevent the erosion of real wages and thus influence the whole climate of collective bargaining." But how could the TUC guarantee that its constituent members would fall in with the broad agreement? Feather said that he thought that the unions would be ready to revive their collective bargaining committee (in which unions submitted voluntarily their wage settlements for scrutiny, but which carried no statutory force) "in an atmosphere of this kind". He added : "We would make our views known about certain things to unions on specific wage claims."

The Labour politicians and the trade union leaders had struck the best bargain they could at this stage. *Economic Policy and the Cost of Living* provided an over-simplified critique of Tory Government policy and then set out the Labour Party–TUC alternative (it is worth noting that the TUC's name appears first in the official document). Under the former heading, the document stated that the "present inflation has been induced and encouraged by deliberate Government policies". These had not only led to higher rents, house prices, fares and food : they had also led to a series of confrontations with the trade union movement against the harsh background of record levels of unemployment. Large-scale under-capacity working in manufacturing industry had led to increased costs. And this was not all. The Government had also chosen to redistribute income and wealth, on a massive scale, to the most privileged sections of the community—those benefiting most from investment income and capital gains, or reductions in corporation tax and estate duty. Yet at the same time it had proceeded to introduce new and increased social changes right across the board, including dearer school meals, and much higher charges for prescriptions and dental and ophthalmic services. In the two-and-a-half years to the end of 1972, food prices rose by 25 per cent, rents by 29 per cent, rates by 30 per cent, fares by 42 per cent, and house prices by more than a half.

The Government's policies "have steadily undermined the

possibilities of co-operation in our economic life", a phrase which gave overt backing by the Labour Party for the TUC's attitude in the deadlocked talks with the Government. The Government, the document stated, had refused to listen. Instead, it seemed to have equated what it described as its electoral mandate with a freedom to ride roughshod over the interests of great sections of the community. "Certainly," it continued, "it was quite unprecedented for a Government in this country to introduce legislation intended to transform the entire legal framework of one of the greatest institutions in our society— the trade union movement—without any attempt at serious discussion of the principles." This, of course, was a reference to the Industrial Relations Act (it could hardly have been directed at the failure of *In Place of Strife*!).

The document went on to refer to a lack of confidence which was reflected in the serious state of the economy. Despite the substantial increase in consumer spending during 1972, and the large increase in profit, manufacturing industry was known to have fallen by no less than 10 per cent—in real terms— between 1971 and 1972. It was argued that by choosing to stimulate the economy through an unplanned and unbalanced consumer boom the Government had brought about a deterioration in the balance of payments, as imports had swept in to meet the demand, while goods which should have been exported had been diverted to the home market. The balance of payments surplus left by the Labour Government had been wiped out, and the trade deficit was growing at an alarming rate.

And the trade unionists? They "are as concerned to keep down the cost of living as anyone else". It continued: "They do not need to be told that what matters is real wages, not paper ones. But the problem of inflation can be properly considered only within the context of a coherent economic and social strategy—one designed both to overcome the nation's grave economic problems, and to provide the basis for co-operation between the trade unions and the Government." It had to be a strategy which took full account of the one irrefutable fact which had been so clearly highlighted by the freeze— namely that wages and salaries were very far indeed from being the only factor affecting prices. It had not been the farm worker, for example, who had been responsible for rising food prices, nor had he shared in the higher profits which had resulted. Likewise it had not been workpeople and their families who had been responsible for rising rents. The document asserted : "And it is surely time it was properly understood that in the composition of consumer prices as a whole, wages and salaries account for only 40 per cent—with profits, rent and other trading income accounting for 25 per cent, and imports and taxes on expenditure, each accounting for between 15 and 20 per cent. Moreover, the level of wages and salaries in Britain is no more than about average for industrial countries—and their rate of increase for the last decade has been below the average."

The document proceeded to outline an alternative strategy to fight inflation. The key, it said, was direct statutory action on prices—above all, direct action on the prices of those items that loom largest in the budget of workpeople, such as food, housing and rents. Food prices must be controlled and the document gave a pledge that "the next Labour Government will create machinery to make this possible, providing subsidies where necessary to curb increases in the price of goods". Special measures would be taken to deal with increases in the price of important basic foods, such as milk, bread, sugar, meat and potatoes, including, where required, the creation of new special purchasing agencies to intervene in the market. But food price controls would be only one part of a wide-ranging and permanent system of price controls.

It was explained that such a system would need, first, to cover the main items on the family budget and affect the various levels of activity, from manufacturing to retailing. But second, the system would be flexible, with powers available to it capable of being used selectively. Inevitably, in deciding to permit or refuse particular price increases, or ordering price reductions, the system would have to concern itself "deeply" with profits, profit margins and productivity. Optimistically, the document ventured the promise : "In this way, the next Labour Government will prevent the erosion of real wages—and thus influence the whole climate of collective bargaining."

A new approach to housing and rents was also promised. The next Labour Government would repeal the Housing Finance Act 1972. Council tenants would be given a better deal—both on rents and on security—and be given much more say in the management of their estates. The aim for private rented tenants would be the municipalisation of privately rented property, with, in the shorter term, much greater security of tenure being given to tenants in furnished accommodation. The Labour Government, it said, while continuing its previous policy of helping those who wish to buy their own house on mortgage, "would end the scandal whereby the richer the person and the more expensive the house the greater is the tax relief". Surtax payers would no longer be eligible for relief at the higher tax rate and all relief on mortgages to purchase a second house would be abolished.

The document then went on to promise the reversal of "regressive social and taxation policies of the present Government, and aim for a large-scale redistribution of income and wealth". It pointed out that at the time, one-tenth of British adults owned between them three-quarters of the nation's private wealth, while 1 per cent of adults owned about half of all ordinary share capital. "This distribution must be changed", it said. "The numerous tax concessions given to the rich by this Government will be reversed; and new taxes on wealth, and also on gratuitous transfers of wealth, will be introduced." The system of direct taxation would also be made more progressive with the tax threshold being regularly raised as necessary to maintain the real value of the personal allowances.

These tax reforms would be supported by a deliberate Government decision to channel resources into the social services. Social charges would be phased out as quickly as possible—prescription charges would be the first to go. "For pensions, our immediate commitment is £10 a week for single retirement pensioners, and £16 a week for married couples— and the basic pension would be updated each year in relation to average earnings, not just to the cost of living." The Labour Government would help to meet the cost of "these urgent social requirements not only by tax changes but also by measures to cut back the level of defence spending to that of our European allies".

Supporting these policies, it was recognised, must be agreed policies on investment, employment and economic growth. "The objective must be faster growth in both national output and in output per man." This depended very substantially on the quality and effective management of capital equipment, as well as up-to-date working methods. Fundamental to the British economic problems was the problem of investment and, more generally, the problem of control and the disposition of capital. "The expansion of investment and the control of capital will thus be one of the central tasks of the next Labour Government." This would mean the development of new public enterprise and effective public supervision of the investment policy of large private corporations. The inference here, of course, was a Planning Agreements system. As the document stated : "For it is these big firms which now dominate the growth sectors of the economy—to the extent, indeed, that no less than half of the nation's manufacturing output is already accounted for by the leading 100 companies, with this degree of concentration growing year by year."

A new approach to regional policy was promised. The next Labour Government would "work closely with the trade union movement on an agreed programme to promote regional development—a programme spearheaded by effective manpower subsidies, a massive expansion in training and retraining, and investment funds for industry linked to greater accountability". A new approach was needed towards "much greater democratic control in all aspects of our national life and towards greater public accountability for decision-making in the economic field". In the control of capital and the distribution of wealth there would be more economic democracy and "the growing range of functions of the trade union movement will bring about a greater extension of industrial democracy". It added : "The collective bargaining process is the essential means whereby the most important factors affecting the livelihood of workpeople can be subject to joint regulation. But these areas must be extended to include joint control over investment and closure decision."

The document said much and at the same time little. As a public relations exercise it was a reasonably successful effort. It demonstrated to the electorate that the party and the unions were again working in unison on a broad front. The objective was to ditch the Tories and then, through co-operation between a Labour Government and organised labour, implement policies to curb rising inflation, stimulate sagging investment and regenerate industry. But the document was evasive over what these policies would be. This was excusable. Many, as yet, were still in the embryonic stage. We will return to these but before doing so a new development in policy needs to be noted.

In January 1973, the month before *Economic Policy and the Cost of Living*, the National Executive and the TUC set up a joint working party for the nationalisation of shipbuilding and associated industries. Its members were, from the Labour Party —Benn, Albert Booth MP, Dick Douglas MP, Bruce Millan MP, Terry Pitt and Margaret Jackson; the TUC—Joe Crawford, David Lea and Larry Whitty; and the Confederation of Shipbuilding and Engineering Unions—Daniel McGarvey and John Service. McGarvey was a veteran, class-conscious nationaliser. The CSEU's demands for public ownership went back years. It was McGarvey, as President of the Amalgamated Society of Boilermakers, Shipwrights, Blacksmiths and Structural Workers, who successfully moved a composite motion at the party conference in 1971 demanding "that a future Labour Government should bring the shipbuilding and ship-repairing industries under public ownership" and also called for it to be "a high priority of the next Labour Government". Motions for the public ownership had also been adopted by the Trades Union Congress and by the CSEU. But the party never actively started to carry out the implementation of the Conference decision until July 1972. It was not until December 1972 that the party's Industrial Committee agreed the joint membership, with the TUC, of the working party.

It was at the same meeting that a sense of urgency crept into the work of the committee because of a major row in November, described later. Before the December meeting was a paper which stated that the Public Sector Working Group had already done a good deal of work on the concept of the state holding company (or, as it was to become, the National Enterprise Board). It was hoped to produce a draft Green Paper in January. The paper added: "An early decision is needed on the NEB. For it is now clear that this body—or bodies, if more than one is set up—is crucial to our whole industrial policy." The Industrial Committee "will therefore need to come to hard policy conclusions on the NEB—its role, its size, its structure— in time for the revision of Labour's Programme".

The Public Sector Group had not been happy with the name "state holding company" for some months and it was in September that they had provisionally decided to call it the

National Enterprise Board. It was felt that "a less defensive line should be taken on the merits and scope of the company". This view, of course, accorded with the belief of some of the Group, that to be effective the NEB would need to be a major instrument of economic policy. But in what light should the NEB be seen? Here the Group ran into disagreement. The Hart-Holland-Mikardo line was that it would be a mistake to use the old IRC as an example to describe the NEB. The Group, however, agreed that their policy document should begin by listing the tasks that needed to be done, such as job creation. This could be done by hammering home the failure of private enterprise, even with past Government aid, to solve the problems. The NEB would then be introduced as the public enterprise answer.

The Public Sector Group had a long discussion in November on the role which might be filled by a revived IRC. Two opposing views were expressed. The first was that NEB should be charged with the whole responsibility for administering Government aid, and IRC should only be revived if experience showed a need for another agency. The second view was that if there were no IRC, the NEB would be landed with lame ducks and be hampered in its main strategy. It was also strongly expressed that the party must not repeat the mistake of the last Labour Government, whose efficiency-promoting IRC had no need to take account of the social consequences of its actions, and where no other agency existed to counteract those consequences in terms of redundancy. The Group thought this highlighted the need for co-ordinating the work of IRC, NEB and the National Manpower Board.

The arguments were resolved by the agreement that NEB and a new, possibly retitled, IRC should be separate agencies, responsible to and directed by the same planning unit or planning Minister. This was so that overall Government strategy was co-ordinated. Additionally, the second agency should concentrate on helping out firms, especially small or medium firms, in which NEB did not wish to take a permanent stake. The Group agreed that as a large base was envisaged for NEB they should consider recommending one planning unit or Ministry, but more than one state holding, the idea being that a decentralised structure was created for different industrial sectors, but overall strategic planning remained at the centre. In this way, if IRC was one of the decentralised units, the party could emphasise the positive overall role of NEB. The group also took a conscious decision to refrain from quoting the Italian Industrial Reconstruction Institute (IRI) in order to avoid arguments as to the merits of IRI's record rather than the role proposed for NEB. Instead, it was decided to emphasise the total foreign experience in this field.* The draft before the Group had stated that "A state holding company bears some resemblance to the IRC", and "The main model for the NEB is the Italian State Holding Company IRI".

The Group therefore saw that the importance of the tasks which the new holding company would be asked to do meant that it had to be brought into existence speedily after Labour was re-elected. As legislation would be required, the first step would have to be the passage of a National Enterprise Act and the establishment of a board to run the new organisation. The board would, like other public corporations, be accountable to a minister who would nominate its members and be able to lay down its strategy. Although there may on occasion be private participation in the undertakings which the board controlled, the National Enterprise Board would itself be wholly state owned. NEB would need a considerable base in order to set about the numerous and urgent tasks which had been identified. If it had to start from scratch and enter industries where it had no experience or stake it would be many years before it got off the ground. Certainly it would have very little to show for itself before Labour had to seek re-election, and therefore would be politically vulnerable. To help create the base for expansion the ownership of BP, Rolls-Royce, Short Brothers and various miscellaneous state shareholdings could be vested with the agency.

The problem about the acquisition of BP, an obviously lucrative asset, was the undertaking given by the British Government in 1914 to BP in which the Government "pledged itself not to interfere in the company's commercial affairs, and undertook not to exercise the right of veto except in regard to certain specific matters of general policy".† Richard Pryke submitted a five-page memorandum to the Public Sector Group in which he demonstrated that the Government was under no

* See Chapter Three.
† BP Annual report, 1970.

such prohibitions and was entitled legally as well as morally to appoint extra directors to the board of BP and to treat the company as a nationalised undertaking. He quoted the letter, dated 20 May 1914, from the Treasury to the Anglo-Persian Oil Company : the Government did not propose to make use of the right of veto except in regard to matters of general policy such as "the control of new exploitation, site of wells, etc.".

Pryke argued that the Government would appear to be entitled without in any way violating the agreement to supervise the company's capital expenditure programme. This surely followed, he said, from the reservation of the right to exercise a veto over new exploitation and the siting of wells. The Group minuted the Pryke Memorandum. Should a Labour Minister cite the precedents of 1914 as a reason for not nationalising BP, the Group would treat Pryke to dinner. "It was further agreed that if BP were nationalised he should similarly treat the Group!"

But BP was not the main point of conflict when the Group's proposals went before the Industrial Policy Committee on 28 November at a meeting in Committee Room 7 at the House of Commons. It was here that Crosland made his major challenge to the interventionist plans of the Group. The focus of the argument was on the public ownership of twenty leading manufacturing companies, one of the big three leading banks and two or three leading insurance companies. It was proposed that these would make up the basic National Enterprise Board portfolio. The plan was presented to the Industrial Committee by Holland.

Holland had won the economic argument for such widespread nationalisation inside the Public Sector Group in October, although he did not secure the agreement of Lord Balogh. Those who had supported him were Judith Hart, Mikardo and Pryke. Margaret Jackson, as research secretary, also gave her support. Holland argued that the state as capitalist could cope with the macro-economic growth promotion problem if it had a package of leading state firms distributed through the many manufacturing sectors. Socialist planning must offer more socialist transformation of the commanding heights of the economy than had previously been attempted if it was to succeed. Twenty new publicly owned firms in modern manufacturing could be added to Rolls-Royce, BP and BAC (with increased shareholdings in the latter companies) and control of major shares of the output, profit and employment of the top 100 manufacturers secured, which accounted for half net manufacturing output. A preliminary dummy run on twenty such companies showed that the share secured could total a third of the top manufacturers' turnover, two-fifths of their profits and nearly half their employment. When Holland had been asked inside the Public Sector Group which companies he had in mind he was stopped in his tracks by Judith Hart. She warned that if names "leaked out" there would be a gigantic political row.

Holland's economic arguments would sometimes lead him into political extravagances or so it would appear. Anticipating objections on electoral grounds, he had once suggested that proposals could be put forward, without specification of the companies, that the Labour Party wished to bring the instruments of economic management more into line with the continental economies by securing an initial public holding package of not more than two dozen firms. Persuaded by Transport House research staff to introduce a decree of levity into the high seriousness of his arguments in order to stimulate more interest, he then proceeded to state in a paper : "As far as the top management of the companies is concerned we have a variety of means at our disposal which we could employ in combination. Twenty-four managing directors can be secured round one table at the same time as an innocuous-looking State Holding Bill is being introduced in Parliament. If they are joined by top trades union leaders as well as addressed by the most senior members of Cabinet, the potential gains to the national economy, their potential role in contributing to the community, their imminent membership of the House of Lords (for laymen), and their membership of the board of the state holding company (for peers) can be made plain to them." Holland continued : "Plus the fact that by the time they leave No 10 the act will be law, the powers of appointment and dismissal to their own boards now residing in the responsible minister through the board of the state holding company on which they will be outvoted." It seemed he was more familiar with Karl Marx than Erskine May.

The meeting of the Industrial Committee in Room 7 was attended by Benn, Booth, Crosland, Dickens, Hart, Heffer,

Holland, McCarthy, McKenzie, Millan, Mikardo, Pryke and Robinson. Heffer had gone along to the meeting to oppose the NEB proposals because he thought them to be a diversion from the true path of socialism and nationalisation. It was only when he sat through the heated argument between Holland and Crosland that he changed his mind, his basic premise being that if Crosland was against the idea then it must have considerable merit.

Holland presented two papers : *Planning Strategy, Tactics and Techniques* and *The New Economic Imperatives.* He emphasised the crucial importance of harnessing the growth of the top 100 manufacturing companies in order to prevent a worsening in regional disparities. He outlined the list of tasks that needed to be fulfilled, such as : provision of a direct vehicle for channelling government expenditure into directly productive activity as a growth promotion or counter recession instrument; reduction of monopolistic pricing by collusive leaders through price restraint below the leaders' normal level of prices; offsetting the multinational challenge by ensuring British ownership of leading companies. There was, he said, a clear need to adopt a fully-fledged Programme Contracts system as an integral part of planning arrangements. (The system would require companies to report on their past five years' activity and thereafter on an annual basis; they would also require leading firms to submit a programme for projects already decided upon or currently being implemented which, in the case of investment in entirely new plants, products and processes, would give the planners a two to four-year fixed horizon for these firms.)

Holland's exposition was too much for the social democrats, Crosland in particular. While the meeting agreed on the tasks that needed to be done—and on the inadequacy of the present machinery and Labour's existing proposals to achieve them— Crosland challenged what proved to be the majority view. He asked why the tasks could not be accomplished with existing machinery and the public enterprises if given a firm government approach. There were those with ministerial and Cabinet experience, he said, who would realise that industrial policy decisions would have to be taken by ministers in Cabinet. Holland replied that there were those with experience who had seen that it was the Civil Service who wrote the strategy options for Cabinet.

Other members argued, against Crosland, that the existing public enterprises were in an "upstream" position in the economy; they were not price-makers and thus were not "foot loose". They tended to be relatively declining sectors or areas of the economy. At the same time their industrial relations had been bedevilled by large-scale redundancies, by losses instead of profits, and erratic government policies. It was manufacturing that set the pace. Existing national industries were, because of their passive position in the economy, quite unable to initiate any broad wave of investment since manufacturing companies, especially medium-sized ones, would refuse to take risks unless other leading companies were investing and growing.

James Dickens asked whether it were possible for such publicly-owned pacesetters to take the risk of investing in development areas. But Holland pointed out that the additional costs to a company of such a policy were usually very small compared to overall costs, though the need for complementary public sector policies to ensure the necesary ancillary services, infrastructures etc.—as suggested in Labour's *Programme*—was recognised. The NEB would play a key role in this field. Both Dickens and Mikardo suggested that there were advantages in extending public ownership on an industry by industry basis. It was generally agreed that the approach outlined by Holland did not preclude other measures of public ownership, while it would help to prevent the state merely accumulating more and more "lame duck" companies.

Derek Robinson emphasised the need to avoid comparing the proposals of Holland against "the criterion of excellence". They would not, he suggested, solve all of our industrial and economic policies, "but they would provide us with a further means of tackling them". Crosland had argued that there was no point in all this bureaucratic intervention at the level of the firm and that it would be electorally disastrous to go to the country on a platform of extensive nationalisation. He questioned Holland on what political and philosophical analysis he based the proposals. Holland gave as one of the examples *The Future of Socialism*, Crosland's own theoretical work. The philosophy of the social democrats was overturned. Benn, for his part, made little contribution to the discussion, but was highly complimentary to Holland afterwards. At the December meeting of the Industrial Committee Benn, in his absence but obviously with his agreement, was installed as the new Chairman, Chalmers not even being nominated for re-selection. 1972 had been a remarkably successful year for the left, but the debate and arguments, particularly over the twenty-five companies, had yet to reach a climax. This was to come six months later.

References

1 *Sunday Times*, 6 August 1972.
2 *The Times*, 1 March 1973.

SEVEN

"Spadework for Socialism"

IN THE EARLY months of 1973 there was a renascence of social democrat activity : a spring offensive. It was agreed that the leftward swing in the party, so apparent at the annual conference, had to be countered. While it succeeded in exposing the inherent divisions within the party, its influence on policy-making proved to be minimal. The inspiration was the commemoration of Gaitskell's death ten years earlier. Its one concrete achievement at the height of the campaign was Dick Taverne's successful stand as an Independent Democratic Labour candidate in a by-election at Lincoln, where he had resigned his seat as a Labour MP. Politicians, political commentators and leader writers, naturally, seized the occasion of the memorial to Gaitskell for reflective analysis on his contribution to British politics. More wistfully, they speculated on what might have been if he had lived.

The fact that Wilson, as Gaitskell's successor, was celebrating his tenth anniversary as party leader, commanded about one-tenth the space. This too, was seen as natural. Wilson's style of leadership did not mirror the Gaitskellite image. His success in transforming the party from one of natural Opposition to one of natural Government may well have been undeniable but, it was argued, at a price. The consensus view was that he was a man led by his party and not leading it, and these activists were moving the party away from the well-springs of the social democratic tradition. Moreover, he was seen as taking a back seat in the "great betrayal" over the Common Market. Gaitskell, of course, had dismayed his friends in 1962 in his opposition to British membership of the Community, but he had his apologists in 1973. Wrote the *Social Commentary* : "Re-reading now his major speech on the subject . . . we cannot help speculating about what his views would have been today . . . how they might have reacted to the major political and economic changes that took place in the Commonwealth in the 'sixties, to the developments in American policy, to Willy Brandt's successes in Germany. We shall never know. But we can be certain that, as always, he would have seen things in the light of the present and future, not of the past . . . he would not have used the 1962 arguments in 1973."

"We shall never know." The feeling of loss by Gaitskell's friends was personal, immense and sincere. On 18 January 1973, some 150 of them held a memorial dinner in the Middle Temple Hall, London. It was a "moving evening", said the *Socialist Commentary*, but overriding the occasion was the vacuum to be filled by a future leader. Roy Jenkins had abandoned the role, having resigned as deputy leader, and few were looking to Crosland to take up the mantle. Both of them paid tributes at the dinner, but it was not the venue for controversy. Jenkins, however, was to find himself at the centre of a party argument two months later because of a speech he made at Oxford. This was after Taverne's success and much self-generated but uninformed speculation from the right that the Labour Party was about to break apart.

Jenkins disassociated himself from any talk of a third party, but he raised the Gaitskellite flag by re-stating the famous phrase of his former leader to "fight, fight, and fight again to save the party we love". That was the right message in 1960, said Jenkins, and he believed it to be the "right message for today". He suggested three rules Labour ought to be applying to policy-making: Was the proposal necessary to create a better society and serve the interests of the broad range of people the party represented? Was there a good chance that it could be carried out and made to work effectively? Was it likely to win support for the Labour Party rather than repel it?

While there was validity in the questions posed, the consensus view was that Jenkins had made an implicit attack on the leadership: if not just on Wilson then on the Shadow Cabinet as a whole. It was sufficient, nonetheless, to ignite fury on the left. The judgment of Barbara Castle was: "Roy Jenkins and Roy Jenkins alone is responsible for starting up all these old rows all over again. Let there be no mistake about who is causing the splits." Heffer denounced Jenkins as one of the architects of Labour's "slide from radical socialist policies between 1964 and 1970". Wilson would not be drawn directly into the conflict, but when pressed on the BBC's "Analysis" radio programme, he stated that party policy was worked out by the National Executive, which was elected by conference, which represented the whole of the movement. Wilson continued : "Now anyone who wants to change that policy is perfectly free, as I used to do year after year, to stand for election. Six hundred-odd constituency parties vote and choose the seven they want on the executive." In case any listeners were missing the point, Wilson added : "So anyone who has got criticism, whatever it may be—even if we don't know what it is—can play his full part by standing for the National Executive, getting elected, whoever he may be, right or left, and play his full part." In other words, Jenkins should show the courage of his convictions and test his case before the party's electorate, something he had never done.

Wilson, by this period, was back in something like his old style after two years of lack-lustre leadership. There was talk of "an ebullient comeback by Mr Wilson" and the readers of the *Daily Mirror* were informed in a messianic banner head-line : "The Second Coming of Harold Wilson". The resurrection of the aggressive Wilson, exuding self-confidence and tactical skill, was partly due to the fact that the Heath Government, with its counter-inflation policies, was running into serious difficulties. But other reasons were seen. James Margach, the highly respected political correspondent of the *Sunday Times*, wrote : "Opposition morale is responding to the unquestioned evidence that after six years of the ultra-cautious, conservative, timid and consensus-motivated Wilson Government the party is moving, in Opposition, towards a much more robust, full-blooded Socialist policy for social and economic change."

But Margach seems to have been carried away by the evidence (certainly it could be questioned) in holding the view that "a substantial shift to the left by a powerful group of leading personalities who were formerly identified with the middle ground". He named them as Callaghan, Healey, Crosland and Edward Short. If they had moved it had not been far and, in any case, it was two years too late to have any dominating influence. Crosland, in fact, with unfamiliar zeal, became a regular attender at the meetings of the Industrial Policy Committee, in order to soften the policies on both the National Enterprise Board and the Planning Agreements system. He did not miss one meeting in the first three months of 1973 and, more often than not, he was accompanied by Dell. Crosland had learned by his mistakes at the November meeting and was determined to put up last-minute resistance before the policy passed out of the Industrial Committee's hands and proceeded on its way to become part of Labour's *Programme 1973*.

Wilson was not involved in the minutiae of policy-making, with its time-demanding month-by-month discussions inside the multifarious committees. However, he had his informal contacts and sources, and was to keep his main challenge until the last minute. In February he was informed by Transport House of the work of the Industrial Committee. The information relayed provided an admirable summary of the strategic themes being pursued by the committee. Wilson was told that the most significant development in the thinking of the committee, and of its various working groups, concerned the need for the next Labour Government to intervene directly in the economy at the level of the firm, especially the large firm. This would be on a selective and discretionary basis. Macro-level planning and demand management just would not be enough. Two new instruments were of especial importance :

Planning Agreements (programme contracts in the papers before the committee) : The aim was to get large companies to agree, in writing, to do certain things, such as an increase in exports and investment in development areas. In return, they would get selective government aid, or would be allowed to go ahead with price increases. Price controls were an essential feature of the planning system. If the firms deliberately failed to keep the "agreement" they could be refused help in the future, or other sanctions could be employed : they could be discriminated against as far as price control decisions were concerned; the state holding company could be used to build up their competitors; or they could be taken over by the SHC.

State Holding Company : This was seen as a key instrument —but it had to be big enough to do the job. This could mean taking over a number of selected leading companies (not necessarily the biggest) in crucial sectors of the economy.

Wilson's immediate reaction to these proposals can be surmised. He was totally hostile to wholesale public ownership of leading manufacturing firms, and was opposed to measures which overtly coerced economic and industrial management. He must have been horrified that the party was being pressurised into introducing compulsory agreements and sanctions upon industry. Governments could no more afford to alienate the captains of industry any more than the generals of the trade union battalions. Wilson was not against intervention, but opposed the magnitude that was being suggested.

In a speech in Leith, in January, he reiterated certain pledges. Wilson promised a ruthless attack on the "Tory gas and oil scandal" to ensure that a "high proportion of the yield of this national asset should go to redress the regional and industrial imbalance" caused by the decline of coal and steel. He called for radical changes in pricing, taxing, selling and royalties, so that the benefits would go to national and not foreign interests. He promised that all land required for urban and essential developments should be taken over by the end of the century. Wilson told his audience: "I favour the widest possible acquisition of land for public use, with the exception of public land owners and working farmers."

When he came to make a speech on industry two months later, in March, to the North East Council of the Labour Party, there was little in it which touched upon the major themes being developed by the Industrial Committee. Party workers were told that the aim must be to extend the socialist principles of "Government by consent to industry". His theme was that "unless radical changes are made in relations between management and shopfloor, it will become increasingly difficult for modern industry to function effectively". The first points he made dealt with the statutory rights of workers to belong to a trade union, and trade union recognition. A further point was nearer the hub of the debate among policy-makers: there would be wider disclosure of information from firms and public agencies; workers should have the right to information on such subjects as manpower and labour costs, ownership and control, and production. For the left, these were essential ingredients for an effective Planning Agreements system.

By April the National Enterprise Board draft had left the Public Sector Group and was before the Industrial Committee for endorsement. In 1973 the total membership of the committee was forty-one, but there were only seventeen members present when the committee met on 5 April. Wedgwood Benn, who had succeeded trade unionist John Chalmers to the chairmanship in December in the left wing coup, was present. For Benn the meeting was only equal in importance to the one which took place the previous month, on 27 March, when he added what was later realised to be the keystone to the interventionist arch, to which we will return.

At the April meeting Crosland, Dell and Sheldon presented their several objections to the draft paper on the proposed state holding company. But they were heavily out-numbered. Perhaps they would have had greater success if some of their like-minded colleagues had put in an appearance, for among those who were absent and could have been expected to lend support were Harold Lever, Lord Balogh, Roy Mason and Reg Prentice. The proposal to take over twenty or more companies in the private sector was obviously the prime target. But Holland, Judith Hart and Heffer stood their ground, and a majority endorsed the case for a large state holding company, given, as it was stated, the tasks it would be expected to fulfil.

Crosland and Dell explored what they believed to be politically or economically vulnerable areas in the paper but failed to convince the committee. It was argued that there was a lack of criteria for choosing companies which should be taken under the umbrella of the National Enterprise Board, but reference was made to earlier documents in which Holland had specified some of the most important of these criteria, and which were discussed at the November meeting. To recapitulate, and to quote from the document before the November meeting : "They must either be actual leaders or potential leaders once their investment rate has been expanded. They must be spread through manufacturing as a whole if they are to secure *both* a *micro*-intra-sectoral effect and a *macro*-inter-sectoral effect."

The minority of the committee suggested that a great deal of creative time and effort might be spent in getting the National Enterprise Board of the proposed magnitude under way, and that a more cautious approach should be adopted. But the majority took the view that there would never be conditions which permitted painless change. The next Labour Government would have to act quickly and boldly. Dell deployed another attack by raising the dilemma of finding alternative managements for the companies taken over. Yet others answered that there need be no real danger of a wholesale "walk-out" of managements immediately after a take-over. As one of them put it, there would instead be a careful and gradual weeding out.

Dell was later to complain that the point he was trying to raise—i.e., the management of the National Enterprise Board itself—was totally missed in the discussion. Crosland was also to register strong objections to the proposal that it would be inappropriate for companies which came under the Planning Agreements system to be referred to the Monopolies Commission. He was against such arbitrary discrimination, which could seriously affect a monopolies and merger policy of a future Labour Government, and he asked that his strong dissent should be minuted.

Crosland and others expressed concern at the possible industrial disruption caused by any large-scale mergers that the NEB might bring into being. But Judith Hart and her supporters suggested that no full-scale mergers as such were envisaged. They argued that the function of the state holding company was to decide strategy rather than tactics, which would be left to the member firms, as it was with many industrial conglomerates. In other words, the NEB was a key institution in any central planning strategy to be adopted by the Labour Government.

One other factor to emerge from the meeting was that the NEB would be expected to make profits and finance the bulk of its own investment programme. There was clearly a conflict of objectives here, considering the tasks it was proposed it should perform. But the majority formed the view that this would not necessarily be the case with most decisions the NEB would have to take. It was thought that such conflicts would be of marginal importance. The committee, with a dissenting minority, recommended publication and this was endorsed later by the Home Policy Committee.

While the draft proposals were published as a Green Paper (in other words there was not specific commitment at that stage), the key proposals had yet to be approved for inclusion in Labour's *Programme 1973*. This was to be debated at the annual conference in October and, if approved, would form the basis of the party's general election manifesto. The NEB proposals, meanwhile, had to pass the final test of endorsement by the Shadow Cabinet and the National Executive Committee. Failure would mean exclusion. But it had to be faced that time was short and the proposals were at such an advanced stage that a major reversal was out of the question. It was a significant triumph for a small group of activists who felt they were, so to speak, plugged into the national grid of Labour movement opinion.

The NEB plan was unveiled officially at a press conference in the House of Commons presided over by Judith Hart. The proposals have been outlined in previous chapters, but the ideology behind them was never more succinctly expressed than in the final page of the Green Paper. It presented both a rejection of the economic policies pursued by previous Labour Administrations and provided what was believed to be the only alternative for future success. It is quoted here in full :

At present, it is the leading private companies which determine the rate and pattern of national growth, through their own strategy and tactics. Before 1980, the top hundred manufacturers will control two-thirds of the key sector in the economy, unless we intervene directly to change the public-private balance. Good behaviour codes, intensified competition legislation, and other indirect policies can do nothing to stop this process, which arises from the dynamics of capitalist competition, rather than from collusion (leading firms exposed to international competition have to grow to survive, and scale economies ensure that they continue to grow).

Similarly, indirect Keynesian monetary and fiscal concessions will neither promote nor direct growth as a future Labour Government would wish, for even leading firms cannot afford to step out of line, in investment or location terms, if their main competitors and suppliers do not do so. The promotion of a broad wave of new investment through manufacturing, and its location mainly in our problem regions, is a public rather than a private responsibility. *But the old planning techniques of 1964–1970 will prove even less effective* [original italics] in future, as the leading manufacturers increase their hold on the market of the domestic

economy, and increasingly go multinational. *Also, the new
planning agreement information will not help us to* harness
the growth of these companies to socialist ends, unless the
government has control of leading competitors, which can
secure a leverage effect on private companies. *New Public
enterprise can bridge the gap* between overall management
of the economy and achieving more effective control over
individual sectors and companies. But this *public-private
linkage can be assured through planning agreements only if
we have the new public enterprise in the first place.* We need
this new tool if we are to match the rapidly changing structure of modern capitalism with new means of intervention.
Unless we face these implications, the next Labour Government will preside over an economy where the power of decision rests with leading private companies, with long-term
implications for the credibility of Labour economic management, and indeed the survival of Britain as an economic
force.

There was little doubt that the group endorsing the proposals
had turned their back on consensus Keynesian demand management principles. But the Green Paper had its weaknesses, which
were never fully answered. The major one, naturally, was that
Judith Hart and her colleagues had not specified which companies they had in mind. There were obvious reasons for this :
first, such speculation would create one of the biggest political
scares since Labour projected a "shopping list" of firms to be
taken over in the late 'forties; secondly, share prices of such
named companies could be pushed up by investors looking for
fat compensation payouts. Judith Hart told the press conference
that shareholders who were bought out would be "adequately
compensated". It was not clear whether private investors would
be encouraged to put their money into the NEB-owned firms on
the style of the Italian IRI, on which the Public Sector Group
had closely modelled its own proposals.

One of the prime justifications for the state holding company was that it could be used for greater and more effective
planning of the economy. More important, perhaps, it would
be used to create jobs in the regions, such as Scotland and the
North-east of England, where traditional industries were in
declnie. But it was an inescapable fact that IRI, which was

under a legal obligation to site 40 per cent of its total investment and 60 per cent of its totally new enterprises in Italy's
depressed South, had not turned out to be the employment
panacea that governments hoped. On the other hand, the Green
Paper was putting forward proposals for an interventionist
agency which went far beyond the powers and remit of the
IRI. After the press conference, the group behind the NEB sat
back and waited for the storm to break about their heads
which, indubitably, it did.

One month earlier, on 11 March 1973 Wedgwood Benn held
a meeting at his London home where he made what became
known as a "presentation". The object was to pull together
the various strands of thought inside the Industrial Committee.
The "presentation" was elaborate, reminiscent of an ops briefing
in the RAF, in which Benn had served, with organographs
drawn in a broad felt tip pen on large sheets of paper to illustrate the Government machine and a projected redesignation
of departmental powers and influence. Among those present
were Holland, Heffer, Margaret Jackson, secretary of the
Public Sector Group, and Geoff Bish, secretary of the Industrial
Committee. Two problems confronted them : one was the need
to create effective Whitehall machinery to supervise the
economic national plan in order to avoid the shortcomings of
the last Labour Administration's ill-fated exercise in planning;
the second was to find the correct legislative formula for enact-
ing the proposals now surfacing from the policy committees and
study groups.

   There was never any satisfactory conclusion to the first
problem. It had already been the subject of heated debate
inside the Public Sector Group which, as we have seen, viewed
the state holding company as central to any economic plan.
Judith Hart had produced a paper in which she suggested a
leviathan Ministry of Planning and Public Sector, under which
would come a Department of Nationalised Industries (fuel,
transport, coal and airlines), the National Enterprise Board
as a separate department, and a Department of Planning.
The strategic economic policies would be hived off from the
Treasury, which would be renamed the Ministry of the
Budget.

   Richard Pryke, who, as we saw earlier, was never happy at

the limitations imposed on the Public Sector Group and thought it should be looking at all the nationalised industries, was naturally a supporter of a Department for Nationalised Industries. He found an unusual ally in Lord Balogh when both criticised the umbrella Ministry of Planning and the Public Sector. Their argument was that it would "appear to be planning everything but the public sector" and would be much too unwieldy. On the other hand, Balogh was opposed to a separate nationalised industry department. More contentiously, he wanted the National Enterprise Board linked to the Treasury. Pryke and Holland registered their strong objections to his suggestion. Lord Balogh appeared to have misread the underlying aim of his colleagues on the Public Sector Group which was to amputate some of the Treasury's tentacles which stretched throughout Whitehall and strangled independent economic initiative.

Similar surgery was argued at Benn's home, but those present finally acknowledged the reality with which they were faced: a vast reorganisation of Whitehall aimed at the diminution of the Treasury's powers would be a lengthy and complicated exercise, and would be strongly resisted by many of the mandarins. The inevitable search for a compromise in such a controversial shake-up would have the effect of delaying what was really the number one priority: the regeneration of industry by state intervention and the shaping of a national economic plan. It was at this meeting that Benn proposed the slogan which, with one minor amendment, became the battle cry of the left: "A fundamental and irreversible shift in the balance of power and wealth in favour of working people and their families". It was to appear in Labour's *Programme 1973*.

In order to obviate the delay Benn suggested, as a basic machinery of Government, that there should be a Ministerial Planning Group. This should include: Prime Minister plus a central policy unit; Treasury with existing functions; and Trade and Industry, which would be responsible for industrial planning, public and private sector supervision, price administration, regional industrial policy, consumer protection, monopolies and mergers, restrictive practices and prices control. The other departments with economic responsibilities would be Employment and Environment. It is easy to see that the trade and industry functions would give departmental ministers super-powers, but this was seen as the only effective counter to the Treasury. The previous experiment with the Department of Economic Affairs had been a failure, particularly after the Treasury had won its battle over the "squeeze" in 1966 and the DEA's National Plan was ruined. But when Benn took his proposals to the Industry Policy Committee on 27 March he encountered opposition and the matter was never resolved. It was argued there that there was no need for the break-up of the Treasury's functions and the formation of a large new planning ministry.

The essential weakness of any discussion on the machinery of government, however, was that the final decisions would lie with the incoming Prime Minister in consultation with his advisers. While relevant, the discussions were no more than a theoretical extension of the policies to which they wanted the party committed. Policy-making was a different matter. Once approved by party conference and enshrined in the general election manifesto the leadership's room for manoeuvre had always been limited: postponements or compromises were expedients, not escapes. Benn and his colleagues were conscious of this. While Benn readily acknowledged that it was the work of others, particularly Holland, that had advanced party industrial and economic thought, it was Benn himself who devised the legislative framework in which it would have to be placed.

He fashioned the concept of an "Industrial Powers Bill", ingeniously side-stepping the anticipated objections to the scale of its interventionism by relating it to Acts and Bills produced by the Heath Government. Two days before the Industrial Policy Committee met, on 27 March, Benn wrote an article in the *Sunday Times* in which he distilled the essence of his argument. He wrote in his introduction: "Below I set out in detail the powers which a Conservative administration that was genuinely and honestly committed to the free enterprise sytem in its election programme, has found it necessary to take in order to run the economy in the way it thought right." He continued: "It is tempting to make political capital out of this change of policy. But to do so would be to underestimate the importance of what is happening, namely that these powers have been accepted as necessary despite a genuine political reluctance which Heath and his colleagues somehow have had to overcome."

It was Benn at his most disarming, but no less politically formidable because of this approach. The whole nature of the mixed economy operating on market forces had been transformed by "this quiet revolution" in a way that was not yet fully appreciated, wrote Benn. In future, industrialists were bound to turn their minds more and more to what the Government felt should be done, and less and less to market forces as a guide to their corporate planning. Benn gave as an example the Ministry of Technology which had been recreated by Heath. The whole argument about intervention, he suggested, had "passed into history books, to be continued—except for statutory wage control which a Labour Government would reject—on the fringes of political discussion".

If this was not making political capital, then the definition of the phrase had somehow been subtly and unknowingly altered. Not only was the argument still very much at the centre of Conservative discussion, but the antipathy towards interventionism eventually grew beyond Heath's control and engulfed him. Within a year of losing the February 1974 general election he was cast out of the leadership of his party. But in 1973 the Bennite line was difficult to refute, and was quintessentially attractive to the left. It was seen to kill two birds with one stone. Not only did Benn's reasoning inflict maximum embarrassment on the Conservative opponents by exposing the bare flesh of an intra-party dispute, but it helped keep at bay those on the Labour right who found many of the proposed interventionist policies unpalatable.

"It would be quite wrong", wrote Benn, "to describe the Government as having adopted Socialist policies. It has not. It has created instruments that a Government of a different kind would certainly want to use, but for objectives that would be markedly different." He gave as an example the absence of Parliamentary control over some of the powers which were "a matter of deep concern" and would be bound to be reopened by the next Labour Government. "If the next Secretary of State for Trade and Industry", he continued, "required powers on this scale—as he certainly will—he should have to go to Parliament for authority to use them. We might well have to develop an amendable Statutory Instruments procedure which would confer the power to act speedily, but would also safeguard the rights of Parliament to do more than 'take or leave it' when the Minister put forward his projects or exercised his powers." Similarly, he suggested that a new Select Committee for Trade and Industry, comparable to the Select Committee for Science and Technology, might be needed "as an additional safeguard against the development of the corporate state which is now causing deep anxiety on both sides of the House of Commons".

In touching upon the corporate state, which was certainly the basis of much comment inside and outside Westminster, Benn was partially contradicting his own thesis. It could hardly be argued that the discussion on interventionism had been relegated to the fringes of political discussion by the action of Heath and his colleagues while at the same time acknowledging the "deep anxiety" about the development of a corporate state. And in any case, some of his social democrat colleagues thought the corporate state argument was specious.

Writing in *Socialist Commentary* at this time, and we can guess to whom the remarks were directed, Bill Rodgers stated : "Another current and rather silly example of loose thinking involves accusing the Tories of turning Britain into a corporate state. In the first place, as a slogan it is ineffective because 99 per cent of the electorate haven't the faintest idea what it means. . . In the second, quite apart from the total unreality of any comparison with Mussolini's Italy, the implication runs counter to the other fashionable cry for more participation." Benn, of course, was a great proponent of participatory politics. Continued Rodgers : "In our corporate state, the story goes, Parliament is increasingly by-passed as governments hob-nob with pressure groups outside and divest themselves of day-to-day responsibilities. But the fullest consultation at every stage with people most affected by decisions is highly desirable as a defence against bureaucracy."

Benn, in his *Sunday Times* article, came to his central point. By burying the argument about intervention, accepting the role for public ownership and plumping for a managed economy the Government had made it possible for the debate to concentrate on the question : "In whose interests is the economy managed?" It would thus be a debate about objectives, and not mere administrative machinery, that would now come into the forefront of public interest. Since the Government had power to control prices and profit margins, and could provide funds for investment itself, many arguments about equality had been subtly eroded. Arguments used against Parliamentary interference with the rights of free enterprise had collapsed now that ministers had taken all those powers into their own hands. The issue lay now between Government and Parliament, and the case for Commons control over Cabinets was very powerful.

Wrote Benn: "Heath has performed a very important historical role in preparing for the fundamental and irreversible transfer in the balance of power and in wealth which has to take place, even if only to allow inflation to be tackled successfully." But inflation was not the only problem, he stated. There were many other pressing social and economic needs that were not met which explained the industrial unrest and the collapse of national confidence, and which remained the most important problem. Concluded Benn: "What we are witnessing is the breakdown of the wartime and post-war consensus which survived for nearly a generation. We must move towards a new consensus, markedly more favourable to Labour, markedly more equal and markedly more democratic. This new consensus, once we have identified it, could last another generation and form the basis for national partnership that would command confidence and release the energies of the people."

When Benn presented his paper on *Industrial Power and Industrial Policy* to the Industrial Policy Committee on 27 March, he not only took along with him his *Sunday Times* article but also his diagrams on the machinery of Government. We saw earlier how little progress was made on the latter, but on the former only one or two members, including Crosland, expressed their dissent. The majority agreed that such powers would be needed in order to supplement other industrial machinery, such as the Planning Agreements system and the National Enterprise Board. The need to prepare a Bill *before* taking office was stressed. What, therefore, was "Heath's Spadework for Socialism", the title given by Benn?

In total, Benn examined seventeen new areas of control brought in by the Government, based upon the Rolls-Royce (Purchase Act) 1971, Industry Act 1972, Counter Inflation Act 1973, Insurance Companies Bill 1973, Fair Trading Bill 1973, Industrial Relations Act 1971, and the Housing Finance Act 1972. "Taken chronologically", he wrote, "these Bills and Acts, together with the Prices and Pay Code, constitute the most comprehensive armoury of Governmental control that has ever been assembled for use over private industry, far exceeding all the powers thought to be necesary by the last Labour Government."

In a single clause, the Rolls-Royce (Purchase) Act gave power to nationalise. Benn saw this as a "stark method of acquisition very different from the elaborate and detailed nationalisation Acts of the past, without generous compensation for shareholders, workers or sub-contractors". The Industry Act essentially restored to the Heath Government the powers it lost when it repealed Labour's Industrial Expansion Act. It gave the Government the right to give financial support to firms and the right of investment by the acquisition of loan or share capital. Under the Counter Inflation Act, the Government gave itself power over prices, profits and large companies, the power to demand information, to amend statutes, to vet investment plans, and power over multi-nationals. In the case of multi-nationals, a highly emotive issue in the Labour movement—posing real and imagined threats to economic planning, the advancement of worker participation and stabilised employment—they could be investigated under the price code on transfer pricing.

The Fair Trading Bill conferred powers to enter premises and inspect and seize goods and documents, although the relevant clause stated that a duly authorised officer of local weights and measure would need the authority in writing of the Secretary of State. The Insurance Companies Bill, as drafted, gave the Secretary of State the power over appointments in that he would not issue an authorisation "with respect to an incorporated company or manager of a company if it appears to him that any controller or manager of that company is not a fit and proper person to be associated with that company". The same bill also allowed the Secretary of State to "require a company to furnish him, at specified times or intervals, with information about specified matters being, if he so requires, information in a specified manner".

Benn went on to suggest that two important legislative innovations had also appeared in other acts. The "wholly new concept" of "an unfair industrial practice" defined in the Industrial Relations Act could be extended, he asserted, to cover many other types of industrial practice, like asset-stripping or inside-dealing. His final point is worth quoting in full for, as we shall see, Wilson was to take personal exception to the Labour policy that arose out of it:

"The Housing Finance Act also includes an entirely new power which could have industrial complications. The Act stated : 'If the Secretary of State is satisfied, after such inquiry as he may think fit, that an authority with respect to whom an order has been made under subsection 1 above have failed to comply with any requirements of the order within the time limited by it for compliance with that requirement, he may order, without prejudice to any other means of enforcing the order, appoint a person (hereafter referred to as a 'Housing Commissioner'). . . The Government has not yet found it necessary to legislate for 'Insurance Commissioners' or 'Production Commissioners' to see that their orders are obeyed. But the concept, once planted in the statute book, is bound to arouse interest."

It certainly did for the policy-makers, for in the original draft of Labour's *Programme 1973* appeared the commitment "to put in an 'Industrial Commissioner' in a similar way to the Housing Commissioner concept introduced by the Tories, to assume control of any company which seeks to frustrate the objectives of the Government". The phraseology is pure Benn, and it serves as an illustration of the influence his paper to the Industrial Committee had been. But Wilson raised strong objections to the phrase when the draft went before the Shadow Cabinet and the National Executive Committee. It would have left him in a vulnerable position because he had already branded the Housing Commissioners, installed by the Conservative Government, as "commissars". In the final and printed version, the commitment read : "To put in an Official Trustee to assume temporary control of any company which fails to meet its responsibilities to its workers, to its customers, or to the community as a whole."

But in terms of intervention and public ownership, the greatest setback to the policy studies was the fate that befell the study group on banking and insurance. It will be recalled that the 1971 annual conference committed the party to public ownership in the field of financial institutions. It was a highly controversial issue and, as was explained in Chapter Two, the party leadership was more than unhappy at the way the study group had been foisted on them. The chairman was Mikardo, and its membership included: Professor Kaldor, Alistair Macdonald, a bank clerk and former Labour MP for Chislehurst, John Roper MP, Frank Welsh, a merchant banker, Ian Wrigglesworth of the Co-operative Party, Peter Jay, Economics Editor of *The Times*, Harold Lever MP, David Lea of the TUC, Muriel Turner of Associated Society of Technical and Managerial Staffs, and academic economists Professor Michael Artis, Professor Robert Field, John Hughes, Roger Opie and Derek Robinson.

The study group met on twelve occasions and eventually a report was produced by the party which none of the members would sign. Wrote Ron Hayward, party general secretary, in a foreword: "Our Study Group on Banking and Insurance produced three models of public ownership of building societies, insurance companies and banks respectively. The models on building societies and insurance companies found general agreement within the study group. The section on banking, however, provoked some considerable controversy within the group. For this reason we cannot present a conclusive report."

The reasons for publication, however, were obvious: the National Executive did not want to provoke a row at party conference by appearing to be ducking the commitment. Hayward put it in more diplomatic language: "We publish the document because annual conference asked for it, and because we want comment from all interests."

But the reasons for the inconclusiveness of the study group's deliberations were best set out in a note sent to the Home Policy Committee by Terry Pitt, Head of Research. It was quite clear from what he said that Mikardo had attempted to steam-roller through the proposals on banking. These were that the London Clearing Banks, Scottish, Northern Ireland and British Overseas Banks, should be nationalised. There should be a British Bank over two commercial banks, a development bank and an overseas bank. The British Bank would have powers to acquire other banks, companies and/or assets.

Pitt informed the Home Policy Committee that of the members of the study group, Barratt-Brown, Jay, Lea and Turner had never attended a meeting. Professor Artis, Hughes, Lever, Opie and Robinson had never attended a meeting which bore directly on the subject matter of the report. Pitt continued:

"At the final meeting Professor Kaldor argued forcibly against the section on banking . . . Ian Mikardo ruled that the report could not be so extensively amended at that stage. He did agree, however, that the study group might continue its work to devise a new model for banking and that a new paragraph in the report saying that the model in the report was one of a number of alternatives under consideration."

The "models" for building societies and life assurance, can be summarised. Building societies would be municipalised under housing authorities, or groups of housing authorities where appropriate. There would be a national authority to deal with national problems. Estate agency, surveying and conveyancing would be the concern of the local building societies, all conducted in the same office. Life assurance and motor assurance would be in public ownership, together with a substantial section of domestic fire and accident insurance. Lloyds would be left "as at present", as would the friendly societies and non-life mutual associations and marine, aviation and transit insurance. There was considerable further scope for regionalisation of insurance companies' offices. Life assurance policy-holders' funds would be invested to the best advantage of the policy-holder.

Pitt informed the Home Policy Committee : "The following members of the study group have told me they will not sign the report because of the section on banking, although they agree with the rest of the report : Lord Balogh, Jay, Professor Kaldor, Lea, Field and Wrigglesworth. Only John Hughes has said he is prepared to sign the report. Ian Mikardo holds the view that the report should not be signed. Ian Wrigglesworth has threatened to issue a minority report on banking, and is likely to get backing from Professors Kaldor and Field." The strength of feeling was more ominous than appeared, for Pitt informed the Home Policy Committee : "An attempt to raise the matter at conference is likely." His conclusions were : "My own feelings are that if handled carefully the dissidents would agree to sign the report in return for a guarantee that their views on banking would win the day, after a period of public debate on the matter. I feel strongly that a poor section on banking would mar the rest of the report and destroy the last vestiges of credibility. It might be better if this were not published."

However, the report was eventually published in August in

order to placate party conference, but with a negligible status, as Hayward indicated : "An analysis of how financial institutions may be reformed to contribute more to the wealth-producing process would aid both the institutions and the Labour Party", he wrote in the foreword, reflecting the compromise formula argued out inside the Home Policy Committee. He concluded : "The public debate on this document will culminate in a debate in the Labour Party's governing body, its annual conference. After conference we shall begin to draw conclusions in relation to the policy of the next Labour Government on banking and insurance."

What happened, in fact, was that the whole issue of banking and insurance was taken over by the Home Policy Committee, which included all senior members of the National Executive Committee, and a report was not published until three years later, in August 1976. By that time Labour was in power and Callaghan, who was then Prime Minister, firmly let it be known that he could not support the proposals. But that argument is beyond the time scale of this book.

EIGHT

Twenty-five Companies

"WE ARE A democratic Socialist Party, and proud of it." The phrase was chosen by Pitt from an early general election manifesto, and it formed the opening to the original draft of Labour's *Programme 1973*, surviving the subsequent revisions inside the Shadow Cabinet and the National Executive Committee. It was a large document, the 56,000 words running to 165 pages of foolscap. Essentially, it was a working document, later to be substantially amended in shape and partly in substance. As an attached note stated : "It is longer than last year's document, and certainly does not yet 'flow' satisfactorily. We do however at last have one document covering several hundred points in place of several hundred dcouments covering one point." The basis of it was the *Programme* of the previous year, revised "in the light of conference decisions and debate".

Before examining in detail those sections of particular concern to industrial and economic policy some broad comments need to be made. As the document stated : "It is not a manifesto, though it contains proposals which will go into our manifesto." But wide qualifications were made : "It makes proposals in some fields which could not be carried through in a single Parliament, and sets out objectives some of which would not be attained in five years through lack of resources." At the same time it was a document "more ambitious than a manifesto, and yet one in which the NEC is well aware of important gaps—some of which are currently under study, and will be reported at a later stage". An example was banking and insurance.

A warning was given about priorities. " . . . Whenever it comes to power, the next Labour Government, because this is the nature of our democratic Party, will have a very long list of commitments—many requiring lengthy legislation, and many requiring substantial money and resources. We therefore make it clear at the outset that Labour will have priorities, worked out in consultation with the whole movement."

It was stated that many of the various interest groups in Britain would find a good deal in the document to encourage them. "We must therefore sound a warning", it continued, "Shelter may be right to demand top priority for housing; the Child Poverty Action Group may be justified in calling for a first call on resources for the large family; the Pensioners Associations and 'Mind' have their own top priorities, as do other groups such as the Comprehensive Schools Committee and the Disablement Income Group. Everyone of these organisations can count on support from the Labour Party, and it may be that they are right in calling for high priority in their chosen fields. But they cannot *all* be first."

The problem of deciding priorities, often a painful process of deciding the allocation of resources between almost equally excellent causes, "is what politics is about", readers were reminded. They were told that the National Executive Committee, after carrying out a great deal of policy work in the past two years and whilst still conducting extremely important discussions with the TUC on economic and industrial policy, saw the following as the major areas to be tackled if Britain's problems were to be solved (there were stylistic revisions to the draft and what appears below is taken from the published document):

Prices. Labour will build upon and strengthen the price controls belatedly introduced by the Tories—extending them to take in prices at *retail* level—and private special subsidies on certain basic foods. We will seek to conclude with the Trades Union Movement a new wide-ranging social contract designed to curb increases in the cost of living.

Pensions. Pensions will immediately be increased to £16 a week for the married couple and £10 for the single person, with the bulk of additional revenue being raised from the employer and through the exchequer. From then on, pensions would be linked to average industrial earnings.

Housing. Labour will repeal the Housing Finance Acts, take necessary development land into public ownership, pursue municipalisation of rented property and institute a subsidy system which aims at parity between help for the owner-occupier and help for the Council tenant. Rents will be held down, land already owned by public utilities will be released for building purposes, and regional or metropolitan House Building Agencies will be set up to guarantee an adequate level of house building.

Education. Educational expenditure will be increased, with a major priority within this sector being nursery schools. The system of direct grant schools will be ended, and the whole education service democratised.

Social Services. Specific reform of the social services would include a disability benefit, reform of the NHS under democratic local control, the total separation of private practice from the health services, and the urgent creation of an Occupational Health Service.

Industrial Relations and Industrial Democracy. Labour will repeal the Industrial Relations Act and restore the role of free collective bargaining. We would also introduce major legislation to extend industrial democracy.

Full Employment. Labour will seek to achieve and maintain full employment in all parts of the country, and to ensure that redundancy will lead to training or retraining, and thus to re-employment.

The Distribution of Income and Wealth. A wide-ranging programme to achieve a massive re-distribution of income and wealth will be set under way. *Tax reform* will include a reform of the income tax system to help the poor and ensure that the rich pay their fair share, and the introduction of a range of wealth and inheritance taxes (this would mean tougher estate duty, a wealth tax and levies on the recipients of inter vivos gifts). In addition we will introduce radical new measures designed to provide workers, and the community as a whole, with a direct and increasing stake in the capital growth of companies.

The Accountability of Economic Power. Government control of, and responsibility for, the economy would be substantially extended. This would mean a major drive to increase investment in manufacturing industry (especially in the regions), an extension of the public sector in the fields of North Sea Oil, Shipbuilding, Financial Institutions, Docks, and a National Enterprise Board, and company law reform to make the private sector more accountable both to the public and to the Government.

Citizens' Rights. Labour would restore and further the democratisation of central and local government; we would legislate to outlaw discrimination on grounds of sex and religion, and give real meaning to the concept of "citizens' rights".

The Common Market. We would immediately institute re-negotiations of the Treaty of Accession to the European Communities. We would ensure that the people of Britain then decided on the course of Common Market policy through a consultative referendum or a further General Election.

At the end of the list was added the following commitment: "Labour pledges itself to the eleven points set out above. As and when success is achieved, we would bring in our other urgent plans for further progress. Labour's aim is no less than a new social order. The people must determine the nation's destiny, and only by economic liberation can they have the collective social strength to decide that destiny."

The warning on priorities was later reinforced by a background paper *Paying for Labour's Programme*, which was issued to delegates at the party conference in October. It was the first time the party had undertaken such an exercise and was also designed with another purpose in mind. It was an attempt to pre-empt the Conservatives, who were bound to cost the commitments and had the Whitehall machine behind them to undertake the analysis. Discussions on the cost of the policies had begun after the initial *Programme* had been approved at the 1972 conference. It was largely the work of the Finance and Economic Affairs Sub-Committee, under the chairmanship of Denis Healey. When the Home Policy Committee met in May, Healey told his colleagues that additional revenue would be needed to carry out the policy and there was limited means of raising it. But he thought "it was not too early to explain these problems now".

A paper before the Home Policy Committee gave basic reasons for using the period of Opposition to tackle the issue of expenditure priorities. They were twofold: first, to be able to present to the party and the country an overall programme which could be seen to be credible; secondly, to ensure that the next Labour Government would come into office with a "systematic sense of social priorities and a viable public expenditure strategy which can withstand the pressures of economic circumstances". The latter point was seen as of particular importance. "Within the lifetime of any government there will be times when tough decisions have to be made on public spending."

National Executive members were reminded that there were at least two major "crunches" of this kind during the five-and-a-half years of the last Labour Government. The paper stated that after the next Labour Government was elected, "there will be an inevitable tendency for its ministers to become preoccupied with short-term problems and to have too little attention and energy to devote to the purposeful planning of priorities". That was why "the opportunity must be grasped now, while still in Opposition, to concentrate our minds on the expenditure options available to us".

When the document was finally published it was admitted that the policies on social policy alone would be enough to soak up the resources available. The total commitments would involve over £5,500 million a year. Shadow minister Reg Prentice, whose views were anathema to the left, wrote in *Socialist Commentary*: "We have to be frank... When the Labour Government is in office, there will be relatively high levels of taxation and local rates and national insurance contributions... We can no longer pay for higher expenditure just by soaking the rich."

Paying for Labour's Programme emphatically rejected the Conservative argument that the extension of public ownership would be prohibitively expensive or lead to increases in taxation and add a new twist to inflation. The Tories did not understand "elementary economic facts". When Government securities were issued to the ex-shareholders of a nationalised undertaking this did involve a nominal increase in the National Debt. But "there is no real net increase in the public debt, for the Government has acquired a new asset to match its new liability". Future payments of interest on the newly-issued Government stock would be balanced by the profits accruing to the Government from its newly acquired undertaking. Previous industries which were nationalised had tended to be bankrupt public utilities and declining industries, and the amount of compensation was in some cases excessive. But "we are now proposing a public stake in the more dynamic and profitable sectors of manufacturing industry".

Just what lay behind some of the above commitments? The draft document not only provides the best insight into the minds of those who had been in at the beginning of the policy-making process but, with the benefit of hindsight, shows which of the many aspirations were dashed. Here we must run the risk of repetition and recapitulate on the agreement that was struck at the beginning of 1973 between the Labour Party and the TUC.

The points were: effective *price control* on the key items in the household budget, especially stringent controls on *food prices*, including the provision of subsidies where necessary; a large and immediate increase in *pensions*; the abolition of *prescription charges*, and a steady progress towards a completely free health service; fair *income tax* treatment for the lower paid, a reversal of the Conservatives' *tax cuts for the rich*; repeal of the Housing Finance Acts, and restraint on *rents*; a big increase in the *housebuilding* programme—fairer treatment for *private tenants*, including municipalisation of privately rented homes; public ownership of *land*; action to save *public transport*, including subsidies to hold down fares; more effective *regional development* policies, including effective manpower subsidies; a massive expansion in *industrial training* and re-training; greater public control of the more powerful private *companies*; development of *new public enterprise*; controls on the international movement of *private capital*; renegotiation of the "crippling" Conservative terms for entry into the *Common Market*; repeal of the *Industrial Relations Act;* "real" moves towards *industrial democracy*.

Stated the draft: "We believe that these policies will go far towards creating the right climate for talks between government, industry and the trade unions about the complementary features of an overall strategy." There was early recognition that the first task of a Labour Government would be to combat inflation. It promised an "active policy to restrain the level of prices in the shops, particularly the most essential items in the family budget". Undertakings were given that Labour would build upon the machinery of price control belatedly set up by the Conservatives". The Prices Commission would be retained and the relationship between this body and the work of the

Monopolies Commission would be examined. (Inserted into the published version was the commitment to subject the Commission to Parliamentary control.) For the larger companies, the draft stated, in referring to the 100 or so "which now dominated the economy", Labour would "employ the full weaponry of price controls as an essential part of our machinery for economic planning".

Effective price controls at retail level would be developed. This would involve publicising and keeping up to date a list of maximum "Fair Prices" for a number of key items in the family budget. The shopper would "police" these fair prices by notifying a local authority *Consumer Price Unit* of any alleged overcharging. The unit would then investigate the complaints, bringing in proceedings if necessary, and publicise the results. Labour would act to curb the increases in the price of food, and especially in the prices of certain basic goods.

The twin pillars for the attack on food prices were: first, a renegotiation of the E.E.C.'s Common Agricultural Policy so that consumers could take advantage of cheap world food prices "should these begin to move back towards levels which existed in the 'sixties". But it was recognised "that world food prices could remain at high levels, and that further increases whilst we are in office will create difficulties for our policies on inflation". Labour therefore believed that the best way to protect the income of farmers was through subsidies to farmers, wherever applicable, rather than high food prices in the shops.

Secondly, it was stated that a Labour Government would be prepared to provide special subsidies on certain basic foods, such as bread, sugar, butter, meat and potatoes. In the short-term, the Government would probably seek to apply these subsidies at the *retail* level; but in the longer-term "we would investigate the possibility of creating a series of Commodity Commissions—to cover home-produced and imported food—as the machinery for applying the subsidy". It added: "The total amount of the subsidy will clearly depend on circumstances, but it will be fixed in relation to the annual agreement reached by the Labour Government with both sides of industry."

There was little change between the draft and the published version in this section, and the same can be said of the paragraphs dealing with "Prices, Profits and Productivity" and

"Prices and Investment". In the former, it was stated that price controls would be used to ensure that, wherever possible, increased productivity resulted in lower prices. Price controls would also be used to curb those profits which were considered to be excessive, or which arose from the "abuse of industrial and market strength". As a justification, it continued : "For we do not believe, given today's concentration of market and industrial power, that high profits can be assumed in any way to represent either efficiency or consumer satisfaction."

The paragraph on "Prices and Investment" opened up with the obvious statement that an important role for profits at the present time was that they provided a large part of the finance needed for investment. Thus, in real terms, the role of profits was to ensure that the nation saved enough from its current output to provide the resources needed for capital investment. But "it is the customer, of course, who is forced to do this 'compulsory saving'—through higher prices". It was further stated : "Since it is the shareholders who own the investment paid for by customers, this is a source of great inequity—and it is seen as such by both consumers and workers. But it can also be a major loophole in any system of price control, for price increases may have to be allowed in order to provide for investment."

Two sets of measures were advanced as a means of closing the "loophole" :

> In certain cases, such as where an item looms large in family budgets, or where it can threaten a "chain reaction" of wage or price increases—a veto on such a price increase may still have to be applied. And if this means that the firm cannot undertake necessary investment, then we shall consider the possibility of government investment to meet the capital needs of the firm—in return for a public stake in the company. Clearly, such decisions would have important implications for taxation and for demand, since the resources will still somehow have to be "saved". But in the context of our broader policy on inflation, these effects would be far less damaging than a sudden price increase on a sensitive item.
>
> In the longer-term, however, the difficulties with self-financed investment remains. Elsewhere in this Programme,

we suggest ways in which the basic inequity can be mitigated. But in addition, we are now investigating alternative methods of providing the necessary savings for investment through the provision of public funds and the creation of the necessary Budget surplus to make this possible.

The longer-term plan for investment could be simply stated : "We shall use the public sector and particularly our new public enterprise, as a direct stimulant to investment, whenever necessary; ... we shall also use the power of public purchasing to stimulate investment in chosen areas and enterprise." The proposed Planning Agreements system was seen as crucial. For companies within the system "we shall provide only discretionary grants to encourage investment, whether in the depressed regions, or elsewhere". Where the amounts were substantial "they will be provided only in return for an equity stake in the company concerned".

The Planning Agreements system, of course, was very much Holland's creation. It was the intention of Holland and his supporters that the 100 or so leading manufacturing companies should be compelled to sign an agreement with the Government, but as we shall see this was one of the measures that Wilson and a Cabinet Committee emasculated when Benn, as Secretary of State for Industry, produced his draft Industry Bill in the summer of 1974. The role of the system is described below, but before we enter into the industrial strategy section one important area needs to be looked at : the trade unions and wages.

Closely following the paragraphs dealing with price control came the following heading : "Prices and Pay". It was a natural correlation but the passage appeared to be governed by prayer rather than pragmatism. "In applying our price controls, we will seek to give effect to the annual agreement reached with the two sides of industry as part of a new *social compact* [author's italics; it was changed to *social contract* in the printed version]. And this will be particularly important in the struggle against low pay—in cases, for example, where the eradication of low pay must mean substantial increases in prices." Nowhere in the succeeding paragraphs was there anything that would cause offence to the trade unions, or alert their suspicions.

The National Executive and the TUC, of course, had worked

together through the Liaison Committee, but despite the close co-operation that had developed it was difficult to remove the belief that the section on wages was an act of blind faith. "We believe that the action we propose on prices will create the right economic climate for a more moderate growth of money incomes than in the past," it was stated. With the Tories' Industrial Relations Act out of the way, with a renewed commitment to policies for economic growth paving the way for a real improvement in standards of living, and with taxation and social policy playing their part in a fairer distribution of the national cake, "the way should be open for a Labour Government to sit down with the two sides of industry to hammer out an agreement for the orderly growth of incomes with stable prices".

However, it was accepted that "a policy of price restraint cannot succeed for very long if wages and salaries are moving out of line with the growth of productivity". It was recognised that labour costs were an important element in prices. What, then, was to be done, if any corrective was needed? The document countered with a different perspective of the relation between wages and costs. Wages were far from being the only element in prices. Council house rents and the prices of houses for sale had both shot up relentlessly, while the building workers' pay was frozen. The same reasoning was applied to soaring food prices when farm labourers and shop workers had received not a penny more in wages.

The conclusion to be drawn from this was that wages were not pushing up the prices of essential goods and services, but quite different factors and "very largely deliberate actions of government policy". It continued : "This is why we put the emphasis on the need to reverse the Tories' regressive social policies and on other measures to deal directly with the problem of prices. Workers can only be expected to moderate their expectations on money wages if firm action is being taken to hold down the cost of living."

It was stated unequivocally : "We do not believe in statutory controls on incomes." Such controls could not be maintained for any length of time without putting intolerable strains upon industrial relations. Moreover, they would threaten to perpetuate all the anomalies and injustices in the framework of pay differentials which were then present. Experience showed that in the long run legislative restraints on pay agreements did more harm than good. The choice was either for a "great compact" (again changed to "contract" in the published version) between government, industry and the trade unions, with all three parties prepared to make sacrifices to achieve agreement on a strategy to deal with the problems of rising prices. The alternative was posed : "An interminable debilitating inflation which will help nobody." The section concluded : "The problem of inflation is perhaps the most difficult area of all in economic policy for any government. Underlying it all is the urgent need to get a grip on prices and deal with the problems of unfairness in pay. There can be no easy guarantee of success. But we believe that the policies outlined above are the essential starting point, without which there can be no real and permanent progress in tackling inflation."

The basis of the economic-industrial strategy, in the words of the printed version, "rests on three major pillars—each one of which is essential to its success". These were : *new public enterprises*—"and most especially the creation of a state holding company, to establish a major public stake in manufacturing industry"; *planning agreements system*—"a completely new system, which will place all our dealing with major companies on to a systematic and coherent basis"; and a *new industry act* —"to provide the next Labour Government with all the industrial powers it will need to meet the economic objectives".

The commitment represented the culmination of the work done inside the committees by the group that had set about to radicalise Labour's programme by fighting for an alternative economic strategy. But although it commanded the approval of the majority of the National Executive it was nonetheless to have strong and influential opponents. We shall see in the next chapter how Wilson, Crosland, Dell and Jenkins registered strong objections, particularly over the proposals to take over twenty-five companies. Because of these objections there was a lurking suspicion that what were thought to be the essential ingredients of the proposals would not be implemented by a Labour Government. This suspicion, in fact, provided part of the driving force of the left to commit the party to as great a degree of intervention as was practicable. Judith Hart revealed to the author later why the left drove the twenty-five companies argument to the point of savage conflict within the party.

The "numbers game", as it was called, was only surrendered after the left were satisfied that the concept of the National Enterprise Board as a major interventionist institution was accepted. One cannot be sure that this was not camouflage to disguise a leftist defeat. But certainly, at the time, after the internal battles had been resolved, the left was expressing a degree of satisfaction with the outcome. The arguments raged throughout the summer up to the party conference. To put those arguments in proper context we need to go back to the detailed proposals.

What was described in the draft programme as the "essential backbone" of an economic-industrial policy was an Enabling Act "giving the Labour Government the powers to act swiftly and selectively, and directly at the level of the firm". It was even more emphatic : "Nothing less, we believe, will be enough." Reference was made to the powers already brought in by the Conservative Government. Labour would "build upon them". It was explained why the powers were needed :

to obtain information, deemed necessary, from individual companies;

to provide any support that may be needed by companies, in return for equity shares;

to invest in individual companies, or to purchase them out-right—compulsorily or otherwise;

to vet the prices, profits, and investment plans of companies;

to issue directives on a wide range of industrial matters, including prices, profits, investment programmes, industrial relations policies and so forth;

to approve, after consultation with trade unions, all major board appointments;

to define and make unlawful a wide range of "unfair company practices";

to put in an "Industrial Commissioner", in a similar way to the Housing Commissioner concept introduced by the Tories, to assume control of any company which seeks to frustrate the objectives of the Government;

to provide for special powers over large and multi-national companies.

We have already seen why Wilson wanted the "Industrial Commissioner" changed, but the printed version also set out the functions of the new-styled "Official Trustee". He would be "put in" to assume temporary control of any company which "fails to meet its responsibilities to its workers, to its customers, or to the community as a whole". But there were other important changes which reveal the concern among some members of the National Executive at the extent of the Compulsory element enshrined in the Policy Committee's thinking. There was a distinct toning down of the power of directives. When the printed version appeared it read : "*to seek agreement* with companies on a wide range of industrial matters, including prices, profits, investment programme and industrial relations policies and to issue, if necessary in the national interest, directives on these matters". On investment in individual companies, the powers remained to purchase them outright, but the phrase was added "preferably by agreement with the company concerned, or if necessary in the national interest, by Statutory Instrument, approved by Parliament". The approval of all major board appointments, was changed to read : "to provide, if this is necessary in the national interest, for *reserve powers* to remove directors in firms with which the Government has a planning agreement."

The phrase "in the national interest" was used on three occasions in the printed version while not putting in an appearance in the draft. One cannot help surmising that during the discussions on the draft it was forcibly stressed that it would be in the *party's* interest to incorporate such phraseology otherwise the Conservative opponents would revel in the jibes of Government by dictat.

One further comparison needs to be made between the draft and the printed text on the proposed Industry Bill, for it certainly appears to contradict the understanding and concern for acting in the "national interest". The draft emphasised that "we shall use the powers under this legislation only after the fullest consultation with our partners in the social contract— both in industry and the trade union movement. And, of course, such powers will always be the subject to the control of Parliament". The printed version reiterated the need for Parliamentary control : "We reject the philosophy of the corporate state." In the party's view, it was stated, industry must be accountable both to the public through Parliament and to its own employees. The worker in Britain had no voice in the decisions that shaped his life. But the printed version pointedly missed out consultation with one of the "partners in the social compact"—industry. And by "partners" the party was obviously referring to the Confederation of British Industry as well as individual firms with whom an incoming Labour Government would have to deal and consult. The printed version read: "We shall use the powers under this legislation only after the fullest consultation with the trade union movement—and, of course, such powers will always be subject to the control of Parliament."

It has never been possible to establish positively whether the omission of the employees' side was deliberate or a sloppy piece of re-drafting. Industry could be expected to put up strong resistance to the proposed powers. But shadow ministers with the experience of Government were hardly likely to have subscribed to the gratuitous alienation of a vital part of the "national interest".

The draft section of planning agreements was left virtually untouched. This is hardly surprising, for it had been so finely sifted during the Industrial Committee stage that any amendments could only have been in the form of disguised substantial changes. In any case, the left and right factions could, and did, read into the wording whatever they wanted. It was explained that under the system would come all major companies, certainly the largest 100 or so manufacturing firms, and all the major public enterprises. The system was explained:

To get up-to-date information, on a systematic and rolling basis, from all companies within the system. This information will concern both past performance and *advance* programme —programmes which can be checked at a later date, against results. And it will cover such areas as investment, prices, product development, marketing, exports and import requirements.

To use information to help us to clarify our planning objectives and to plan for the redistribution of resources needed to meet these objectives.

To get the agreement of the firms within the system—the written Planning Agreement—that will help us to meet certain clearly defined objectives (e.g. a certain number of new jobs in a Development Area); the tactics which will be needed to achieve these objectives will then be left to the companies themselves.

To provide for the regular revision of these agreements, in the light of experience and progress.

To provide a basis for channelling *selective* Government assistance directly to those firms which agree to help us to meet our planning objectives; and to enable us, therefore, to dispense altogether with most of the general aids—at least as far as large companies are concerned.

To provide a *systematic* basis for making large companies accountable for their behaviour, and for bringing to heel those which refuse to co-operate using, where necessary, both the extensive powers under our proposed Industrial Powers Enabling Act, the activities of our new and existing public enterprises, and the powers of public purchasing.

To publish and publicise a detailed annual report to the nation on the record of the companies within the system, and on the progress—or lack of it—towards meeting our economic objectives.

Discretion being the better part of valour—or perhaps it was common sense anticipating industry countering against "jack-boot Government"—the printed version had large companies being brought "into line" rather than "to heel". The Industry Powers Enabling Act became the Industry Act. Shadow ministers were aware, even if others on the National Executive affected not to be, that Enabling Bills, or reference to them, provoked the most bitter resentment in Parliament. Whatever the protestations, they carried the odour of dictation by the executive of the legislature. The pledge of "re-assertion of Parliamentary responsibility" may have been enshrined in the *Programme*, but this was not felt likely to convince MPs jealous of their rights. The Conservatives naturally would have made great propaganda points.

One final amendment was made in the printed version. This was to remove the clause dealing with the dispensation of most of the general aids (under the paragraph dealing with *selective* Government assistance). The active interventionists would have liked this to have stayed because it fitted in with their aim to impose sanctions on those large companies which would not sign a planning agreement. But there was no reference to this in the printed text. In fact, another strongly interventionist phrase was also omitted. This came in the concluding paragraph on the Planning Agreements system which stated that, because of the "modest number of firms involved", there would be no need for an elaborate apparatus for a planning system of this kind. (In parenthesis, it should be noted that this seemed wilfully unrealistic considering that the top 100 companies, some of which were leading multinationals, were expected to account for not less than two-thirds of net output in manufacturing by 1980; the manpower resources to negotiate and back-up an agreement would be considerable.) The published document recognised that a "powerful planning Ministry would still be needed, in order to bring together the various responsibilities for price control, planning agreements, investment, regional development and so forth. . ." However, the draft went further but met with objections : "But it is already clear that we will need within the planning ministry a separate unit staffed by a new 'breed' of civil servant—one able and willing to lean on, and if necessary *direct* [original italics] the managers of large firms which refuse to help us meet the need of the nation." This sentence was dropped from the printed version.

Nye Bevan once described Britain as an island of coal surrounded by fish. Coal, of course, had been nationalised, as had steel, gas, electricity and the railways. They represented some twenty per cent of Britain's gross national product. Labour now planned to nationalise all development land and also all mineral rights "which should be clearly within the control of, and should be exploited for the financial benefit of, the community as a whole". While Bevan's "fish" were outside direct legislative control (although fishing limits could be construed as a form of public ownership), the sea was not and the document carried the commitment to "bring North Sea Oil into public ownership and control". This was argued on the grounds of the total failure of the terms of royalty payments, licence fees and other taxes and "to bring a fair share of revenue to the state is universally recognised".

Moving back to coastal waters, there was a commitment to nationalise shipbuilding and ship-repairing although the report of the working party on the best methods, mentioned in an earlier chapter, was still awaited. It was published separately in June 1973, which was too late for inclusion in Labour's *Programme 1973*. The report called for a National Shipbuilding Corporation which "would need eventually to control all large shipbuilding and repair operations". This meant, in effect, the nationalisation of virtually all yards of significance. It was stated that the NSC would also need powers to acquire and regroup, where necessary or desirable, marine engineering establishments in particular, and possibly other supplying industries, or associated enterprises. Ultimately, all the major marine engineering groups should be brought within the NSC structure.

The aircraft industry was only touched upon in the *Programme* but in the light of subsequent events—the Labour Government's Aircraft and Shipbuilding Industries Bill—it is appropriate to explain the development here. The pressure on the party came from the same source as that on shipbuilding, the Confederation of Shipbuilding and Engineering Unions. At the forefront of the campaign was the Amalgamated Union of Engineering Workers which sent the Labour Party what was described as a "most interesting document".

In 1973 the TUC, as well as the CSEU, committed itself to the nationalisation of the industry, and arising out of this the Labour Party agreed to a joint working party with the other two bodies. A joint statement was issued the following year, in June 1974, after Labour had come to power. The demand was put forward for a British National Aerospace Corporation. It was stated that the public ownership of the aircraft industry would be covered by statute in the following way : a publicly-owned aircraft corporation would include the basic airframe constructors (British Aircraft Corporation and Hawker Siddeley Aviation) and guided weapons manufacture; and the statute should also permit the BNAC to diversify its activity where appropriate.

The draft and printed programme gave reasons for expanding the public sector. The experience of the last ten years had shown "very clearly that economic planning in the national interest has been continually frustrated by the inability to exercise effective control over those vital economic processes which determine our national well-being". Accepting the leftist critique of past attempts at indicative planning, it stated : "In particular, the level of investment in industry has shown itself to be highly resistant to incentives, exhortations and the limited measures of control over private industry which are at the disposal of Governments."

The need to extend the public sector into manufacturing was justified with the comment : "Yet it is investment within the productive and manufacturing sectors of the economy which largely determines the level of employment, resolves or continues regional imbalance, and governs the hard realities of our balance of payments." It continued : "It is intolerable that the 'arbitrary exercise of economic power', as Tawney described the private enterprise system, should be permitted to frustrate the national will for full employment, regional justice, and success in exports. It is now plainly evident that private and public interests do not by any means always coincide, and that only direct control, through ownership, of a substantial and vital sector of the growth industries, mainly in manufacturing, which hold the key to investment performance, will allow a Labour Government of the future to achieve its essential planning objectives in the national interest. An expanded public sector is a key instrument of the planning process."

The National Enterprise Board was to be the principal instrument for the extension of public ownership and economic planning. The proposals in the printed version (there was little deviation from the original draft) are here set out in full :

The National Enterprise Board is a new and more flexible instrument of national and regional planning. It will, for the first time, provide an instrument for exercising control in the area of profitable manufacturing industry. It offers opportunities to pursue new paths in job creation, in more effective regional policies, and in the achievement of greater public accountability over a wide area of society. In a separate Green Paper we have outlined the full range of potential tasks which could be tackled by the NEB under clear Parliamentary control if it is sufficiently large and is given sufficient scope. These are, briefly : job creation, especially if in areas of high unemployment; investment promotion; technological development; growth of exports; promoting government price policies; tackling the spread of multinational companies; the spread of industrial democracy; import substitution.

The structure proposed for NEB consists of a base in existing State shareholdings such as BP, Rolls-Royce and Short Brothers, with a substantial addition of companies from the present private sector. Its value in securing the wider acceptance of Government economic targets and forward planning would only be felt if its holdings are spread across leading firms throughout the different sectors of industry. Firms in any given sector are strongly influenced by the investment planning, plant building, and pricing policies of their most feared competitor (not necessarily the largest firm in the sector). Fear of losing their share of the market can be a more effective stimulus than the wise words of Government. For the range of tasks suggested, some twenty-five of our largest manufacturers (Category 1 firms) would be required, very early in the life of the Board. These companies would be selected on the basis of the use to which their resources could be put.

NEB would itself be wholly State-owned, and would always take a controlling interest in its participating firms. As it is intended to invest in potentially the most profitable areas of industry, NEB should, in the long-term at least, make profits it can re-invest, and should, over the years, extend its influence over a very substantial area of the economy. This influence could be used to tackle some of the problems of regional and general economic and industrial policy more directly than hitherto. As it develops its particular usefulness for regional planning we expect it to work closely with regional authorities especially in Scotland and Wales.

From the viewpoints of changing the balance of economic power, of increasing equality, and of more Government directed planning, NEB makes a valuable addition to the public sector. We need this new tool if we are to match the rapidly changing structure of modern capitalism with new means of intervention. Unless we face these implications, the next Labour Government will preside over an economy where power of decision rests with leading private companies, with long-term implications for the credibility of Labour economic management, and indeed the survival of Britain as an economic force.

The declared intention was unmistakable. In the end the battle between the left and right was fought over only twenty-six words, those referring to the twenty-five companies. What happened inside the Shadow Cabinet and the National Executive is related in the next chapter.

NINE

Victory and a Veto

THE HOUSE THE left built was opened for official inspection by the Shadow Cabinet on 14 May 1973. Shadow ministers had been sent copies of the draft *Labour's Programme 1973* three days earlier. The 14 May meeting, in Wilson's room in the Commons, was in preparation for a joint meeting to be held with the National Executive at the Churchill Hotel, Portman Square, London, two days later. Some of the shadow ministers had already had a preview because they were on the National Executive and had participated on the various committees. Others were privately informed what to expect by their colleagues. There was much in the document with which they agreed. It was when they came to examine the proposals on economic-industrial policy that the inevitable confrontation between the majority of the Shadow Cabinet and the National Executive was foreshadowed. The shades of political conviction deepened and it became impossible to prevent the private disagreements becoming a public battle over the future direction of party policy. The overwhelming concern of shadow ministers and, for that matter, the Parliamentary Party, was that Labour, while posing a radical alternative to the Heath Government, should not be so rash as to trip over ideology and ruin the chances of winning the next general election.

Outside Westminster politics, however, the Labour activists in the constituency parties and in the trade unions, together with the democratic socialists on the National Executive, were not prepared to abandon a socialist programme they had successfully pushed forward over the past two years. Their increasing dominance inside the party was reflected in the votes at the annual conference in October 1972 for membership of the National Executive Committee. Foot, after many years of self-imposed exile on the periphery of party power politics, stood for the constituency section of the NEC and topped the poll, a clear indication of the enormous affection with which he was held in the Labour movement. Since 1970 the constituency section with its seven seats had been a left wing stronghold, with Denis Healey, the only moderate in the section, only just succeeding in holding off a challenge from Eric Heffer by 4,000 votes. The retirement of Lady (Eirene) White, another moderate, created a vacancy in the women's section, and the delegates elected in her place Joan Maynard, secretary-agent of the Thirsk and Malton constituency party, an official of the National Union of Agriculture and Allied Workers, and Marxist in outlook. (Thirsk and Malton is a largely rural constituency and the militancy of the activists was mainly directed towards agriculture; after the Second World War it helped lead the fight over the "tied cottages" of farm workers and, if it wasn't that particular issue, there would be demands at Labour Party conferences for the nationalisation of agricultural land.)

The continuance of this shift leftwards has to be contrasted with what was taking place inside the Parliamentary Party. When the PLP voted for the Parliamentary Committee (Shadow Cabinet) in November 1972, Shirley Williams and Reg Prentice tied for first place, Crosland was third and Foot fourth. The others elected, in order of votes cast, were: Callaghan, Healey, William Rosse, Fred Peart, Lever, Merlyn Rees, with Benn, Peter Shore and John Silkin tying in twelfth place. Benn, it will be seen, was low down in the ballot, and only he and Foot could be identified with the left. The supremacy of the moderates was best symbolised by the fact that Barbara Castle failed to maintain her place, having joined the Shadow Cabinet the previous year when three pro-marketeers—Jenkins, George Thomson and Lever—resigned. Mikardo described the results as demonstrating a further widening of the gap in outlook and attitudes between the Labour Party and the Parliamentary Labour Party. "It almost looks", he complained at a meeting of the Camden Fabian Society, "as though some Labour MPs—and especially those with an elitist, condescending attitude towards the rank and file of the party—are taking a perverse pleasure in throwing down a gauntlet of defiance to the party members and annual conference."

We can see from this disposition of the various forces that all the ingredients were there for a struggle of unilateralist and Clause Four proportions. The catalyst was that section in the

draft document dealing with "A New Economic Strategy".
The Shadow Cabinet meeting lasted nearly six hours and the
moderates launched their counter-attack. The strongest criticisms came from Crosland, Lever and Shirley Williams. They
argued that the public ownership proposals represented a crude
throwback to the Labour Party thinking of the 'thirties. A
more sophisticated approach was needed in the light of modern
economic management techniques and fiscal instruments of
control. In other words, a development of Keynesian principles
which the left had set out to prove was an unstable foundation
upon which to build a socialist programme and a successful
Labour Government.

Crosland argued that the document involved too many commitments, and Lever had a sustained blast at the proposal on
twenty-five companies. The entire nationalisation package
offered a hostage to the Conservative Party. He said the proposals to take over twenty-five companies would ruin Labour's
chances in every constituency in which the named companies
when they were named) were major employers. Unilever was
mentioned as an example. He said it would be easy to imagine
the Conservatives going around every shop selling Birds Eye
food and telling them they were threatened with nationalisation. While this may have been Lever at his most fanciful, the
gravamen of his argument, and that of the other right wingers,
was not lost. Benn, for his part, struck out in defence of the
document. Whatever the number of companies finally designated, it was essential that a Labour Government should pass
enabling legislation swiftly. Wilson is not remembered as having
made a key contribution to the argument at that time, but then
it was assumed he was keeping his counsel.

Not all of the discussion centred on the economic strategy.
The draft carried substantial sections on housing, transport,
health and welfare, education, and, not least, the Common
Market. The Shadow Cabinet, as ever, was split on the latter
issue, although the debate on that particular section was not
prolonged : the pro-marketeers realised that they could gain
little at that stage, and the anti-marketeers knew that they
would have the majority of the annual conference on their side.
The demands posed in the document should be familiar :
major changes in the Common Agricultural Policy, new and
fairer methods of financing the Common Market, "the retention

by Parliament of those powers over the British economy needed
to pursue effective regional, industrial and fiscal policies", and
the safeguarding of the economic interests of the Commonwealth and the developing countries.

Crosland and Lever, together with Denis Healey who joined
in the argument, carried their campaign to the Churchill Hotel
when the joint meeting was held two days later. Lever kept
to his main thesis that economic policy could be carried out by
a future Labour Government through demand management
and taxation policies. His contribution was much the strongest
of the moderates. Crosland and Healey accepted the need for
some forms of public ownership on pragmatic grounds, but
argued against the specific proposals contained in the document. Judith Hart, together with Benn, stoutly defended the
interventionist programme, although she appeared to be in a
conciliatory mood. In order to preserve the principle, she
accepted the view that it was not essential to mention the figure
of twenty-fiive companies. But she insisted that the scale of
operations of the proposed National Enterprise Board should
be maintained. Mikardo, on the other hand, kept to his line
first expressed inside the Public Sector Group when it discussed the issue in October 1972, that it was a mistake to
specify the number of companies in which the NEB would
have a controlling interest. While he fully supported the interventionist ideology behind the state agency, he was on the side
of the moderates rather than the left when it came to the
numbers game.

Shadow ministers left the meeting mistakenly believing that
the battle had been won. They had heard Wilson propose that
the next Labour Government should set up a Royal Commission
inquiry into the Stock Exchange, and were quite happy about
that. The left were also delighted, although it did appear to
some that this was a tactic to undermine the work of the study
group on financial institutions. Wilson reminded his colleagues
of a remark once made by Harold Macmillan, the former
Conservative Prime Minister, who described the Stock Exchange
as a "casino". He did not, however, recall a comment of his
own about Royal Commissions, that they "take minutes and
sit for years", although it could have been at the back of some
suspicious minds. An inquiry into the Stock Exchange did not
commit a future Labour Government to anything. There was

not even a tentative mention of the terms of reference. As for the twenty-five companies, ministers lulled themselves into a false sense of security. They judged from the drift of the debate that the paragraph would be deleted when the National Executive met two weeks later to give the draft programme the final stamp of approval. They could not have been more wrong.

The National Executive met at the Churchill Hotel on 31 May in an exhausting session which lasted over eleven hours. There was not a full turn-out, seven of the twenty-nine being absent, including Ted Short, the deputy leader, who was in his cottage in the Lake District, believing that all the issues had been resolved. The others were two left wing backbenchers, Mikardo and Renee Short, and four moderate trade unionists, Andy Cunningham (General and Municipal Workers Union) who was to achieve his own notoriety in the Poulson corruption case, Jim Diamond (British Iron, Steel and Kindred Trades Association), Len Forden (Transport and General Workers Union) and Joe Gormley (National Union of Mineworkers). The voting strengths of the opposing factions became even more complicated because as the meeting dragged on beyond 7 p.m.—and by that time the Executive had been in session for over nine hours—some members began drifting away. Barbara Castle left after arguing, particularly with Terry Pitt, head of the Research Department, over pensions policy in which she partly persuaded the National Executive to her view-point. This lasted for nearly two hours and Barbara Castle thought she had done her prime task for the day, not anticipating there was a more important vote to be taken. Alex Kitson, the left wing representative for the Transport and General Workers Union, departed early in the evening to attend a reception at the Russian Embassy in preparation for a Labour delegation which was to visit the Soviet Union later in the month. Others who disappeared were two moderates, Tom Bradley and Fred Mulley, a Labour frontbench spokesman on transport, and one left winger, John Forrester of the Amalgamated Union of Engineering Workers.

When it came to the debate on the National Enterprise Board, therefore, it looked as if the moderates were in a dominant position. They had already had one important victory on the industrial section of the document when the Executive, by eleven votes to three, had succeeded in deleting a paragraph on re-nationalisation.* Wilson had tried to avoid a battle by asking Pitt the previous week to delete the sentence on twenty-five companies, but Pitt informed him that this was not possible. Earlier drafts had included the sentence and, as head of the Research Department, he did not have the discretion to make omissions. It was up to the National Executive to decide what changes should be made. This episode is important because it makes Wilson's behaviour at the meeting all the more puzzling. Quite clearly he was desperate to have it removed and yet did nothing when his best opportunity arose. As a result, his subsequent actions ensured even greater controversy within the party.

Wilson warned the National Executive that the inclusion of twenty-five companies would be a hostage to fortune at the next general election. He stated twice that the party's manifesto committee, when it eventually met, had the right of veto. This was not strictly correct, but he had not said his final word on the possibility of a veto and this will be dealt with later. Wilson had the support of both Callaghan and Healey, and those on the opposite side of the argument were primarily Judith Hart and Benn. Healey had been told by Wilson of the Leader's conversation with Pitt, and, having looked around the table and sized up the balance of forces, pressed for a vote. He moved an amendment deleting from the section on the National Enterprise Board the offending two sentences : "For the range of tasks suggested, some twenty-five of our largest manufac- turers (Category 1 firms) would be required, very early in the life of the Board. These companies would be selected on the basis of the use to which their resources could be put." He had little doubt that the moderate faction would win.

Healey, however, had miscalculated. When the hands went up for those in favour of his amendment he saw, to his astonish- ment, that Wilson was not casting his vote. Five voted with Healey : Callaghan, Shirley Williams, Foot, Walter Padley, a representative of the Union of Shop, Distributive and Allied Workers on the Executive, and Sidney Weighell, of the National Union of Railwaymen. Six of those present, therefore,

* The success was short-lived. There was a row inside the National Executive when it met in Blackpool before the annual party conference in October, when the left succeeded in having the "without compensation" sentence reinstated. Although Callaghan described the policy as "legalised robbery", the left wing amendment was carried by seventeen votes to six.

were in favour of the amendment, and there were ten others still to cast a vote. When Bill Simpson, leader of the boilermakers and the party chairman that year, who was in the chair at the meeting called for the dissenting vote, seven hands went up : Benn, Judith Hart, Frank Allaun, Joan Lestor, Joan Maynard, Peter Doyle of the Young Socialists, and John Cartwright, who normally aligned himself with the moderate faction and was the representative on the NEC of the Co-operative and Socialist organisations. Simpson did not exercise his right to vote and abstained along with Chalmers and Wilson. While Healey was privately fuming at Wilson's abstention, the left were in a triumphant mood. They had scored a victory by the default of their opponents. As for the centre-right, they only had themselves to blame.

The vote of Cartwright and the abstentions of Wilson and Chalmers need further explanation. Why should Cartwright, a moderate on nearly every other issue, join the left to support the twenty-five companies, a proposal which did not really command his sympathy? The answer is that Cartwright acted in a fit of pique at something Healey had said and, at that particular moment, thought it the best way of retaliation. Cartwright is a strong Co-operative Party man and was nominated for the National Executive by the Royal Arsenal Co-operative Society, the only Co-operative Society in the country, incidentally, which is affiliated to the Labour Party. Cartwright's background being the Co-operative movement, he took great exception to a remark of Healey when he said : "Do we really want to nationalise Marks and Spencers to make it as efficient as the · Co-op?" Healey, in being characteristically provocative in his argument, was guilty of over-kill, and in doing so was seen to cast a gratuitous slur on the Co-op movement. This was too much for Cartwright, who also did not entirely approve of the sentiments expressed by Healey and Wilson on public ownership generally. Cartwright, as a consequence, became one of the militant seven.

Chalmers abstained because he was in a difficult position. His union, the Amalgamated Society of Boilermakers, Shipwrights, Blacksmiths and Structural Workers with McGarvey, a doctrinaire nationaliser, as its President, was in favour of the proposal. Chalmers, however, thought the party would be creating problems for itself if the twenty-five companies proposal remained. His only way out, therefore, was to abstain. Wilson's attitude, on the other hand, was entirely different. He was vehemently opposed to the proposal and, as we have seen, made efforts behind the scenes to get the sentences removed. But Wilson also had an over-riding belief that the leader of the party should not participate when a vote was called inside the National Executive Committee. He consistently maintained this view throughout his thirteen years as leader of the party. The only occasion that readily comes to mind when he broke his own rule was when he cast his vote in favour of Ron Hayward in the 1972 election for the party general secretary. Nonetheless, it is also true that Wilson expected the Healey amendment to be carried. His anger at losing was shown the following day.

Wilson's reaction to the events at the Churchill Hotel was not entirely characteristic. As leader of the party, he well knew that the majority of the Shadow Cabinet were not in favour of such an overt declaration of state intervention. Moreover, if Labour won the next general election the Cabinet would have no intention of carrying out the proposal. Why, therefore, should the party land itself with such a doctrinal albatross? The only people to gain would be the party's Tory opponents who would make heavy party political propaganda. While most of his shadow ministers shared the same belief, there were some, including Ted Short, who nonetheless felt he over-reacted the following day by issuing a statement denouncing what had taken place. By stating publicly that he would veto any such plan he exacerbated rather than alleviated party tension. His statement is printed here in full because it was one of the toughest he ever issued to the National Executive as leader of the party:

The Labour Party's National Executive Committee by a majority of seven votes to six—those in the majority comprising less than a quarter of the full executive—yesterday adopted a proposal to nationalise an unnamed twenty-five of the 100 biggest companies in Britain. In view of the inaccuracies in the unauthorised disclosure of what I said, I want to put on record the warnings I gave to the meeting, first about the proposal to renationalise without compensation, and second, about the twenty-five companies. The warnings I gave were that, while the National Executive Committee was master in its own house on any recommendation it chose to put to conference, the election programme set out in the party's manifesto was constitutionally the responsibility of the Executive and the Parliamentary Committee meeting together.

A substantial majority of the Parliamentary Committee had already made clear its position both on compensation and on the twenty-five companies, and I emphasised that in my view the Shadow Cabinet would not hesitate to use its veto at the appropriate time. It was inconceivable that the party would go into a general election on this proposal, nor could any incoming Labour government be so committed.

The National Executive Committee's decision would be included in the policy document to be issued next week and would be before conference. The political reality of the determination of the issues on which the party will fight the election is as set out in my statement to the Executive.

Wilson could not have been more categoric. He was correct in saying that the manifesto is drawn up at a joint meeting of the Shadow Cabinet and the NEC which selects items from the programme approved by the party conference. His one great problem, however, was that if the conference approved the twenty-five companies proposal by a two-thirds majority, he would be in considerable difficulty if he exercised the veto. Undoubtedly a storm would be created—the last thing he would want on the eve of a general election. Renee Short, one of the left wingers who had not attended the Churchill Hotel meeting, pounced on the Wilson statement and at the same time declared her support for the twenty-five companies proposal. "Mr Wilson is attempting, in my view, to pre-empt Labour conference decisions on policy documents in an unseemly manner", she said. "The whole Labour and trade union movement is painfully aware of the stark fact that the policies of the right wing have been tried and found wanting every time we have a Labour Government."

Wilson issued his statement without consulting any party officials and undoubtedly he annoyed Hayward, the general secretary, who insisted that they should meet. Hayward informed Wilson that the statement had been unnecessary and that it had created an unhappy situation which need never have arisen. By that time, of course, the damage had been done, although Wilson was given some public support by Jenkins. The day after the statement was issued, Jenkins told a meeting in Bath : "It is vital that the next Labour Government should not arouse hopes which it cannot fulfil and not take on commitments which it cannot meet."

The scene was now set for one of those furious debates in which Labour politicians indulge in public soul-searching, an exercise which enlivens consciences, engages political commentators and can enrage the average Labour voter. But the argument was not confined to the politicians. The proposals for the NEB brought to the fore Wilfred Beckerman, Professor of Political Economy in the University of London, who was a former adviser to Crosland. On the other side were Holland, progenitor of the NEB and Planning Agreements, and John Kenneth Galbraith, from Harvard University. One final irony has to be mentioned relating to the Churchill Hotel meeting. Wilson insisted at a subsequent meeting of the National Executive Committee that, in future, the NEC should have a quorum without which no voting would be valid. The figure settled on was fifteen, that is slightly more than half of the twenty-nine membership of the NEC. It did not escape the notice of some members of the NEC that there were sixteen people in the room when the NEC voted on the twenty-five companies and that some had chosen to abstain.

Before Labour's *Programme 1973* was published on 7 June, Benn entered the lion's den of big business and financial institutions when he addressed a conference on the future of the City of London organised by the *Financial Times* and the *Investors' Chronicle*. "There was never any magic significance in twenty-five", he said, "although it might be noted in passing that if Slater-Walker can acquire twenty-nine companies in a single year, 1972, a government target of twenty-five over a far longer period does not sound excessive." Benn went on to state that it was not the number but the principle of "really substantial extensions of public ownership into manufacturing that does matter". He added : "Put this way, as it should be, the case is very powerful indeed. I am sure the next Labour Government will want to move forward on these lines."

Benn attempted to convince his audience that there was no

split in Labour's ranks or a leadership crisis, but there were "disagreements on a narrow range of issues". He then proceeded to make oblique criticisms of his moderate colleagues in the Shadow Cabinet: "Whatever the merits of these arguments may be, some people assume automatically that if the Labour Party put them forward in the next election we would be heavily defeated. I wonder. Do the British people really want a society in which industrialists and bankers have more power over Britain's economic future than the governments they elect? Can we ignore the fact that many workers—right up to management level—are also now more worried about takeover bids and asset stripping which are inseparable from private ownership?"

Benn was to run into trouble inside the Shadow Cabinet later in June because of that speech and other comments he made, but he demonstrated that not only was he in no mood for compromise but was publicly encouraging the state interventionist left. Wilson, on the other hand, embarked on a policy of undermining what he and others believed to be the worst aspects of the NEB proposals. He made clear at the press conference, which launched the *Programme* on 7 June, that he had no quarrel with the policy document, the "best the National Executive has brought forward" since he had been a member, apart from the twenty-five companies issue. He had nothing to add or subtract from the statement he had issued. Questioned about whether he had second thoughts on his use of the word "veto" the previous week, Wilson looked across at Callaghan and said: "We have sat on many manifesto working parties over the years, and there has never been a vote on any issue. Everything has been done by agreement." [1] Callaghan parried another questioner who wanted to know whether the figure "25" could be deleted by the party conference that year. The party treasurer replied, half facetiously, that the press conference was not held to discuss the relationship between the Parliamentary Party, the NEC and the conference, although the party was quite willing to have one for that purpose. Wilson intervened to say that many people who had expressed anxiety about his veto statement had probably not read the document. "They will be vastly reassured when they study the document as a whole", he said. "It does not stand or fall by those two phrases alone."

On the general matter of public ownership Wilson said there was no question of firms coming under public control except by agreed procedure or parliamentary legislation. A Labour Government would, however, take specific powers to prevent British firms coming under the control of multinational companies. Wilson was to pursue this line of thought in a speech he made the following day, 8 June. There was too much concentration of industrial power in too few hands without public accountability, he told Northumberland mineworkers at Tynemouth. He went on to acknowledge that the document was a "conscious recognition that the new commanding heights of the economy lie in giant industrial and financial corporations, national and multinational, responsible to no authority except, and then only in times of crisis, their shareholders." He commented : "The multinational companies owe no loyalty, no duty, to the national policies or the needs of the British national community." But then he went on to warn, in almost Morrisonian language, that while the Labour Party was democratically discussing its proposals for changing the unattractive and unacceptable face of capitalism, and not by cosmetics only, "we must be equally vigorous in examining the problems of existing publicly owned industries, and equally radical in making changes which are necessary in their structure, organisation and accountability to the public need".

Wilson was not as intransigent as Morrison, who in 1948 called for a halt to further nationalisation and asked for a period of consolidation. But the juxtaposing of the private and public sectors, nonetheless, must have been calculated with the listener left to decide where the party leader would place the emphasis. However, he did give some credit to the work that had been done on the impact of multinational companies on economic planning. And it was at this point that the readers of the *New Statesman* were treated to the vituperative correspondence of Beckerman and Holland.[2] It lasted throughout the month of June.

Beckerman began by pointing out that Holland had stated in the *Guardian*, 24 May, what he believed to be the general philosophy underlying the projected extension of detailed public intervention in industry. Commented Beckerman : "Reading it, and some of the documents in the case, one can see why even the more left wing members of the Executive, such as Ian Mikardo, preferred to steer clear of such patently muddled proposals. In fact, so grotesque is much of the reasoning behind them that if we were living in the Vatican or Renaissance Italy one would have assumed that the whole thing was a put-up job designed to make Tony Benn and Judith Hart look foolish, and that their backroom boy, Mr Holland, was a paid agent of their political opponents."

Holland countered the following week : "Professor Beckerman clearly sees himself as the economists' Bernard Levin. No jibe is too low and no distortion too gross to caricature an opponent. But Beckerman lacks Levin's skill. His scathing attack in last week's NS thrashed much hot air, completely missed my case, and captured his own. It was abusive, but largely self-abuse. This showed both in his analytical myopia and his refusal to research the facts." And, later : "Beckerman is hopelessly ignorant of such new use of state holdings and planning agreements in Italy, France and Belgium."

What, then, was the academic argument about ? The respective contributions were lengthy and we can only go into the essentials here. Beckerman noted that Holland, in his *Guardian* article, had stated that the merger boom of the last decade or so had led to an increased degree of industrial concentration, "which is almost certainly true". "But Holland," said Beckerman, "then argued that the giant firms, being in a more or less monopolistic position, were the price makers rather than the price takers, so that they were able to finance the bulk of their investment from retained earnings and hence were relatively unaffected by fiscal or monetary incentives." Stated Beckerman : "Why this should require detailed state intervention of the particular type proposed is a matter which I shall come to later, but even this starting point raises a number of prior questions."

Beckerman argued that no account was taken of increasing competition from imports in domestic markets. It was arguable that the merger boom had been partly a defensive reaction to this increased competition. Was there any evidence that the rate of profit had been rising in the economy on account of industrial concentration ? Continued Beckerman : "In fact, as I pointed out in the NS some months ago, there is no evidence of a long-run change in the post-tax rate of return on capital in Britain one way or the other over the last twenty years. But there has been a fall in this rate over the last few years (which I ascribed to temporary phenomena), which contradicts the Holland suggestion that the increasing concentration of power has been reflected in firms' pricing policies and liquidity positions."

Holland's retort to this was that Beckerman was a liberal capitalist in an era of monopoly leadership at home and multinational competition abroad. Beckerman, he said, assumed that demand management of private enterprise would secure social and economic harmony but admitted exceptions to this, such as monopoly profits, economies of scale, and differences between the private and social costs of labour or imports. Therefore, in the view of Holland: "What he fails to grasp is that the monopoly-multinational trend has transformed these old exceptions into today's rule." Holland instanced scale economies as not being exceptions to moponoly power or multinational operations. They were the underlying cause, he wrote. At the same time multinationals were forced to follow their leaders abroad to find labour or tax havens or they would lose global power. Holland argued: "This makes British labour less competitive than cheap labour abroad. It also undermines government trade and fiscal policies, since multinationals charge themselves high import prices from foreign tax havens to syphon out profits."

Cheap labour was mentioned by Holland at this point in reply to another of Beckerman's allegations. Beckerman had said that some of the alleged implications of the trend towards larger companies "hardly need to be taken seriously". He mentioned in particular the argument that "their multinational operation gives such companies access to labour abroad in such countries as Hong Kong, Singapore and Brazil" where labour costs are much lower, thereby blunting the incentives provided by labour subsidies in development areas in Britain. Chided Beckerman: "The notion that labour in Brazil is a close substitute for labour employed building a ship on the Clyde is too funny to require further comment."

Beckerman correctly stated that Holland seemed to have some idea at the back of his mind that the features of the larger firms had "seriously undermined the Keynesian monetary and fiscal policies" (a quotation from Holland). He kept coming back to the point, said Beckerman, again quoting Holland: "At national level the parallel blunting of fiscal and monetary incentives also has produced a credibility gap in the effectiveness of indirect or Keynesian economic policies" and that the Keynesian policies had been eroded by the multinational trend.

It was difficult to understand what Holland understood by "Keynesian" policies, Beckerman asserted. Most economists would interpret this blanket term to refer to aggregative policies to influence the pressure of demand in the economy, in the belief that the unaided working of the private sector would not automatically produce the desired level of demand. Beckerman said this had nothing to do with the longer-run rate or pattern of growth of the economy by means of structural changes, and few people would expect that Keynesian policies would ever be cast in such a role. (Beckerman gave as an exception their incidental indirect effect on investment rates, and hence longer-run growth, arising out of increased entrepreneurial confidence in the government's determination and ability to prevent massive and prolonged unemployment.) He added : "Hence, since Keynesian policies had no role to play in engineering structural change, it is difficult to see how this role could have been eroded by the growth of larger firms."

Holland replied : "Beckerman shows a schizoid unawareness of the dependence of macro-policies on a competitive microframework." Commenting on the Beckerman view that Keynesian policies only had an incidental effect on the longer-run growth in the economy, Holland said : "What he ignores is that the long run structural changes such as the monopoly-multinational trend have a *crucial* effect on Keynsian policies." In 1930 the top 100 companies controlled only a fifth of the key manufacturing sector, "but today they control more than half and are set fair for two-thirds before 1980". This changed consumer sovereignty over many producers into producer sovereignty over consumer prices.

The Beckerman-Holland dispute occupied several columns in the *New Statesman*, covering the twenty-five companies, planning agreements and state intervention generally. All of it was highly relevant to the arguments being conducted between the Shadow Cabinet and the National Executive. Apart from the fascination of two economists rigorously defending their arguments in highly personal terms (academics when pressed can be more bitchy than politicians), the correspondence had the distinction of getting to the centre of the debate. None of it, however, hit the headlines, as did the continuing feud of the politicians. But before returning to that, let Galbraith round off the academics' argument. In a letter to the *New Statesman* at the time, he wrote :

> Among the righteous it is now established that General Motors and ICI, as presently constituted and owned, are the final work of men and God. Shareholders, it is agreed, are without power or function. However, nothing should be allowed to disturb their peace and increment. Certainly there should be no suggestion that their ownership (and increment) should be transferred, however, gracefully, to the public at large. Proposals to the contrary induce cries of outrage and this is understandable. The privileged protect their privileges by holding that the personally inconvenient is unthinkable. It would be a shame, however, if the controversy over the proposal to take the large British corporations into public ownership should lead people, either in Britain or abroad, to overlook the remarkably progressive way in which *Labour's Programme for Britain 1973* brings the problem of the large corporation into full economic and political focus. In taking note of corporate power, including supernational power; of how corporate purpose diverges from public purpose; and in accepting the need for public control of corporate pricing as an aspect of general economic policy, this document improves on past discussion of corporate power in Britain and vastly on the perception of the problem by parties of the left. And it improves equally on the stylised trivial discussion and non-discussion of the problems of corporate power in the universities and accepted text. For this, however damaging its electoral effect, surely some will be grateful.

But politics is about power, and the politicians, or at least the social democrats, were madly exercised about the damaging electoral consequences. Dell thought that the National Executive had produced a monster. "As far as I am aware," he said, "the authors of this idea have not provided any figure of the number of the NEB's employees." [3] They could not do so, he continued, because the twenty-five companies had not yet been specified. But the figure would be very large indeed. It was not just the twenty-five but Rolls-Royce, BP and other companies in which there were existing Government shareholdings, or in which Government shareholdings were obtained as a result of any financial aid provided. All these were to be gathered under the umbrella of the NEB. Dell stated : "The NEB would thus be by far the largest industrial enterprise in Europe and probably in the world. It would be many times larger than the Italian IRI on which it is supposedly modelled. It would be many times larger than any existing nationalised industry. The management problems of this conglomerate are to be imagined."

Dell went on to state, correctly, that the apparent purpose of "creating this dinosaur" was to put it in the power of a Labour Secretary of State for Trade and Industry to achieve directly the objectives which the last Labour Government had failed to achieve by incentives and by other forms of inducement which it could exercise. But it would not be the Secretary of State who decided what this body did, Dell said. It would be the NEB and its subsidiaries. Whatever control the NEB could in fact exercise over its subsidiaries, it would certainly be an effective shield between them and any minister. The fact of public ownership would not make it responsive to ministers' wishes. It would have its own ideas of the public interest and the power to act on them.

Dell concluded : "I believe that we do need in this country a paragovernmental agency equipped to manage part of the public intervention in industry which is an inevitable characteristic of our industrial society. But there are two essential conditions. The first is that its relationship to government and to Parliament must be a great deal better thought out than was the case with the IRC. Secondly, it must not be so large and so powerful as completely to over-balance the relationship between itself and the democratically elected government. The NEB in the form in which it is now proposed should be rejected on democratic grounds if no other."

Crosland was even more forthright. He condemned the proposals as "half-baked" and protested against an "idiotic" attempt to "bamboozle" the public and called for a "return to sanity". Crosland told a meeting at Rotherham, Yorkshire, on 9 June that the nationalisation proposals had damaged Labour in three ways. First, by diverting the public attention from the events that should have been disastrous for the Tory Government—another 10 per cent rise in house prices in the first quarter of the year, a further rise in food prices, "an open threat to mutilate the railways", and the Lonrho affair.* Secondly, the row over them had tragically excluded publicity for the more relevant parts of the party programme, including tax reform, land policy and housing. Thirdly, the programme risked deceiving the public by suggesting that nationalisation automatically furthered the basic socialist aims of equality, justice and democracy. The public knew perfectly well this was not true, "and so do the workers who have suffered from pit closures, steel redundancies and the rundown of the railways". Crosland added : "What we cannot justify is a blanket threat to every large firm in Britain—good or bad, socially responsible or not, progressive or reactionary—based on the misleading assumption that a change of ownership of itself will produce miraculous results."

The matter was not allowed to rest there. The *Tribune* Group of left wing Labour MPs criticised Wilson, declaring that his enunciation of the right of veto by the Shadow Cabinet was "unacceptable in a democratic socialist party". Norman Atkinson, one of its leading members, stated in a speech on 13 June that : "I would like to see in the first Queen's Speech of the next Labour Government the announcement to take over British Leyland, Courtaulds and the General Electric Company." Heffer found the attacks on the *Programme* by leading members of the Parliamentary Labour Party "astonishing". Crosland, he told a meeting in Oxford, had used harsh language, especially as he had advocated competitive public enterprise in his books. "It is certainly not half-baked", he said. "On the contrary, it is very well thought out. If the scheme is half-baked then so too were his [Crosland's] proposals." The rejection of the proposals by leading individuals in the party was irresponsible. "It has given our enemies precisely the opportunity they wanted to denigrate the proposals

---

* The so-called "Lonrho Affair" involved secret payments of funds and caused a well-publicised boardroom row, involving a court case and a special meeting of shareholders. The "scandal" had its attendant political implications. Heath, as Prime Minister, delighted the left with his description : "It is the unpleasant and unacceptable face of capitalism, but one should not suggest that the whole of British industry consists of practices of this kind."

and the programme as a whole", he declared. "It reduces the party membership and the conference to mere ciphers."

Another significant voice, which so far had remained silent on the issue, decided to join in the row which by now was patently out of the control of the party managers. It was that of Bill Simpson, the party chairman, who, as we saw, abstained in the 7–6 vote in the Churchill Hotel. Simpson was important because he was a prominent trade union moderate and had a clear knowledge of what his unionist colleagues were thinking. His displeasure at the pronouncements of some of the leading members of the Parliamentary Party was unmistakable : "I believe the opposition within the party to the National Executive Committee's proposals stems more from imagined political considerations rather than the economic realities of the proposals." He declared : "Some people say that the take-over of twenty-five firms is a half-baked idea. It is certainly not. It has been well thought out by people who have not only worked in and studied industry here, but have also looked at the economic realities of other European countries." He sug-gested : "Let the party conference decide and let us unite behind that decision. Let us debate it under the TV cameras at Blackpool and accept the democratic decisions of the conference."

But the conference was four months away, a period too long for any politician actively engaged in party affairs to keep quiet, if this was what Simpson was implying. Simpson, in any case, was hardly consistent in his view on public ownership and its political effect. The following week, as general secretary of the foundry workers' section of the Amalgamated Union of Engineering Workers, he attended the AUEW annual con-ference at Eastbourne. Before the delegates was a motion demanding : "This national conference instructs the National Executive council that they must insist that the Labour Party in their election programme and manifesto adopt a policy which calls for the nationalisation of all major industries with-out compensation." Simpson argued that the public would have to be convinced of the need for more nationalisation, and cast his section's votes against the motion. It was carried by 37 votes to 32. The union, however, did not press the issue of compensation at the Labour Party conference.

By this time all but the Labour Party activists could be

forgiven for wondering what was happening inside the Labour Party. The point was not lost on Judith Hart. She complained at the Prestonpans Labour Club: "The excitable headlines and emotional comments of the last three weeks have obscured the real issue which the movement will have to consider at the conference." Her speech was made on 24 June and in one section she focused her sights on Dell. It was not a policy to get up a huge industrial conglomerate on the nationalisation model of the public corporation, she said. The essence of the proposal was to give a Labour Government a new planning instrument. It would not be remote from Government. It would not require a vast new management structure. Judith Hart explained: "The National Enterprise Board will take the sector leaders of profitable manufacturing industry into public ownership and control. It will do so in order to exercise direct influence on their strategies for investment, for prices, for exports and for location of new plant in the regions. To be effective it must be on a substantial scale and that means that at the end of a five-year term one-third of the turnover of the top 100 manufacturers, who account for about half of our net manufacturing output and two-fifths of their profits and about half their employment, should be invested with the board. To provide such strategic leadership through public enterprise would mean the takeover of some twenty to twenty-five companies, dependent on their size." Behind the proposal, she added, lay the conviction that no Labour Government could hope to achieve its social purpose if it relied entirely on demand management.

Turning to the critics of the proposal in general, Judith Hart asked whether they thought the British public was in love with the bureaucratic private corporation which employed them? Did they think that they have some deep affection for Slater-Walker and Lonrho? Was there in the hearts of the British electorate a deep approval of tax havens, golden handshakes, and irresponsible economic power? Did the average British elector, be he white collar or blue collar, identify with directors in the boardroom whom he never sees and who are totally unaccountable to him? "If the Labour Party", said Judith Hart, "were ever to accept the ethos of capitalism, ugly faced and narrowly motivated, as the necessary electoral framework for its own policy-making, it would be the end of the Labour Party as we know it."

Shadow ministers who did not share Judith Hart's views objected that they were just as anxious to change the face of capitalism as she was, and not by "cosmetics only", to use the Wilson phrase. But they argued that holding a Damoclean sword over the whole of manufacturing industry was more likely to be treated as an indication of potential electoral suicide rather than evidence of intended major surgery. The Shadow Cabinet, in fact, had had a further important discussion on the public ownership proposals four days before Judith Hart made her speech. It was at this meeting that major differences between Foot and Benn appeared. Both of them were critical of Wilson in issuing the threat to use the veto; and so was Healey who, while agreeing with virtually every word of the Wilson statement issued after the Churchill Hotel meeting, said it had been unwise to raise the question of a veto. It was inevitable that it would precipitate a major squabble inside the party.

Foot, however, parted company with Benn over the twenty-five companies. Foot was all in favour of extending public ownership but he felt the declaration of a specific number of companies had been unnecessarily damaging, both inside the party and in its standing with the electorate. It must be remembered that Foot's over-riding ambition was to get a British withdrawal from the European Community and that this could not be achieved without the advent of a Labour Government. Foot sometimes wondered whether Benn, also opposed to Britain joining the Community, wanted to win the next general election : he felt Benn was doing the party harm with his "open discussion" policy which only distracted and dissipated Labour's attack on the Government. Benn, in fact, was as anxious to win the general election as Foot, and the latter knew this : their real argument was about electoral strategy. It seemed, however, that Wilson had secured himself an important ally on the left. This could be crucial at the party conference in October.

References

1 *Guardian*, 8 June 1973.
2 *New Statesman*, issues dated 8, 15, 29 June and 6 July 1973.
3 *Guardian*, 6 June 1973.

TEN

Wilson's Escape Route

WHEN WILSON WENT to Blackpool for the party conference at the beginning of October he took with him a plan to sterilise the argument over the twenty-five companies. The number was more than a fixation. He had never approved of the concept of the National Enterprise Board—although, as will be shown, he unwittingly betrayed the fact that he did not fully comprehend it—but there were other over-riding political factors that had appeared. Politicians and trade union leaders alike realised that it could be the last Labour conference before Heath called a general election. Wilson said as much in a confidential note to the National Executive Committee attached to his proposal on nationalisation. The imperative, therefore, was to demonstrate a united party, ready to put before the electorate an alternative strategy to that of the Government, which had just embarked on consultations for a further year of controls on prices and wages. These considerations were to have an important bearing on the outcome of the conference, but they did not prevent the National Executive decisively rejecting an initiative by the Shadow Cabinet in general and Wilson in particular.

Wilson had called a meeting of his Shadow Cabinet colleagues the week before the party conference. His objective was to prevent decisions taken by delegates getting out of control and undermining general election strategy. The fact that he had to resort to such stratagems is an indication of his lack of confidence in the support of the trade unions who commanded the conference with their block vote. His proposal, on the surface, was simple and straightforward. Wilson suggested, and the Shadow Cabinet agreed, that he should propose to the National Executive a joint meeting between the two bodies before the conference began to select from the *Programme* those items that should be included in a general election manifesto. There would also be a series of meetings after the conference to continue the process of selection. Under the party's constitution such joint meetings were established procedure, but Wilson's proposals incorporated a new element. The conference had not yet approved any of the proposals in the *Programme* and, quite clearly, the first joint meeting would be the one that determined the scope of any manifesto. The tactic was obvious. Wilson and the Shadow Cabinet wanted the meeting to pre-empt any adverse decisions taken by the conference.

But there was the question of the party's commitment to increased state intervention and to public ownership. What could be done about that? Wilson told the Shadow Cabinet he would propose to both bodies that they should agree on an immediate statement on public ownership in respect of all land required for development, minerals, North Sea gas and oil, local authority ownership of rented property, ports, shipbuilding and ancillary industries, aircraft, as well as sectors of the machine tool and road haulage industries. The proposed statement would deal with the new public enterprise in the regions and the return to public ownership of franchises, licences and assets transferred to private ownership by the Conservatives. It would also include the adoption of the Planning Agreements system set out in the *Programme* and the enactment of the Industry Act with the powers agreed in the document. Equally, the establishment of a wholly state-owned National Enterprise Board would be endorsed with the functions and structures laid out in the *Programme*.

Whichever way one examines the statement it was a formidable commitment. Shadow ministers felt they would have no difficulty in getting the agreement of the National Executive. Customarily the National Executive meets on the Friday and Sunday before the conference begins to determine the NEC's view of the various resolutions. Wilson proposed at the Friday morning meeting, held in the conference headquarters hotel, that the joint meeting should be held immediately after they had completed the business for the day—that is, mid-afternoon. Shadow ministers who were not on the National Executive therefore turned up at the Imperial Hotel in readiness for the joint meeting. It proved a wasted journey. The National Executive turned down the proposal, although it endorsed the idea of joint meetings after the conference. Wilson also failed to get his proposed public ownership statement through the NEC, but it was agreed that further consideration be given on the Sunday.

Wilson's note to the Friday meeting stated that he had made it clear in a succession of widely attended public meetings all over the country that he regarded the *Programme* as the best the party had put forward since 1945. "In particular, that it represents an up-to-date statement of the principles of our Socialism, which is particularly relevant to the economic and social problems of the mid-1970s." He continued : "The fact that this has been carried through at a time when the Party was facing the strains of internal division over the Common Market and the inevitable soul-searching following the election defeat reflects great credit on all those concerned with its preparation." It was the relevance of the *Programme*, combined with the low standing of the Government (even among its supporters), which had led to the campaign by the party's opponents to denigrate the document and also to magnify the differences inside the party.

He then came to his central point : "It is their aim to distract conference and the country from the 99 plus per cent on which we are agreed by elevating the importance of twenty-six words on which there is a disagreement." Those twenty-six words referred to the NEB taking over control of twenty-five companies in manufacturing industry. Wilson continued : "I believe there is a real duty on both the National Executive Committee and the Parliamentary Committee [Shadow Cabinet] to seek to resolve these minimal outstanding differences so that the conference can be the success that all of us want it to be, so that we can go forward on an agreed programme. It is my view, therefore, that the two bodies bearing the duties laid upon them by the Constitution, namely the National Executive Committee and the Parliamentary Committee, should now proceed to our agreed selection of those parts of the programme which are to head the manifesto."

The "minimal outstanding difference", as everyone knew, was the pivot on which the whole argument about the future direction of the party turned. Constituency parties had sent in over sixty resolutions on public ownership, thirteen of them specifically endorsing the twenty-five companies proposal and others demanding even wider state intervention. In the end, it was the scope of the resolutions that was to save Wilson in his attempt to keep party unity, but this was not apparent at the Friday meeting. He first encountered hostility on his proposals for a joint meeting that afternoon and withdrew it after fifteen minutes' discussion. The argument against his proposed joint statement on public ownership was that it was unconstitutional. Only the National Executive, and not the Shadow Cabinet, could present statements to the conference, and the left wing democratic socialists expressed opposition to its content. Unable to resolve the issue, the rival factions on the National Executive agreed to have another look at the statement on the Sunday. Wilson, in the meantime, proposed two amendments to the statement, having omitted to mention the public ownership of the construction industry and also the creation of a Co-operative Development Agency to "encourage rationalisation and modernisation in Co-operative Societies and help provide capital for new and existing development". Both were mentioned in the *Programme*. Wilson left the meeting and called the shadow ministers, who had been waiting in the lobbies of the hotel, to a meeting in his room. They were told the joint meeting was unacceptable, but a further attempt would be made to get a statement on public ownership.

The weekend before a party conference sees the start of actual lobbying by delegates. There are fringe meetings, private groupings to discuss tactics on resolutions, trade union delegations' caucus meetings to decide what line should be taken on various debates, and the "compositing" meetings. The latter is a ritual with a mystique all of its own. With the conference lasting only five days it is plainly impossible for all the motions submitted for debate to be taken. (In 1973 there was a total of 436, excluding amendments, covering every conceivable subject, from prices and incomes to inflammable materials, from multinational companies to a pneumoconiosis.) There is a traditional practice, therefore, that those who have tabled similar resolutions be brought together to agree a composite resolution. After much argument, for none of the delegates want to see their own concocted subtleties and emphases subsumed in generalisations, there is usually an agreed compromise. In the case of public ownership in industry where there were over sixty resolutions, these were narrowed down to three composites, incorporating varying degrees of scope and commitment. By the Sunday afternoon these were ready for the National Executive Committee to consider what recommendations it should make to the conference: acceptance, rejection, or a request for remission because of political or administrative objections.

In the meantime, further words were expressed on the Sunday morning about public ownership at an eve-of-conference meeting organised by *Tribune*. Foot appealed for caution. The first thing to be achieved was winning the general election. After that the party could set about ensuring that the new Labour Government was held to the decisions taken by the party conference. Mikardo, on the other hand, said the party's new commitment to nationalisation should not be limited to the takeover of the top twenty-five or even the top 250 companies; the programme should commit the next Labour Government to a "continuous process of nationalisation" which would over a period of two or three Parliaments bring four-fifths of the economy under state control.

Figures have a fascination for Mikardo. When he doodles on the margins of his papers at meetings he fills them with banks of statistics: multiplying, dividing, subtracting. It became a habit early on in his life. When he first joined the National Executive, a number of the social democrats thought he was quietly taking notes of what they were saying for the benefit of journalists after the meetings. They arranged to have a discreet look at what he was jotting down; and were bewildered by the sight of columns of numbers. Mikardo's fascination, as we have seen, did not go as far as wanting twenty-five written into any political commitment. What he had to say at the *Tribune* meeting, therefore, was of considerable interest. Although those in the audience were not in a position to realise it, Mikardo foreshadowed what was to happen at the National Executive meeting that afternoon.

"The fact is," he said, "that those who wanted twenty-five companies written into the policy were not really advocating the nationalisation of just twenty-five companies. In normal circumstances one would have said that the proposed National Enterprise Board has got to take a big slice of the economy and continue to add to it. Why did anyone seek to quantify it at all? It was because there was a lack of confidence in the leadership. It was thought that if it was not quantified someone might try to duck out from the obligation—such were the sad memories of 1966. Therefore you must tie him [Wilson] down by putting a figure on it, so that later on you would be able to measure with precision whether the Labour Government had carried out the undertaking or not."

When the National Executive came to discuss the three composite resolutions on industrial public ownership in the afternoon there was little difficulty in accepting two of them. The technical and supervisory section of the AUEW wanted the conference to support the proposals by the National Executive for early nationalisation of important parts of the British economy. The second resolution, to be moved by the Association of Professional, Executive, Clerical and Computer Staff (APEX) stated: "This conference, recognising the need to change the balance of public and private power, expresses its belief that the next Labour Government should extend public ownership, and that the National Executive Committee, when drawing up the election manifesto, should commit the party to a programme which is capable of being carried out in the term of office of the next Labour Government." Given the climate at the time, it was a moderate proposal, allowing considerable latitude to the next Labour Government. To reinforce the point, the resolution added: "Conference rejects the concept of shopping lists of industries and companies for social ownership."

The third resolution, however, was wholly at odds with the general platitudes of the other two. It came from the fiercely militant constituency parties of Brighton Kemptown and Liverpool Walton. It wanted the conference to endorse the proposal to take over the twenty-five of the top 100 companies "but considers that the Labour Party must go further". The extent of the resolution's ambitions was set out in fifth paragraph: "Conference calls on the next Labour Government to nationalise by means of an enabling act approximately 250 major monopolies together with land, banks, finance houses, insurance companies and building societies with minimum compensation of proven need and the renationalisation of all hived off sections of public owned industries without compensation; all under democratic workers' control and management."

Such extravagances went far beyond the sympathies of most of the National Executive Committee, on electoral, if not entirely doctrinal, grounds. The resolution was the escape route for Wilson and the Parliamentary Party. The conference officials who assisted the drafting of the composite based on resolutions submitted could not have provided (one hesitates to say, without conclusive proof, engineered) a more convenient way out of the dilemma. If the resolution had stuck to twenty-five then the left would have been obliged to support it or lose face. In any case, there was a reasonable certainty that the majority of conference delegates would have supported such a resolution. But when the figure was multiplied tenfold it entered an unreal political world. Acceptance of such a resolution by the National Executive would not only have delighted the Tory opponents but undoubtedly would have alienated many moderate Labour voters. Wilson and the social democrats knew this, but more importantly, in this context, so did Benn, Hart, Castle and all the others who had fought the Shadow Cabinet in the numbers game.

They decided to recommend its rejection and at that point Wilson expressed his satisfaction. He even said that in view of the NEC's decision he would withdraw his proposed statement on public ownership which they had before them and incorporate it in his speech. After six months of heated argument over the issue, which had threatened to drive a huge wedge between the Parliamentary Party and the party activists, the tension was eased. The problems were still there but they were now of manageable dimensions. Few at the time gave any thought to the irony of it all. Fourteen years previously Gaitskell had sought to draw the party back from its Clause Four commitment and had lost. This time round, a strongly militant faction, and there was no denying the uncompromising Marxist commitment inside the two constituency parties involved, had attempted to push the party too far in the opposite direction, and also had failed.

The argument over the scale and functions of the National Enterprise Board, however, had not been resolved. As Judith Hart said at a meeting on the Sunday: "I do not want the twenty-five companies to be regarded only as a symbol of this year's conference decisions, polarising right and left, raising the conflict between the NEC and conference on the one hand and the Shadow Cabinet on the other. What is at issue is whether we can give the National Enterprise Board the tools to do the job." She continued: "If we are not prepared to do that, the whole proposal becomes intellectually dishonest. To carry out the tasks which are set out for the NEB, it must be given a substantial basis in profitable industries, through public ownership of leading firms in the key sectors of manufacturing. The strategic leadership which is needed demands a scale of the order of twenty to twenty-five companies, depending on their size. Vague commitments can and do mean all things to all people."

Judith Hart knew, although she did not say so on that particular occasion, that she and her supporters of the NEB were confronted with a technicality which was going to make their continued campaign all that more difficult. Neither of the two acceptable composites contained a reference to the size of the NEB, and *Labour's Programme*, where it was set out in those contentious twenty-six words, was not being voted on by the conference. The rejected Brighton Kemptown resolution would not be carried by the conference—by Sunday night it was known that the two major unions, the Transport and General Workers Union and the Amalgamated Union of Engineering Workers, would oppose it—and therefore no binding decision would be made by the delegates. The social democrats could go to the manifesto drafting meetings in a stronger position than they ever dared hope. The left may have been the dominant influence in building the *Programme* but some of their over-ambitious colleagues at Brighton Kemptown and Liverpool Walton had, so to speak, bolted the door.

Heffer, who first became the MP for Liverpool Walton in 1964, was not exactly helpful to his own constituency party or the advocates of the NEB when the resolutions were debated at the conference on the Tuesday. He told delegates: "I am sorry to have to get involved in arguments of this kind, because when I listened to the speech of Harold [Wilson had opened the debate] and began to tot up the industries or individual companies that we were going possibly to take over in the construction industry—I am all for that—in pharmaceuticals—I am all for that—if you look at the list, it seemed to add up to much more than twenty-five. So let us not have an argument about this question of twenty-five, let us unite entirely round the question of extending public ownership in order to carry out our basic historic tasks."

Delegates applauded Heffer, but he had obviously only given

a superficial examination to Wilson's speech, for the party leader had barely touched upon *manufacturing* industry in his list of categories for public ownership. There was land, the docks, aircraft and shipbuilding, which existed mainly through the injection of state financial aid, sections of machine tools, and those other sectors listed earlier, but this was nothing like the size and scope which the National Enterprise Board concept envisaged. And when we look at Wilson's speech for his view of its functions it is manifest that he was unwilling or had failed to comprehend the arguments that had taken place.

"Its first duty," he said, "is to act as a holding company to control and manage state assets already in public ownership. Until now the assets in coal, gas, electricity and so on, have been held by the Treasury in a passive sense. They will now be vested in the National Enterprise Board who will have a much more active and dynamic role. And, as I have said, one of its first duties will be to socialise the existing nationalised industries, in the sense at least of bringing into being a real system of industrial democracy, bringing the general level up to or above that of practices now followed and also providing an exemplar for other industries to follow."

We know that this is not what the Public Sector Group had in mind, nor what the argument was over inside the Industrial Sub-Committee, nor what had been approved by the National Executive Committee. The last thing they wanted was the new public interventionist body encumbered with the ailing service and basic nationalised industries. The party leader had got it wrong. Wilson got a little nearer the mark when he said : "But I must once again emphasise that the role of the National Enterprise Board is not confined to the duties of a public holding and management agency. That is not how it was conceived by the National Executive. It will act also as a means to a further substantial expansion of public ownership through its power to take a controlling interest in relevant companies in profitable manufacturing industries."

The question that had to be asked was : What did Wilson mean by "relevant"? What was politically possible, as he and the Shadow Cabinet saw it, or economically essential as part of a future Labour Government's general strategy? There was more than a faint suspicion among the left that the issue had been sidestepped. This was reinforced when Wilson added :

"My own view on the twenty-five companies proposal has been stated. I am against it. The Parliamentary Committee is against it. I will leave it with these words, that the Parliamentary Committee charged by the constitution with the duty of sitting down with the [National] Executive to select, from the Programme adopted by the conference the items for including in the election manifesto, entirely reserves its constitutional rights on this matter and there could be nothing more comradely than that."

Wilson was applauded for this section of his speech and the voting at the end of the debate was to reinforce the overwhelming impression that delegates did not want to get tied down to numerical arguments. Wilson was supported by Jenkins: "It is no good taking over a vast number of industries without a clear plan as to how and by whom they are going to be run. It is no good pretending a transfer of ownership in itself solves our problems." It was left for Benn, who wound up the debate, to restore some of the torn fabric of the proposed National Enterprise Board: "When we are sent back to power, as I believe we surely shall be, we are ready to give instructions for the completion of the Industry Bill with the powers contained within it, and to establish the National Enterprise Board, not to be an ambulance for lame ducks, but to move into the area of profitable manufacturing industry which is at the heart of that proposal." But Benn, who was replying to the debate for the National Executive, had to call for the rejection of the Brighton Kemptown resolution on the grounds: "We are not ready for Composite 34, and if Conference takes its decisions seriously we ask it not to pass that resolution." It was defeated by 5,600,000 votes to 291,000. The other two resolutions, from the AUEW and from APEX, were both carried.

The conference should not be left without discussion of prices and incomes, where it was vital to get some form of agreement with the trade unions if a Labour Government's economic strategy, whatever it may be, was to be creditable. The main resolution down for debate was from the AUEW. This instructed the National Executive Committee to oppose any Government's attempt to freeze wages and instructed the National Executive Committee to "oppose the unjust law by calling on the Trades Union Congress to reject further talks with the Tory

Government and to join with the National Executive Committee in leading the Labour movement in opposition to the Prices and Incomes Policy of the Tory Government and to the capitalist system which interests are served by these attacks on working people".

Hugh Scanlon, President of the AUEW, in moving the resolution made it clear from the outset that his union rejected any so-called incomes policy that directly interfered with the principle of free collective bargaining. But he also recognised, in the militancy of the resolution, that his union was asking for something which had already been rejected by the TUC. In order to avoid embarrassment both for the unions and the Labour Party, he therefore recommended successfully that it should be remitted—"for we recognise that we would be putting the [National] Executive in an invidious position indeed if in effect we were saying to them 'Go back to the TUC General Council and ask them to do something different from that which Congress has already decided' ".

No one deluded themselves that the problem had been resolved by this device. It was Tom Jackson, the moderate general secretary of the Post Office Workers' Union, who was prepared to go to the heart of the debate : "There is a yawning gap in the policy statement which we have before us this morning and that gap is the very field where dissension and trouble will start between the trade unions and the Labour Party if the Labour Party is elected to the Government next time. That is the area of wages, where the document says little or nothing, and this, as far as we are concerned, is a place where real difficulty can start."

The reference to prices and pay was on page twenty-four of Labour's *Programme 1973*. "In applying our price controls," it said, "we will seek to give effect to the annual agreement reached, after talks, with the two sides of industry as part of our new social contract. And this will be particularly important in the struggle against low pay in cases, for example, where the eradication of low pay could lead to necessary price increases." Such a statement was not committing either side. The subsequent paragraph on incomes again reflected hopes rather than commitments. "We believe that the action we propose on prices, together with an understanding with the TUC on the lines which we have already agreed, will create the right

economic climate for money incomes to grow in line with production." On the other hand: "We accept that a policy of
price restraint cannot succeed for very long if wages and salaries
are moving out of line with the growth of productivity." The
Programme reiterated that the party did not believe in statutory controls on incomes, but there were some who saw a
qualification in the subsequent sentence: "Such controls cannot be maintained for *any length. of time* [author's italics]
without putting intolerable strains upon industrial relations and
threatening to perpetuate all the anomalies and injustices in
the present framework of pay differentials." It appeared to be
a concealed escape clause if a future Labour Government ran
into economic difficulties and short-run controls had to be
imposed.

Denis Healey, in winding up the debate, stated that the one
thing which had emerged very clearly was that the key to controlling inflation was to control prices. Another factor was that
no machinery for controlling prices would work, and certainly
not work justly, unless the Government's whole economic
strategy was right. Labour made price control its first priority,
"but we cannot get control of prices unless we get control of
Government itself". And it was he as much as anyone else who
reflected the prevalent mood of the conference: "The time has
gone for theoretical logic chopping, it is no good behaving like
a college of angels in the sixth circle of paradise. Our job is to
get power, and we join battle armed with the most radical and
comprehensive programme we have had since 1945. Its aim is
honestly stated, to bring about a fundamental and irreversible
shift in the balance of people and their families."

Both the democratic socialists and the social democrats left
the conference satisfied that they had won the essential arguments. "We've kept the Red Flag flying here!", proclaimed
Tribune in its end-of-conference edition. "Now on to the biggest campaign for public ownership", it intoned in a sub-
headline which suggested that the battle may have been won
inside the conference but convincing a Labour Government
might be a different matter. The social democrats, on the other
hand, felt they had shaken off the albatross of twenty-five
companies and that the commitment to widespread public
ownership would be of the choosing of a Labour Government in
which they would be dominant. What had come out of the

conference was that the prospect of a general election and the chances of regaining power had occupied minds and defused internal diatribe.

But a lot of questions had been unanswered. Would a Labour Government bring about that irreversible shift by massive state ownership, which the left believed essential? And would it be able to strike a bargain with the trade unions over wage increases? As Healey said about a national plan for redistributing incomes: "We are plunged immediately into the problems of incomes policy, and I believe that during the coming months we must discuss this problem with the trade union wing of our movement to see if we can reach agreement on a voluntary policy for incomes which takes account of taxation too." We will see later what happened inside the tripartite Liaison Committee when Labour came to draw up its draft general election manifesto.

Shadow ministers returned from the conference to Westminster and what they believed to be the real world of politics. While it is true that Labour lost a parliamentary seat at the Glasgow Govan by-election to the Scottish Nationalists and failed to make any improvement in their vote at Berwick on Tweed (the Conservative seat was captured by the Liberals), there was a general recognition that the Heath Government was running into enormous economic problems and that Labour would benefit. The Government had an energy crisis due to the increase in prices by the Arab oil producing countries, soon to be followed by a state of emergency because of overtime bans by mineworkers and electricity power workers in pursuit of claims for increased wages. Shadow ministers detected a smell of death emanating from the Heath Government.

It is little wonder then, as an example, that Callaghan should lose his temper with the Transport House apparatchiks and their National Executive backers. The Home Policy Committee, where the incident occurred on 13 November, had before it the first draft of *Labour's First Five Years*, the document which would go before the joint Shadow Cabinet–National Executive meeting and would form the basis of the general election manifesto. Callaghan told the Home Policy Committee that Transport House was making too many policies and not devoting energies in getting across the ones already agreed. He implied facetiously that he was not sure whether the committee was responsible for, or to, the home affairs department at the party headquarters. Pitt, as head of research, defended himself and his colleagues, by saying it was their job to provide policies for discussion. If there were any propaganda problems then these should be taken to the committee responsible.

The incident, seemingly trivial in itself, illustrated how the Parliamentary Party was sickened with the degree of policy-making undertaken by the Labour Party. The conference had taken its decisions and the National Executive should call a halt. It was a theme to which Jenkins warmed. "We must make clear that in a national crisis we are concerned with the nation's interests and not just with party politics", he told a meeting in Wolverhampton on 16 November. "We must criticise the Government where they deserve to be criticised, but not from a whole series of contradictory points of view... We must fill in the gaps in our own policies and concentrate on those aspects of them which are and can be relevant to the nation's problems."

Labour's First Five Years went through four drafts and appeared before joint meetings of the Shadow Cabinet and the National Executive Committee on 12 December and 11 January. The tripartite Liaison Commitee met between these dates and it was during these three meetings that the Labour Party at last faced up to the problems of an incomes policy. But before looking at what occurred we must return, briefly, to the last attempt in Opposition to have the public ownership proposals dropped from the draft manifesto.

The move came from Reg Prentice, who by this time had climbed well out on to the right wing of the party by campaigning for moderates to stand up and be counted in the fight to release the (alleged) Marxist grip on the party. Prentice argued at the first joint Shadow Cabinet–National Executive meeting that some of the proposals would alienate many Labour voters, although he favoured the public ownership of development land. He had qualified support from Shirley Williams who said the policy should be more specific about intentions. She returned to the argument developed over the past two years by Dell, Crosland and Jenkins, that the party should state, for instance, what areas of the aircraft industry would be taken into public ownership. But most of the social democrats present realised the joint meeting was neither the time nor place for re-opening the battle. Wilson aborted further discussion by stating there could be no going back on the decisions taken at party conference.

The main concern of the meeting was the absence of any reference to incomes in the draft document. It was generally agreed that the party would leave itself open to challenge if it had nothing to say on an issue which was already bedevilling the Government. Ted Short, deputy leader, came up with a formula which appeared to satisfy the mood of the meeting, although it did not survive for long afterwards. He suggested that the document should incorporate the passage on incomes in *Labour's Programme 1973* (which was quoted earlier in the chapter). It was felt that there should be further exploration of the problem before the next joint meeting—Callaghan, Foot, Benn and Castle were to form a working group. In the meantime there was to be the Shadow Cabinet–TUC–National Executive Liaison Committee on 4 January.

The trade union side, although prominent leaders such as Jones, Scanlon and Basnett, of the General and Municipal Workers Union, were absent, was to prove difficult. Wilson, Callaghan and Healey explained that at a recent Parliamentary Party meeting the view had been expressed that the campaign document should say more about incomes, relativities and the link between prices and incomes. It was widely recognised within the Labour Party that there was no easy incomes policy which could be introduced. The public had to be convinced that this problem could only be solved by real consent and national co-operation. The Labour Party, it was said, was concerned about inflation and such problems as public sector pay; it would welcome a statement from the TUC which said that they would, not that they might, respond if the collective bargaining climate changed.

Those who represented the TUC side included Sir Sidney Greene, chairman of its Economic Committee, and Len Murray, assistant general secretary. In a lengthy response the trade unionists explained that there was a definite feeling on the TUC General Council that there would be a broad understanding with the Labour Party. This was the reason for the adoption of the joint statement "Economic Policy and the Cost of Living" the previous February. However, the politicians were told that the TUC was not going to give an absolute pledge on wages. The TUC Economic Review stressed that it was wrong to focus attention exclusively on rises in incomes, and that it should be on the other side of the equation : on increasing productivity and output.

The trade unionists argued that the calls for an incomes policy were often made without specifying the reasons for one, and without stating what interventions in collective bargaining were needed. The TUC's view was that statutory incomes policies did not make a significant change in relativities and were only counter-productive. On the other hand, tax changes and social security benefits could have a very real effect on living standards of the less well off.

They felt it was necessary to state these factors, as had been done in 1970, to provide a realistic background to what the TUC could say. Greene, Murray and their colleagues hoped that the phrase "incomes policy" would be forgotten. The TUC, they explained, wanted to talk about industrial efficiency and manpower utilisation, which was part of the process of collective bargaining. The politicians were reminded that the joint statement adopted in February 1972 had referred to the Donovan Commission on trade unions and employers' organisations and the complexity of collective bargaining which necessitated voluntary arrangements. However, the TUC side said it was reasonable for the Labour Party to put to the TUC that if the party made significant moves in implementing the agreed objectives then they would expect all parties to conform to these objectives. The trade unionists, who were manifestly reserving their position, agreed they would examine the campaign document and, where necessary, respond.

Callaghan and his three colleagues found a formula on incomes that was included in a revised draft document which went before the Shadow Cabinet on 8 January, and later to the National Executive. "After so many failures in the field of incomes policy under the Labour Government, and even more seriously under the Tory Government's compulsory wage policy, only deeds can persuade", it stated. "Only practical action by a government to create a much fairer distribution of national wealth can convince the worker and his family and his trade union that an incomes policy is not some kind of trick to force him to bear the brunt of the national burden." There then followed a passage which was the *quid pro quo* between a future Labour Government and the trade unions; in other words the kernel of the Social Contract. It said : "But as it is proved that the Government is ready to act—against high prices, rents, and other impositions falling most heavily on the low paid and on pensioners—so we believe that the trade unions *voluntarily* (which is the only way it can be done for any period of a free society) will co-operate to make the whole policy successful."

When the document was approved by the National Executive and the Shadow Cabinet on 11 January, Callaghan agreed at a press conference later that day that the voluntary policy as outlined would not "have much effect" on the level of wage claims, "but it would on the level of wages settlement and that is what matters". In order to secure the co-operation of the trade unions—and it cannot be over-stated that this was a major plus for Labour when the general election came—the party undertook to fulfil the series of commitments outlined in the *Programme*.

Between the publication of the *Programme* and the February general election, the Labour Party commissioned Market and Opinion Research International to carry out a highly confidential poll of the electorate on how it valued the various promises. Not surprisingly the commitment to increase pensions immediately, by £10 for the single person and £16 for the married couple, came top of the poll with 74 per cent. The curb on property speculators won 49 per cent support (among trade unionists it was 54 per cent) and the limitation on rent increases won the approval of 47 per cent (with Labour supporters 62 per cent in favour and trade unionists 54 per cent).

But when one examines the response to Labour's promises on public ownership the figures reveal a marked drop in support. The nationalisation of North Sea oil and gas attracted 24 per cent among all those questioned, 30 per cent among Labour voters and 34 per cent trade unionists. The figures for the nationalisation of development of land were : 17–26–25. As for commitments to nationalise shipbuilding, ports, aircraft industries, etc., the response was : 7–12–12. The proposed National Enterprise Board suffered an even worse fate : 6–6–7. This apathy, if not outright opposition, towards further public ownership among Labour voters appears to be confirmed by a poll conducted by National Opinion Polls. It showed that 44 per cent of Labour supporters were against the introduction of more nationalisation, 37 per cent in favour and 19 per cent did not know.

The left blamed the lack of enthusiasm on the fact that the case for public ownership was highly complicated and needed considerably more articulation. Without the "fundamental and irreversible shift in the balance of power and wealth", the next Labour Government would go the way of its predecessors. In the next and final chapter we will see what happened to the *House the Left Built.*

ELEVEN

Power but No Glory

NEARLY FOUR YEARS after losing office Labour returned to power on 4 March 1974, the Heath Government having failed to secure an overall majority in the February general election and being unable to reach an accommodation with the Liberal Party to sustain it in power. Wilson returned to Downing Street, Callaghan went to the Foreign and Commonwealth Office, Healey became Chancellor of the Exchequer, Jenkins was appointed Home Secretary and Crosland Secretary of State for the Environment. As for the two prominent left wingers, Foot was made Secretary for Employment, a bold if surprising stroke which ensured the support of the trade unions, and Benn returned from whence he came, the Department of Industry. He lasted just over a year before Wilson decided enough was enough and moved him to less politically vulnerable quarters, Energy.

Wilson, on becoming Prime Minister, told separate meetings of the Parliamentary Labour Party and the National Executive Committee : "We are going to carry out the manifesto and I regard myself as custodian of the manifesto." There were few who believed, however, that Labour could survive long as a minority Government. The combined forces of the Opposition parties could defeat it at any time and a general election within the year was inevitable. Nonetheless, the Queen's Speech to Parliament on 12 March detailed a full legislative programme, with the Government demonstrating its determination to honour its side of the Social Contract.

The Industrial Relations Act 1972 would be repealed and it fell to Foot, as Employment Secretary, to bring in new legislation : the Trade Union and Labour Relations Bill. This redefined the employers' associations and the trade unions, gave trade unions greater freedom in drawing up their own rules and procedures, made legal the negotiation of closed shops and broadened the legal immunity of unions in respect of strike action. But the Government did not have an overall majority and the Conservatives were able to incorporate safeguards into the Bill before it passed on to the Statute Book. The main changes related to the closed shop provisions protecting employees expelled or excluded unreasonably from unions by legal safeguards, and employees could choose which union they joined. Moreover, where employees objected to belonging to a union on reasonable grounds they could not be forced into membership. The definition of reasonableness, of course, evoked highly subjective responses and the trade unions were far from satisfied. It was when the Government attempted to amend these Tory qualifications in 1976 that the unions were once again brought into the centre of the political battlefield.

In carrying out the manifesto commitments, the Queen's Speech also stated that measures would be taken to ensure fair prices for certain key foods, with the use of subsidies where appropriate, and price inflation would be restrained. On industry: "My Ministers will hold consultations on measures to encourage the development and re-equipment of industry. A Bill will be laid before you to consolidate and to develop existing legislation to promote national industrial expansion. High priority will be given to the stimulation of regional development and employment. They will develop an active manpower policy and bring forward legislation for protecting the health and safety of people at work."

Benn was not involved in the drafting of the Queen's Speech and would have preferred less anodyne references to industry. The first hint of this came in a speech to the Young Socialists at Clacton on 13 April when he said: "*We have begun the task* [author's italics] of translating the policy agreed at conference and expressed in the manifesto into specific worked out proposals for the National Enterprise Board, the planning agreement, the Industry Act and the extensions of public ownership." In other words the Queen's Speech did not go as far as the manifesto commitment. But Benn felt he had a mandate to take what he believed to be the correct course. As he told the Young Socialists at the annual conference: "Our industrial strategy for Britain is set out in the Labour *Programme*... The party consciously chose this policy and it is this policy that I am now directly engaged in preparing." It was a speech that was not thought to be controversial at the time but in fact had important ramifications.

The task of providing the Industry Bill fell to Benn and the three junior ministers appointed with him to the Department: Heffer, the Tribunite backbencher who was made Minister of State (Brian Walden having turned down Wilson's offer of the job), and two parliamentary under-secretaries, the left-inclined Michael Meacher and a dour, moderate Scot, Gregor MacKenzie. Benn gave Heffer the responsibility of chairing the departmental working party created to draft a consultative Green Paper—later changed to a more declaratory White Paper—on which the Bill would be based. Other members on the committee, apart from the junior ministers, included: Francis Cripps, a Cambridge economist whom Benn had appointed his economic adviser, Frances Morrell, formerly with the Fabian Society, who became Benn's political adviser, two senior civil servants, Alan Lord, a financial expert at the Department, and Ronald Deering, who had vast experience of regional problems as a former regional director, and, as a temporary civil servant, Stuart Holland.

Holland's route on to the committee was somewhat circuitous. He had not been taken on by Benn as an adviser, as many thought he would, but became part-time economic adviser to Judith Hart, who had been made Minister for Overseas Development, an area in which she had specialised for many years and had widely acknowledged expertise. Holland, therefore, had a foot in Whitehall, with one still at Sussex University where he was a research fellow and lecturer, and was able to join the Heffer working party. Ever since the National Enterprise Board and planning agreements proposals had been approved by the party's National Executive Committee Holland had been active among constituency parties and shop stewards' meetings promoting the ideas as major instruments of socialist planning. He therefore seized opportunity, offered by Benn, to help steer the proposals on to the Statute Book.

The ministers had taken to the Department copies of the general election manifesto, *Labour's Programme 1973* and the Green Paper on the NEB, but progress inside the working party was slow. Its members met two or three times a week, but there were suspicions among members that the civil servants, or some of them, viewed the working party and the whole project as no more than a propaganda exercise. These civil servants, it was thought, believed that the work was being undertaken in preparation for a second general election which the Government would have to call in the autumn in an attempt to secure an overall majority. Moreover, some highly placed civil servants, including Sir Anthony Part, the permanent secretary, believed the proposals were so politically interventionist that they would alienate every section of industry and that without that support the Government's industrial strategy would be doomed. One prominent industrialist who privately withdrew his co-operation very early on was Sir Frederick Catherwood, who had been offered the chairmanship of the National Enterprise Board soon after Labour returned to office.

Catherwood was a natural, almost ideal choice. He had been director general of the National Economic Development Office in the previous Wilson Government and had the respect and confidence of industry. He was a known Labour sympathiser, although it was less known that he had worked on party policy committees, and for many years had supported the case for a paragovernmental interventionist agency. By chance, he had offered his resignation as Chief Executive of the Laing Group of Companies on the day of the February general election, not because of any disagreement but because he wanted more freedom and new challenges. When Labour assumed office, Sir Anthony Part invited him to the Department and suggested he may be interested in the chairmanship of the NEB which would be included in the Government's programme. Catherwood, as it happened, knew Holland and was familiar with the ideas in the NEB Green Paper. Although he did not agree with all of them, he was attracted by what could be done with such an agency. He believed that if it was carefully managed, and did not blunder around industry like a rogue elephant, it could make a significant contribution to much needed industrial expansion and investment. Catherwood informed Benn that he was interested and then later changed his mind.

Sir Fred had no quarrel with the Government's declared intentions for industry in the Queen's Speech, but he was somewhat concerned when he read reports of Benn's Clacton conference speech. It appeared to him that the Industry

Secretary wanted to embark on the full and immediate implementation of party policy. When he sought clarification from Benn, his fears appeared to be confirmed. He informed Benn that such an approach was so highly political that the NEB would never get the co-operation of the Confederation of British Industry or of individual firms. In these circumstances Catherwood was no longer interested in the job when it became available.

The matter did not end there, for Catherwood discovered that his name was still being floated as the chairman-designate as late as June : much to his embarrassment as he felt the rumours would ruin his prospects of an attractive job in industry. He called on an old friend, Sir Douglas Allen, head of the Home Civil Service, to see how these stories, which were thought to emanate from Benn's Department, could be dispelled. Allen gave a remarkable reply : Sir Fred was told not to worry as Wilson was soon to announce that Sir Donald (now Lord) Ryder, chairman of Reed International, the twenty-fourth largest firm in the country, was to be appointed Industrial Adviser to the Government and the chairman-designate of the NEB. By this time Benn had lost control of the White Paper on industry, his over-enthusiasm and ambition having given the Prime Minister the excuse to wrest it from his grasp. Sir Donald Ryder's appointment was a symbol of the diminution of Benn's influence, and those who were aware of what had happened treated the failure to hold Catherwood as a sad loss.

Benn rarely attended the Heffer working party, although he was involved in regular discussions on its progress during the customary ministerial meetings in his department. Early on, Heffer was to show his frustration at the slow progress of the working party and on 1 April produced a draft paper setting out the programme for a Green Paper. They went through each item to be included : the National Enterprise Board, pricing policy, the Official Trustee, and planning agreements. Heffer's aim was to have the draft ready before the Whitsuntide so that Benn could read it during the Parliamentary recess. The target date was reached, but it became not only the time when the draft left Heffer's hands but marked the beginning of disenchantment with his boss and colleague. We will see why later, for Benn at this stage was being exceptionally active in providing the rationale for the Government's plans to intervene more directly in industry. At the beginning of May he released figures showing that over the past four years—from April 1970 to April 1974, which covered the period of the Conservative Administration—the Government had paid out £3,075 million in subsidies to industry. This assistance to private industry, he said, had been running at the rate of £2 million a day. Addressing a May Day rally in Bristol, he said this meant that the £3,075 million paid out could be compared with the £6,375 million paid in tax by companies in the last four calendar years. Therefore, in one sense, the Government had been returning to industry about one-half the taxes it had paid to the Government.

Benn went on to draw another comparison. During the same period, dividends paid out on ordinary and preference shares amounted to £6,508 million. Thus, in another sense, the Government had been financing just under half the payments of dividends to shareholders. Benn stated that in publishing the figures he was not suggesting that the money was provided for the wrong purposes, nor was he hinting that amounts should be cut; he was not blaming past Governments for paying the money nor criticising the industrialists who took it. What then, was his reason? The Secretary of State for Industry explained : "I am saying that these figures throw new light on the argument that private enterprise, free from public support, exists in Britain in the form in which we are told it exists. I am also saying that the national purposes for which these policies were developed have not been achieved."

Not surprisingly, Benn's approach did not have the unqualified support of the more moderate members of the Cabinet. Healey, Chancellor of the Exchequer, for example, was categoric at the beginning of May in his assurances to the Confederation of British Industry that the Government wanted a "private sector which is vigorous, alert, imaginative and profitable". He told the CBI at their annual dinner : "I can assure you that the Government has no intention of destroying the private sector or encouraging its decay". What he could not say was that the Government, or some sections of it, was more intent on at least partly destroying Benn's interventionist plans, and that the Treasury was playing a leading part.

Early on in the life of the Government, Healey had issued

a Treasury minute stating that the public ownership proposals were highly inflationary and that a deflationary policy was essential. The Treasury was not represented on the Industry Department's working party but it became evident (they *were* more than suspicious, as one minister put it) that discussions inside the working party were being recounted to Treasury officials through the Civil Service grapevine. Ministers became conscious that the Treasury was waging a skilful campaign against the proposals to be incorporated in the draft White Paper. Having failed to halt the progress of the working party, there appears to have been a change in the Treasury's tactics in May. Instead of the plans being too inflationary, the Treasury began to argue whether, given the economic climate, the Government could afford such institutions as the National Enterprise Board.

It was these kind of tactics which helped Benn to decide to fight out in the open, as well as inside the Cabinet Committees where he was nowhere near getting wholehearted support. Hence, for example, his May Day rally speech at Bristol. He employed another tactic which did not assist his relationship with Wilson. The tripartite Liaison Committee between the TUC, the PLP and the National Executive was kept in being when Labour came to power, with senior ministers participating. Early on it was decided that Cabinet ministers should submit, in broad outline, the work of their departments and the stage the various policies had reached. It was a demonstration of the Social Contract at work. The first three Cabinet ministers to submit documents were Shirley Williams, Secretary of State for Prices and Consumer Protection, Barbara Castle, Secretary of State for Health and Social Security, and Benn. All three departments were of paramount interest to the trade unionists because they covered vital areas of the Social Contract : prices, pensions, industrial regeneration and investment. Benn's confidential document went much farther than most, in two senses. It was more detailed, and it leaked and became public knowledge.*

In reality, there was nothing much that was new in the document. All the proposals were contained in *Labour's Programme 1973*. But the document now had the imprimatur of a Cabinet minister and was seen as the declaration of Govern-

* To the author, *The Times*, 23 May.

ment policy. The draft White Paper had yet to be approved by the Cabinet and here was Benn saying that the NEB would "rationalise the industrial structure in each main sector in line with the longer-term public need, rather than short-term considerations". Moreover, it would "act to reduce the growth of monopoly power by inserting public enterprise competition where needed". And if this was not enough to cause anguish in boardrooms and anger at the CBI, the NEB would "counter multinationals by empowering a tougher bargaining stance for government, particularly over new investment location". One other example—the document ran to several hundred words— was the ringing declaration that "the basic objective of the planning agreements system is to secure the conformity of leading companies with national economic priorities in return for supporting requested industrial development, giving financial assistance, etc.". The basis for such agreements "will therefore include such criteria as price control, the level of home and overseas sales, the regional distribution of employment, domestic employment levels, industrial relations practices and product development".

The Confederation of Industry was appalled, and so were many of Benn's ministerial colleagues. But matters were developing inside the Department of Industry and in the Cabinet which were to change the whole tone of the White Paper. Aspirations were one thing, application was another. Heffer had called a whole-day meeting on 23 May to finalise the draft document and submit it to Benn. Those on the working party saw that Heffer had been careful in the drafting of the document in an attempt to ensure that nothing should be said which Wilson would find politically offensive. Although all the major policy measures were enshrined in the draft, they were seen to be couched in moderate language and, in consequence, should be acceptable to the Cabinet. It was noticeable that while the draft carried a strong determination to press forward with the policies, there was no overt criticism of capitalism and the private enterprise system.

Benn studied the draft during the recess—he called a meeting of close associates at his home, although Heffer was unable to attend—and then had a meeting of ministers in his room at the Commons. Significant changes were made. In he words of one of the working party: "He had radicalised the introduction. It looked as if parts of it had come out of Kings Street [headquarters of the Communist Party in London]." While this was no doubt an exaggerated spontaneous reaction, there is little doubting that Heffer, whose temper is rarely on a long leash, exploded in anger at what he saw. He argued that the balance of the whole document had been unhinged and that it would never get past Wilson, a view partly supported by Gregor MacKenzie. Benn could not, initially, be persuaded to see the force of this argument. Heffer, however, had worked himself up into a rage and could not be dissuaded from his opposition. He even asked at one point, mistakenly allowing personalities to intervene, whether Benn was more concerned with popularity inside the party than with getting policies through Cabinet and subsequently Parliament. Though it is not likely that Heffer would have employed such provocative language in less heated moments—in fact it was a distortion of Benn's position and what he was trying to achieve—he succeeded in getting some modifications to the revised draft. Nonetheless, Heffer left the meeting with the feeling that Benn's new approach would backfire, and in this he was to prove correct in important details.

When the draft went before the Cabinet's public enterprise committee, which included most of the senior Cabinet ministers, Wilson moved in and took command of the document. From then on it was in the hands of the Cabinet Office. One of the essential ingredients of the planning agreements system, argued throughout the period when Labour was in Opposition, was that it should carry a degree of compulsion, otherwise it would be ignored by industry. When the White Paper emerged from the Cabinet the system had been changed to one that would operate on a voluntary basis: a "Planning Agreement will not be an agreement in the sense of a civil contract enforceable by law", to quote the White Paper. It explained that the heart of the system would be a series of consultations between Government and companies, leading to an agreement about plans for the following three years. These would be reviewed and "rolled forward annually". In the course of the consultations, the Government would assess with the company its needs for assistance to support and reinforce agreed company plans. There would be special reference to selective assistance for new

employment projects in the regions. From the White Paper :
"In particular, if in the course of these discussions it becomes
clear that in order to align the company's plans with national
needs some financial assistance is required beyond that which
would in any case be available to the company by way of capital
allowances, regional development aid and regional employment
premium, the Government will be ready to provide the kind of
discretionary financial assistance by way of grants and loans
for which the Industry Act 1972 now provides." When the
Bill was published at the end of January 1975 it closely followed
the lines of the White Paper, excepting that whereas the White
Paper had devoted four pages to planning agreements the Bill
contained only one clause. This guaranteed that firms entering into such agreements would not suffer a cut in the value of
regional development grants during the life of an agreement.
It was all that remained of the original selective assistance
proposals.

There were other retreats from the party policy and draft
proposals in the White Paper. As Heffer, who was sacked for
his stance over the referendum on the Common Market (of
which more later), was to write the following year : "Most of
its teeth have been drawn. I am not going so far as to say the
NEB is a toothless animal. That would be wrong, but it is
hardly the sturdy bulldog that was originally devised in the
Green Paper and later endorsed in the party *Programme*."
The Party *Programme* had stated that "it was necessary to
put in an 'Official Trustee' to assume temporary control of any
company which fails to meet its responsibilities to its workers,
to its customers, or to the community as a whole". The White
Paper threw in qualifications : while "The Government wish,
however, to retain other means of dealing with factory closures
in the private sector on those occasions when, for social and
economic reasons, it is desirable to find some way of keeping
a plant in operation while Government Departments and other
interests concerned consider whether and in what manner a
permanent solution to the resulting problems can be found",
the conclusion was that "such a proposal inevitably raises
difficult issues of company law and will need further study
before decisions can be taken by the Government". When the
Bill appeared the proposal for an Official Trustee had been
dropped.

These modifications to the draft White Paper by the Cabinet in August led to Benn's isolation. The moderates, led by Wilson and Healey, had successfully carried through their determination, first voiced in Opposition, to muzzle any attempt to have the Government's economic-industrial strategy so demonstrably interventionist that the confidence and co-operation of industry and management would be lost. Planning Agreements was a perfect example. Healey had expressed the view in Opposition to a party sub-committee that such a system was the only policy he had been offered which could help him as a future Chancellor of the Exchequer to get to the root of the inflation problem, through information on the cost and profit structure of big business. But he and his colleagues called a halt on compulsion : the Government dare not risk alienating industry by coercion. At the time of writing only one Planning Agreement has been signed between the Government and Chrysler.

Wilson and his economic ministers all agreed during the summer and autumn of 1974 that investment, or the lack of it, by industry was one of the major problems facing the Government in getting the economy moving. They nonetheless rejected the clamour of the left for direct intervention with State cash and corresponding control. Harold Lever, who was Wilson's economic adviser with a seat in the Cabinet, came up with the idea of a new form of investment bank. This proposal had its attractions : not only would it take over the role the party policy-makers had designated for the National Enterprise Board, but it would also reduce its scope to that of the old Industrial Reorganisation Corporation. Although the investment bank was discussed inside Cabinet it never materialised, but the proposal was seen by the interventionists as another attempt to turn the party's industrial strategy full circle.

The expected general election was called by Wilson for 10 October and Labour was returned with a majority over the other parties of three seats, hardly an overwhelming vote of confidence by the electorate, more a cautious recognition that Labour had the benefit of the doubt instead of the Tories. The voters appeared to accept the skilful exploitation by Labour that a return to Conservative policies would resurrect confrontation politics with the trade unions. Labour had its Social Contract with the unions and the Government's determination to carry out its side of the bargain was amply demonstrated in the Queen's Speech. It included proposals to set up the NEB, introduce capital gains tax, take into public ownership development land, offshore oil and gas, and the shipbuilding and aircraft industries. The catalogue of nationalisation proposals stands in stark contrast to the legislative programme of the 1964 Government when Labour, on a similar majority, dared not even expose itself to defeat on the renationalisation of iron and steel. It was both an indication of party feeling and the power of the trade unions: this time there could be no prevarications, or "betrayals" as left wing critics would have described them.

Before the publication of the Industry Bill Healey produced his third Budget as Chancellor in November against a gloomy background of the economy running into sharp recession, with industry running out of cash, production levelling out below the figures of the previous year, and inflation continuing to rage. He made an extra £1,000 million available for investment by private industry, but at the same time swung a deflationary axe against public expenditure and limited the increase in demand on resources to an average of more than $2\frac{3}{4}$ per cent a year over the succeeding four years. The revenue support for nationalised industry prices, running at £1,000 million a year, was to be phased out as soon as possible. Although the 10p piece he picked up in St James's Park on the way to the Commons to deliver his Budget may have been a personal bit of good fortune, Healey's statement was an indication of the grim times that lay ahead for the Government and the country.

The Industry Bill, when it was published at the end of January, showed that there had been other major changes from the White Paper apart from those outlined earlier. The provision for compulsory disclosure of information by firms to Government and trade unions was no longer connected with planning agreements, although it had been forcibly argued in Opposition and by the interventionist-minded ministers in Government, that the linking of the two was essential. The Confederation of British Industry had mounted a powerful campaign against them both, although by separating the disclosure power from what were to be voluntary planning agreements made the disclosure provisions more general, which seemed a peculiar way of attempting to minimise the fears of the CBI.

Industry proved to be enraged by the disclosure provisions, stating that they could damage the commercial interest of the company, upset existing methods of consultation with employees, and inhibit decision-making. Holland, in fact, had persuaded Labour policy-makers that the linking of planning agreements to disclosure of information would guarantee trade union support for the proposal, ensuring the co-operation of management with the work-force and thereby strengthening shop-floor bargaining power. But the CBI was not going to be pushed easily in that direction.

Throughout the argument on the Industry Bill, as it proceeded through the committee stage in Parliament, there was an air of unreality with both sides often taking up extreme positions. The left thought the Bill was no more than a pathetic substitute for securing control of the commanding heights of the economy" whereas the Tories and their advisers from the CBI gave the distinct impression that they were sitting in the ante-room to a Marxist-run state. On the question of disclosure, for example, the Conservatives raised all sorts of horrors which did not really exist. Continental experience showed that there was no foundation for companies' fears that they would be harmed by being forced to disclose information to the trade unions, providing there were proper safeguards. In several countries, for example, West Germany, the law demands disclosure to employees, and therefore trade unions, on such matters as investment plans, which British firms believed they needed to keep secret.

The more interventionist-minded among Labour politicians voiced their criticisms at the watering down of the Bill and were not placated by the protestations of the CBI or the Tories that it would bring down the curtains on competitive private enterprise. Nonetheless they happily quoted a remark of Wilson, made at the Merseyside Productivity Council on 7 February 1975, that in his view the NEB was "the biggest leap forward in economic thinking and policy since the war, above all in the investment context. In addition to filling the gap left by the abolition of the Industrial Reorganisation Corporation . . . the NEB adds a new dimension to economic management. For when private investment is inadequate to ensure a high level of employment and modernisation, public investment is enlisted." This is what the left had been saying all along, but they turned a deaf ear to other remarks made by Wilson at the same meeting. With the CBI's objections in mind, Wilson stated: "So much of the uninformed criticism of the Bill is based on fears, imagined, fantasised or fabricated, that all this puts unlimited power in the hands of a single Minister [i.e. Benn] assumed to be operating in some underground monastic cellar impenetrable by the light. This attitude is based on total ignorance of how modern government works. There can be no question of this power being used for any significant acquisition except by a collective decision of one of the most powerful standing committees of the Cabinet [the Industrial Committee, of which Wilson was chairman]."

It became apparent to those supporters of Benn that Wilson was running out of patience with his Secretary of State for Industry, if not on personal terms then by his speeches and actions which appeared to the Prime Minister to be further undermining the spirit of co-operation that the Government needed from industry and commerce. If more evidence was needed by the left that this was the case then it was given in oblique fashion on 7 May. "Wilson to Clip Benn's Wings" was the headline of the *Daily Telegraph*'s authoritative story by its Political Staff: "If Mr Benn imagines that he is going to have *carte blanche* to run the National Enterprise Board as an instrument for the wholesale nationalisation of industry through acquisition of State shareholdings he will be sharply disillusioned by the Prime Minister."

The report went on to state that Wilson meant to show Benn exactly who is boss by making clear that appointments to the National Enterprise Board when it was set up would be made by the Prime Minister after consultation with the Chancellor of the Exchequer, the Secretary of State for Industry, and the chairman of the NEB himself (then Sir Don Ryder). In addition, under the Statute when it became law, the Board would be free to act within the terms of the Statute and of any guidelines laid down; the nature of the matters where the Board sought to consult the Government and the line taken by the Government would be supervised by, and would be under the general direction of, the Prime Minister. If this was true there seemed little doubt that Wilson was intent upon cutting Benn's wings, as the *Telegraph* put it. But as Wilson at the time was in Bermuda attending the Commonwealth Prime Ministers' conference, what credence could one place on the authoritativeness of the report? Then it dawned. Wilson had been accompanied on his tour by a number of British political journalists, one of whom was Harry Boyne, the then Political Correspondent of the *Telegraph*. The story not only rang true but was taken to toll the demise of Benn as Secretary of State for Industry.

However, the development of these tensions has not to be seen in isolation. Overlaying them was an even more formidable obstacle to Labour unity, inside and outside the Government. This was over the vexed and divisive issue of British membership of the European Community. Should Britain stay in or withdraw? The Government was committed by the terms of its general election manifesto to consult the British people through a referendum after renegotiating with its European partners. The left saw the two problems as inseparable : unless there was a withdrawal from the Community Britain would be unable to pursue the kind of strategy that was essential to regenerate British industry. The Treaty of Rome, particularly its preamble, demonstrably served to strengthen the capitalist ethos and in consequence throw up barriers against the encroachment of socialist policies and State interventionism. Benn was to lay great emphasis on this aspect in the great debate on membership whereas other anti-marketeers treated it with a degree of circumspection. It was a return to the old dilemma : in attacking the EEC when many of the proposals in the Industry Bill were drawn from continental experience, the democratic socialists among the anti-marketeers ran the risk of being charged with inconsistency of thought.

Ever since Labour had returned to power in March 1974 Callaghan, as Foreign Secretary, together with Roy Hattersley, his overtly ambitious Minister of State and social democratic pro-marketeer, had been undertaking the renegotiations with the eight countries in the Common Market. At the outset, Callaghan and the Cabinet's European Committee had produced a master-stroke to counter the campaign for British withdrawal. They had decided—and this was a manoeuvre never properly anticipated by the anti-marketeers throughout the long period of intra-party feud while Labour was in Opposition

—to renegotiate within the terms of the Rome Treaty. In others words, there was to be no fundamental challenge to the political-economic-social philosophy on which the European Community was founded. The Common Market Agricultural Policy, for example, would have to be changed, but the British Government was not saying it would have to be scrapped. Wilson and Callaghan appeared to be giving a favourable declaration of intent to the EEC and the anti-marketeers were left high and dry.

As early as December 1974 the anti-marketeers were fighting a rearguard action as reports came across the Channel which indicated the successes that Wilson and Callaghan were having in European summitry. Benn in particular among the anti-market ministers began a counter-offensive. He told a private meeting of Labour backbenchers in December that because of British membership ministers were supplicants and not decision-makers. "We are no longer masters of our own fate in industrial and regional policy", he stated, much to the annoyance of his ministerial colleagues who favoured continued membership. Benn told the backbenchers that they must realise that the powers and position of the Department of Industry were totally different from when he was there in the late 'sixties. The Industry Bill had yet to appear, but Benn informed the meeting that the Government was having to have constant consultations with the European Commission and it was most likely the Commission would see the proposed Bill before Parliament. Put another way, Benn was giving a further demonstration of the weakening of Parliamentary sovereignty because of the EEC. "You can take it from me," he said, "that at all levels there are consultations on the Bill."

Saying these things at a private meeting was one thing but going public was another. Wilson had yet to give his dispensation which allowed ministers to break ranks over Europe and abandon collective responsibility. Benn aired his view publicly at the end of December, at the very moment when the renegotiations were at a delicate stage and before the Cabinet had considered the new terms that Wilson and Callaghan had succeeded in achieving. In a letter to his constituents in Bristol South East—a convenient device of politicians who ensure that national newspapers get a copy—Benn said : "Britain's continuing membership would mean the end of

Britain as a completely self-governing nation and the end of
our democratically elected Parliament as the supreme law-
making body in the United Kingdom." Benn was not the only
minister, inside and outside the Cabinet, to share this view, but
the others did not feel that the appropriate time had been
reached to voice their misgivings and fears about continued
membership. That moment came when the Cabinet had its
final meeting on the acceptance of the terms on 18 March. The
split was wider than expected : sixteen voting for the terms
and seven against. All the latter were aligned with the left :
Foot, Benn, Shore, Secretary of State for Trade, Barbara
Castle, Secretary of State for Health and Social Services, John
Silkin, Minister for Planning and Local Government, Eric
Varley, Secretary of State for Energy, and Willie Ross,
Secretary of State for Scotland.

In an unprecedented action in post-war politics they issued
a declaration within five hours of the Cabinet meeting ending.
In it they stated : "We believe it is in the true interest of our
people to regain the essential rights which permanent membership of the Common Market would deny us; the right of
democratic self-government through our own elected Parliament; the right to determine for ourselves how we impose taxes
and fix food prices; the right to pursue policies designed to
ensure full employment; and the right to seek co-operation
with other nations in a worldwide framework." They went on
to state that they intended to campaign for the withdrawal of
the United Kingdom from the Common Market "and we
invite our fellow citizens to join us". The following day 132
members of the Parliamentary Labour Party, including twenty
more ministers—Heffer and Judith Hart among them—signed
a Commons early day motion opposing the terms. The same
day, eighteen members of the National Executive Committee—
that is, a majority—signed a motion attempting to commit the
party to actively campaign against the Government's decision,
a provocative and, as it turned out, abortive plan to deprive
Labour's pro-marketeers of the use of the party's organisational
facilities during the referendum campaign.

In all thirty-eight ministers voted against the Government's
recommendations when they were debated in the Commons
in mid-April, but Heffer was the only casualty. He was sacked
as Minister for Industry for speaking during the debate and

therefore breaking the ground rules laid down by Wilson that ministers should not speak against Government policy inside Parliament, although they were free to participate in the anti-market campaign outside. Heffer was helping to pilot the Industry Bill through the committee stage and returned to the backbenches. His dismissal provoked a threatened boycott of the committee's proceedings by other Labour backbenchers but it was called off after Heffer had stated that he did not approve of the protest. What none of them could possibly know at the time was that their planned walk-out was to serve as a dress rehearsal for a more dramatic revolt two months later when Wilson removed Benn from the Industry Department.

By this time—that is, in May—Labour politics were hopelessly divided. There was real disagreement over the Government's handling of the economy, the left was demanding a more rigorous application of party policy inside the Industry Committee, and there was the referendum on Europe. Although Benn was not alone in his opposition to the European Community he was now being portrayed as Public Enemy Number One. In the view of many politicians and the majority of political commentators he was mischievous, perhaps dangerous or even mad. Benn's eyes became the object of close attention by the cartoonists: they stared out from beneath arched eyebrows or appeared to revolve. It was a malicious and grotesque distortion of the man and the political creed he was promulgating, but at the same time he could hardly plead innocence. Benn thrived on ideas and ignored the risks of sometimes pushing them to the limits at inopportune moments.

There was the occasion in April, as an instance, when he presented a confidential paper to the party's Industrial Sub-Committee (which continued with its work while Labour was in office) advocating that a new industrial programme was necessary to double the amount of investment in manufacturing. Few disagreed with him on this. But his suggestion that a main source of funds could be insurance companies, pension funds and other financial institutions created a furore when his paper, inevitably, leaked. In fact, it was not an entirely new idea among party policy-makers. The suggestion had been made as early as February 1972 at the "conference of experts" but had not got very far on the grounds that such a proposal could be misunderstood and alienate the small saver and, indeed, some of the trade unions whose members had money tied up in pension funds. But the greatest offence was that the document came at a time when Wilson and his other economic ministers were attempting to placate the fears of the Confederation of British Industry and the City.

Benn was also prepared to raise the stakes in the referendum campaign. While he and other anti-market ministers issued a statement declaring that continued membership of the Community threatened to ruin Britain and that acceptance of the Treaty of Rome was "economic surrender", it was Benn who raised the spectre of unemployment, later to be backed by Foot. Benn argued that 500,000 jobs had already been lost because of British membership and that if the trend continued there would be mass unemployment. While this is not the place to examine the arguments of the real causes of unemployment which burdened the Government in succeeding years, Benn can justifiably argue that there was some validity in his predictions. At the time of his pronouncement Healey was stung to reply, issuing a statement through the Treasury, that those who sought foreign scapegoats "for our shortcomings were escaping from real life by retreating into a cocoon of myth and fantasy".

On Thursday 6 June nearly 26 million people voted in the first referendum ever to be held in the United Kingdom. The results was an overwhelming victory for the pro-marketeers: 17,378,581 (67.2 per cent) voted Yes and 8,470,073 (32.8 per cent) voted No. The Government's policies were safe and Britain would remain in the European Community. But would Benn remain in the Cabinet? No one doubted the survival of the other anti-market Cabinet ministers: Foot, Shore, Silkin, Ross, Varley and Castle. But what about Benn? There was an immediate clamour that there should be no victimisation, with Jack Jones, of the Transport and General Workers Union, lending his not inconsiderable influence: "Any move of Mr Benn away from the Secretaryship of Industry, and I think I can speak for the TUC, would be a grave affront to the trade union movement... It is vital if we are to maintain a degree of industrial unity that he stays where he is." Jones added: "We have a very great deal of confidence in Tony Benn, and I know Harold Wilson is aware of this. We would like him to stay where he is. It is best if we do not have victimisation."

But it turned out that Jack Jones was not around when his presence was needed.

Benn spent the weekend at his home in London, pondering his fate. On the Monday he answered questions in the Commons and then received a summons from Wilson. Benn was told he was being moved, that his Cabinet job would be interchanged with Varley's at the Department of Energy and that he had to give his reply by 8 p.m. that night. On his return from seeing Wilson, a movement started to rally Benn supporters, messages going to Barbara Castle, Foot, Mrs Hart, Mikardo, Meacher, Hayward, general secretary of the Labour Party, and Jones. That night, all of them (apart from Jones who could not be contacted) made their way to Benn's private ministerial room in the Commons, where they found Benn, his wife and two eldest sons and Frances Morrell. Judith Hart informed them that Wilson wanted her to move from the Ministry of Overseas Development to be Minister of State for Transport and she had refused.

The one key element was Varley's position. Had he been informed by Wilson and was he prepared to take on Industry? Varley, it transpired, had been attending the opera at Covent Garden and had been summoned by Wilson during the performance. Varley's reply had been that he would only take the job if Benn was prepared to make a straight swop. Judith Hart, in the meantime, had been recalled by Wilson and informed that she could stay at Overseas Development (he later changed his mind again), but Wilson wanted to know what Hayward was doing in Benn's room, clearly worried that he had a revolt on his hands. Foot, who was by far the most influential of the left wing ministers and had developed a close political relationship with Wilson, offered to act as mediator. He went to see Wilson and reminded him of the promise that there would be no recriminations after the referendum campaign.

By this time the 8 p.m. deadline set by Wilson for a decision by Benn had been passed. Foot's mediation was helpful in that the Prime Minister extended his time-limit for further reflection, provided there was no leakage of the discussions that were occurring. Wilson told Foot that if anything got out and Ian Aitken (Political Editor of *The Guardian*) had the story in the following day's paper : "The whole damn deal is off." It never leaked and the to-ings and fro-ings were to last for another twenty-four hours. Support was coming in for Benn from a number of constituency parties, who submitted resolutions to the party's National Executive Committee, although they had no inkling of the rising drama at Westminster. Their surmises were a reaction to press speculation.

The following day, Tuesday 10 June, there was a universal cry at Westminster : "Where is Benn?" It was voiced officially by the Conservatives through Michael Heseltine, their front-bench spokesman on industry. Benn had not turned up for the morning session of the Industry Bill committee and Heseltine was wanting further elucidation on a matter which the Industry Secretary had raised during question time the previous day. Benn had told the Commons that the Government would consider the publication of a further White Paper on industry "in the course of the review of the Bill which we have undertaken to carry out". Labour MPs had interpreted this as an intention to change the Bill to meet the demands of the Confederation of British Industry. Having failed to get specific assurances from Meacher, the Industry Parliamentary Secretary, inside the committee, the Opposition wrote to Benn saying : "We are very disturbed to hear there may be a further White Paper in relation to the Industry Bill. This would seem to suggest that there could be fundamental changes made to the Bill which is currently being discussed in committee." In these circumstances "we would appreciate it if you would make a statement to the committee this afternoon".

But Benn never appeared before the committee again. That afternoon, the Labour backbenchers, noticing Benn's continued absence, staged a walk-out, all the while being encouraged by Joe Ashton, a blunt Yorkshireman, a committee member, and, more to the point, Benn's zealous parliamentary private secretary. Though few of the backbenchers realised it at the time, they were being brought into the private battle with Wilson to keep Benn in his job. A deputation was sent to Bob Mellish, the Government Chief Whip, informing him that they had no intention of returning to the committee unless Benn turned up. Whips were sent to hunt around the Palace of Westminster for him, but Benn was holding out in his private room and the telephone was not being answered.

By this time, however, the tide was turning against him. His options were to accept Wilson's offer, resign or remain obdurate and be sacked, but as the day wore on it became clear that there was insufficient support to sustain him in his present position. Resignation would be a nine-day wonder or it could inflict enormous damage on party morale. Either way Benn would not emerge with much influence on his side. He would certainly not make sufficient impact to change Government policy. And, in any case, one essential ingredient was missing to ensure positive success : after Jones's initial warning against victimisation, the unions had not rallied round to lend support. After hours of fighting a rearguard action, Benn conceded defeat early that evening and Wilson announced his Cabinet changes that night.

Benn went to Energy and Varley to Industry. Judith Hart resigned rather than accept a lower job as Minister for Transport, the bitter irony not being lost that her successor as Minister for Overseas Development, Reg Prentice, was kept inside the Cabinet, where Judith Hart had not been. In her resignation speech in the Commons later she said the CBI and the Conservatives had served notice on the Government that it must sacrifice the industrial policies which she had helped to shape. "If the Government seek to solve the nation's economic problems by capitalist methods—and I trust they will not do so—and abandon their socialist policies they will fail to resolve the crisis and will betray the Labour movement."

The day after the Cabinet changes were announced Varley, in his new role, began examining amendments to the Industry Bill which Wilson insisted should be incorporated, partly to meet the wishes of the CBI. They were to include further modifications to the disclosure of information. It had been an eventful week for Varley. In particular, he was never to forget that moment when Wilson interrupted his enjoyment of a performance at Covent Garden. The opera was Verdi's *La Forza Del Destino*—The Force of Destiny.

Appendix

By the summer of 1972 the political and industrial wings
of the Labour movement had laid down the foundations of the
Social Contract (see Chapter Five). The detailed analysis below
is based upon comparison between Labour's *Programme 1972*
and the TUC *Economic Review* which were published that
year. It covers three areas: "Broad Agreement", "Broad
Agreement Expected" and "Difference of Approach".

BROAD AGREEMENT

Economic and Industrial Policy

Commitment to Full Employment
Programme: The commitments included "the complete abolition of long-term unemployment", and a long-term aim to
see that "in every part of the country there are at least as
many suitable jobs as there are workers seeking employment". It stated that "full employment will only be achieved
by a government which understands that active public intervention in the economy is the only way to success. The
achievement cannot be the responsibility of private
industry..."
Review: A general commitment was made to "full employment" and the "right to work". It called for "the need of a
five-year perspective".

Methods to Achieve Full Employment
Programme: Appropriate methods of demand management
would be used with the emphasis being on public spending.
A pool of public spending commitments would enable projects to be brought forward wherever necessary. These
policies would be supported by selective and interventionist

industrial, regional and manpower policies (see below); plus willingness to change exchange rate rather than forego full employment. "Moreover, we would not accept any kind of international agreement which compelled us to accept increased unemployment in order to maintain a fixed parity."

Review: A very similar approach, though divergence of view on certain details (see below).

Note : Both the TUC Congress in September and the party conference in October 1972 called for reductions in the working week, additional public holidays, longer annual holidays, and earlier retirement on full pension.

Manpower Policies

Programme: A National Manpower Board would bring together, under one organisation, job replacement, training and retraining, and manpower planning. A general training levy would be introduced together with the compulsory notification of vacancies and the statutory advance warning of redundancies.

Review: Very similar approach, although rather less integration of the various services was suggested. Unlike the *Programme*, the National Manpower Board would also have the power to authorise public works projects. It would have its own "vote" of public expenditure.

Regional Planning

Programme: Detailed proposals involving differential man-power subsidies and taxes (taxes to be levied in congested zones); regional capital grants, with a large element being discretionary and selective, and being given in return for equity shares. New public ownership, including the state holding company. The party was also considering new regionally based machinery, with executive powers.

Review: A similar emphasis was placed on labour-related sub-sidies, plus regional capital grants related to the jobs created. A public investment agency, similar to the state holding company, was suggested. In addition, "Development Auth-orities" were proposed, based on the regions, "with sufficient powers and initial funds . . . to promote industrial develop-ment" in the regions.

Investment

Programme: The reintroduction of investment grants would
be considered. But discretionary grants would in any case
be introduced, with equity stakes being taken in the companies concerned. The power of public purchasing would be
used to stimulate investment in chosen areas and enterprises
backed by an expanded public sector—especially the use of
the SHC. In addition an agency similar to the old Industrial
Reorganisation Corporation may be needed to help schemes
of rationalisation. It also contained proposals for a return to
the 1965 system of Corporation Tax and the public ownership of banks and financial institutions.

Review: The suggested public investment agency would channel
all special and selective grants to the private sector, in return
for equity or loan capital. The agency would also use
Government procurement to stimulate demand especially in
capital goods industries, e.g. machine tools. It also called for
the extension of the public sector : the shipbuilding, aircraft
and pharmaceutical industries were specified.

Industrial Power

Programme: In addition to the wide powers suggested to plan
and intervene, specific proposals were made on multinational
companies, and extra powers on mergers and monopolies.
The reform of multinationals was "particularly urgent". It
stated : "We shall seek to ensure, for example, that the
Government has the right to appoint public directors to the
resident subsidiary companies of non-resident multinationals,
and to the main boards of resident multinationals."

Review: Demands for further controls over the exercise of
monopoly power, mergers and the operations of international
companies. There had to be a recognition that large-scale
enterprise was often monopolistic and that meant the
Government had an active responsibility to oversee planning decisions of such corporations. To this end, the powers
of reference to the Monopolies Commission should cover all
large firms over a certain size, not merely those who were in
a position of technical monopoly.

Industrial Democracy

Programme: Insistence by the state that the best standards current at the time should be generalised throughout industry, supported where possible by statute, regulations and the purchasing power of the public sector; the statutory right of every worker to belong to a trade union; the statutory right to recognition by employers of the trade unions; statutory rights on a wide range of facilities for accredited trade union representatives, such as access to the work place and to interview members, compensation for loss of earnings, and facilities for conducting meetings.

Substantial improvements in training and education for representatives with new courses through Industrial Training Boards, firms, unions and technical colleges.

Disclosure of information on a much wider basis, both from the firm and from the relevant public agencies. Workers should have the right to information on, for example, manpower and labour costs, ownership and control of the company, the projected work-load, pricing policies, and development, production, and investment data. Statutory trade union safety representatives, and joint safety committees, along the lines of Labour's Employed Persons (Health and Safety) Bill. A deliberate Government initiative to encourage the development of joint systems of control.

A statutory consultancy service should be able to carry out "industrial efficiency audits".

Experiments in new forms of workers' participation should be encouraged—especially in the public sector—and appropriate institutional and research facilities should be available to help appraise these experiments.

Review: The TUC document, being an *Economic Review*, carried little on industrial democracy. But as trade unionists sat upon the party's policy-making committees, there was little in the proposals with which the TUC would disagree.

Public Ownership

Programme: In general, industries heavily dependent on public support would be considered ripe for public ownership. An extensive programme of new public ownership was envisaged —including the reversal, where practicable, of Conservative Goverment measures such as licences and "hiving off" of those sectors of nationalised industries (airline routes an example). The expansion of the manufacturing powers of public enterprise and public ownership measures in the field of ports, pharmaceuticals, financial institutions, shipbuilding, aircraft, North Sea gas and oil and mineral rights. A Co-operative Development Agency would encourage rationalisation and modernisation of Co-op Society. Plus the interventionist powers of the SHC.

Review: Much as above. Where firms relied on "continuous subvention" nationalisation was considered directly relevant.

Taxation

Programme: Conservative changes on interest-rate relief, unearned income, share option schemes, etc., would be reversed. Tax loopholes would be plugged, helped by a special unit within the Inland Revenue. A tax on wealth and on *transfers* of wealth, would be introduced. On *indirect* tax, Value Added Tax harmonisation, to the pattern of EEC versions (with impositions on food, fuel, etc.), would be resisted. On *direct* taxation, tax rates would be made significantly more progressive with the tax thresholds being kept well clear of the poverty level. A system of Child Endowments would replace the system of tax allowance, eliminating the need for the Family Income Supplement. Trade union contributions would be given tax relief. The system of corporate taxation would be reshaped to favour retention rather than divided payments.

Review: The TUC approach was very similar regarding direct and indirect taxation, corporate taxation and the taxation of wealth, although there were some differences of detail on direct taxation; for example, on the replacement of the then tax allowances.

BROAD AGREEMENT EXPECTED

ECONOMIC AND INDUSTRIAL POLICY

Capital Accumulation

Programme: Attention was drawn to the trend to further inequality which arose from the growth of corporate wealth financed from retained profits. Apart from the extension of public ownership, three other proposals were suggested : the investment of a proposed National Superannuation Fund in equities; for the state to purchase equities on a large scale, offset by the issue of Government fixed interest debt; and the setting up of a National Works Capital Fund—run by workers—financed by annual distributions of shares from the private sector. The party was opposed to any kind of profit sharing scheme. The idea behind the Fund was that every worker gained an equal capital entitlement for each year he or she worked. The capital for the body would be derived from companies being required to transfer annually to the central fund, in the form of equity shares, a certain percentage of their wage bill or of the market valuation of their companies. The scheme at that stage was in the early stages of consideration. The party had set up a Capital-Sharing Study Group in 1971.

Review: Little comment was made on this. Earlier reviews, however, especially that of 1969, had emphasised the seriousness of the problem of capital accumulation. Changes in taxation were suggested as a partial solution in the 1969 Review.

Price Controls

Programme: Wide ranging price controls were suggested (as part of the planning system), bearing most heavily upon certain *key prices*. Special attention was paid to the problems of the public sector. In addition many retail prices would be subject to indirect control via a statutory list of "fair prices" inspectorate. A proposed National Consumer Authority would have responsibility for the whole field of consumer protection.

Review: Very little was said on price controls, but the party view was very much in line with TUC policy.

Incomes

Programme: "We therefore intend to supplement our strict price controls, in both private and public sectors, with a voluntary incomes policy." The objective, it was stated, must be to ensure that the growth of the nation's wealth was accompanied by steadily rising real incomes, with sharper rises for the lowest paid. The voluntary policy would be worked out with the TUC. On *pay*, there would be "no statutory intervention in wage negotiation", and "no discrimination" against workers in the public sector. Stress was laid upon the need to ensure that *equal pay* was made effective by the end of 1975. *Property incomes:* The prices policy was seen as the principal means of preventing excessive *profits*, backed by a firm anti-monopoly policy, continuous industrial intervention, and expanding public enterprise. There would be the redistributive tax policy. Private *rents* were to some extent covered by the proposals to strengthen the fair rent system and the municipalisation of private accommodation. Nothing, however, was said in the *Programme* about *dividend* control.

Review: The need to adopt *threshold agreements* was stressed, and also the need to attack low pay through the adoption—via collective bargaining—of reasonable minimum rates. A composite resolution carried at the TUC Congress re-affirmed opposition to wages restraint in any form. It declared "that no consideration can be given to any policy on incomes unless it is part of an integral strategy which includes control of rents, profits, dividends and prices, and is designed to secure a redistribution of income and wealth nationally and globally".

Economic and industrial policy formed the basis of what was to become the Social Contract. But it was not the only area where there was a convergence of views between the political and trade union wings. The policy was a means to achieve an end. Out of better economic management, it was hoped, would flow a more socially just society. The aspirations in the fields of social security, housing and education, for example, could be met. While this study is essentially about economic and industrial policy, total neglect of other areas would give an unbalanced portrait of the policy-making process. This is a convenient point to touch upon those areas and, again, relate party thinking to that of the trade unions.

BROAD AGREEMENT

HEALTH AND WELFARE

Occupational Health and Safety
Programme: Contained a commitment to create an Occupational Health Service with statutory powers financed by a

levy on industry. In the interim it was suggested that part of the Industrial Injuries Fund could be used.

Review: This tended to emphasise safety at work rather than the health service as such, although the two were clearly related. There was a call for better legislative backing for factory safety and for a contribution from industry. The review also called for a statutory system of joint safety organisation, very much in line with Labour's policy.

Family Allowances

Programme: Proposal for a system of Child Endowment, which would effectively increase and extend family allowances (including the first child).

Review: Similar proposals.

Housing

Programme: Both the *Programme* and the *Review* condemned the Housing Finance Act 1972. The party and the TUC conferences called for its repeal. The congress resolution supported non-implementation; the party conference called for the repayment of fines. It was this policy which led to the "Clay Cross rebels".

Furnished Tenants: Both the party and the TUC called for security of tenure for furnished tenants; this was a party commitment.

Private Dwellings: Again both sides were in agreement that the municipalisation of privately rented accommodation should be encouraged.

Owner Occupation: Both parties agreed also in this area. Both suggested similar solutions; for example, the limiting of tax relief on mortgages.

Programme: Called for as many houses as were needed, but no specific figure. The party conference, at the request of the National Executive, turned down a resolution calling for a target of one million houses a year.

Review: Called for targets to be set and the resolution of the congress stated a target of 500,000 houses a year. Another resolution wanted the end of the sale of council houses (which was also accepted at the Labour Party conference). The TUC congress also called for the freezing of rents, which was not accepted by the party in the terms proposed. The

TUC wanted to make "gazumping" illegal. This was not discussed by the party or by the conference. The trade unionists also wanted loans and mortgages at 2 per cent. The party view was that mortgages were still being investigated, along with other aspects of housing policy.

Education
Pre-school
Programme: Nursery education for all, beginning with areas of greatest need. Department of Education and Science would be required to tell education authorities to produce plans. The Urban programme for priority areas would be extended.

Review: Stressed need for expansion, at least as speedily as recommended by the Plowden Committee on Primary Education. The committee proposed that an additional 400,000 places should be provided in nursery schools and classes in the ten years from 1967 to 1977.

Secondary Education
Programme: Promised to end the system of selection by legislation and to require local authorities to prepare development plans for comprehensive education throughout compulsory school life. In future building programmes, local authorities would be asked to give priority to those projects which include, as one of their purposes, the ending of selection.

Review: Proper development by local education authorities of comprehensive secondary education. Abolition of selection.

Day Release
Programme: Offered education for all in the 16–18 age group. Legislation would give the right to continue education to all in this age group. It should not be possible to employ under 18s without making provision for their education and training. Obligation to release for education should exist until end of academic year in which age of 18 reached.

Review: The introduction of universal and compulsory day release for young workers up to the age of 18. The reform would assist in remedying some of the deficiencies of secondary education and be of particular benefit to those leaving school at or near the statutory minimum school-leaving age.

Adult Education
Programme: Labour would plan for a comprehensive adult

education service, to be provided by local authorities, colleges, polytechnics, and universities and voluntary bodies like Workers' Educational Association. "The task of the next Labour Government will be to lay the foundations so that eventually opportunities for education are available to everyone throughout their adult life."

Review: Called for expansion of activities, although the TUC definition of adult education included only WEA, evening classes and extramural work of universities.

BROAD AGREEMENT EXPECTED

HEALTH AND WELFARE

Short-term Benefits

Programme: Dealt with sickness, unemployment and other National Insurance benefits, and suggested some specific reforms the party would be considering. Since most of them came from the TUC it was not thought likely there would be differences of opinion. They included the extension of maternity grants to all mothers, regardless of National Insurance records; restoration of the previous entitlement to payment for the first three days of National benefits: abolition of those parts of the Social Security Act 1971 involving cuts in supplementary benefit for those in industrial dispute, and the repayment of supplementary benefit; a review of the amount of the cuts in supplementary benefit of those disqualified for other purposes; changes in the short-term sickness, unemployment and widows benefit, so that those in receipt did not lose because of claims in the previous year; a review of the appeals machinery for dealing with cases of disqualifications.

Urban Aid

Programme: Confirmed party's policy of extending the urban aid programme and the idea of "positive discrimination" in favour of areas where the "cycle of deprivation" was particularly acute.

Review: Did not deal with the subject, although trade unionists were expected to be in support of party policy.

Chronically Sick and Disabled

Programme: Outlined a policy to alleviate hardship—financial and otherwise. Two objectives were stated : further provision must be made for the extra expenses incurred by disabled people and their families as a result of handicap; compensation would be paid for loss of earnings whether loss was total or partial.

Review: Did not deal with subject, but again a common approach was expected.

Land

Programme: Land needed for development should be publicly owned. Study group created to prepare detailed policies.

Review: TUC was working on a policy in this area, but no mention of land in *Review*. Both party conference and congress called for public ownership of land.

DIFFERENCE OF APPROACH

Pensions

Programme: Suggested a revised "Crossman" type scheme with earnings-related contributions and benefits. The *Programme* stated the party would see what emerged from the Chancellor's proposals for linking tax and social security before deciding the precise machinery by which to implement Labour's determination to provide an adequate earnings-related scheme. It reaffirmed the main principles on which the Crossman plan was based and on which any future schemes would be based, i.e. annual adjustment of pensions; a redistributive formula enabling low paid workers to qualify for an adequate pension; full rights for women; preservation of pension rights on change of job. The party would also work out proposals for overcoming a major defeat in the Crossman Plan, its long twenty years' period of maturation.

Review: Broadly supported *some* of the principles in the Crossman scheme, but the TUC strongly argued for a "redistributive formula in favour of the lower paid employees, met by a substantially increased Exchequer contribution". It also wanted a large increase in existing benefits, again financed from taxation.

Index

Bold figures indicate biographical information.

Abbreviations